W9-BUM-623

The Bishop's Voice

Selected Essays 1979 - 1999

The Bishop's Voice

John Shelby Spong

Compiled and Edited by Christine M. Spong

A Crossroad Book
The Crossroad Publishing Company
New York

The Crossroad Publishing Company
370 Lexington Avenue, New York, NY 10017

Printed in the United States of America

Library of Congress Cataloging-in-Publication Data

Spong, John Shelby.
The bishop's voice : selected essays, 1979-1999 / John S. Spong ; compiled and edited by Christine M. Spong.
p. cm.
Includes bibliographical references.
ISBN 0-8245-1592-7 (hardcover)
1. Spong, John Shelby. 2. Episcopal Church. 3. Christianity.
I. Spong, Christine M. II. Title.
BX5995.S77A5 1999
230′.3–dc21 98-52206

1 2 3 4 5 6 7 8 9 10 04 03 02 01 00 99

for

THE PEOPLE OF

THE DIOCESE OF NEWARK

where the "signs of the Kingdom"

are always arising and renewing our lives

in wonderful and diverse ways

Contents

Part Two: Religion and Politics

Part Three: Religion and Church

Part Four: Conversations with Other Faiths

Part Five: Religion and Life

Part Six: God, Jesus, and Christianity

Introduction

In the spring of 1998 the Crossroad Publishing Company invited the Right Reverend John S. Spong to publish in book form a selection of his monthly columns from the Newark diocesan newspaper, *The Voice*. These monthly essays, written over some twenty years, ranged across the theological, political, moral, and personal landscape. The publisher had known Bishop Spong since 1970 and had worked with him on other publishing projects. He anticipated that the bishop's impending retirement would create a desire to have these essays in a more permanent form. The bishop responded favorably by saying that while he did not have the time to give to this project, his wife would be an ideal person to take on this task. She not only knew her husband in a deep personal way, but she had also worked with him on the diocesan staff from 1984 to 1990 and since their marriage in 1990 had been even more closely involved with his writing and lecturing activities, serving as his primary editor and overall manager. The publisher was pleased, and so it was that in May 1998, we agreed to move forward with a selection of the most interesting and most representative essays. This volume is the result of that process.

How does one make a selection from the more than 220 articles published over a period of twenty years? After that choice is made, how should they then be organized to make the most interesting presentation for the reader? Is it enough to choose one essay on a particular issue or is it better to choose an issue and then select every article written about it? Can one presume that the person reading this book will know the author of the essays? And, again, can one presume that the reader will remember the historical context when noting the date of the particular essay?

It was fascinating to read in the order in which they were written all 220 articles and to see that the seeds of the author's later essays were already planted when he came to the diocese. It was also easy to see that they fell into various categories: theology, justice, the institutional world of religion, personal issues. It was relatively easy to make the decision to cut certain essays which were either too narrowly focused or some cases in which there was no longer "life" in the topic. It took four readings with the cuts becoming more and more painful as I got down to the suggested number. How could I not include the article on that wonderful young man Chuck Packard, cut down in the prime of his life by a drunk driver? Which of the articles on homosexuality would be the best to be in this collection?

At the end of the selection process, it became clear that part 1 should reveal the very human face of a very public bishop through the essays he has written about the people who have been important to him. I particularly like the essays on his family members because they are now my family and they have been a gift beyond measure. "Christine" was included at the author's request! The essays about John Hines, John A. T. Robinson, and Desmond Tutu had to be included, not just because they were his mentors, but because each of them was and, in Desmond's case, is a great leader and an example for us to admire and to which to aspire. The final three essays are about our diocesan family — Harry Smith, Wanda Hollenbeck, and Ray Roberts. Each in his or her own way has had a profound effect on this bishop and this diocese. I never fail to weep when I read about Ray Roberts. He was my friend, and yet I never knew him. We had lunch six months before he died when he was still hoping to sail on the *QEII* to visit his beloved England one more time. I was there to comfort Jack when he came home in despair the night Ray died.

In part 2 on politics and religion the interplay between right-wing politics and right-wing religion during this period is quite fascinating. Looking back from the vantage point of the fall of the Berlin Wall and the break-up of the communist empire, it is interesting to read "Lunch at the White House." It is also of interest to see what has happened to Lt. Col. Colin Powell and Alan Keyes in the following years. The politics of Lee Atwater in "Diagnosis: Spiritual Vacuum and Moral Decay" have been carried to even greater excesses since then. It is a shame his dying words have not had such an impact. After the 1998 elections the publisher asked the bishop to add a brief comment to "Mr. Clinton: It's Time to Name the Demon" and this has been included.

In part 3 the first essay is an introduction to the bishop by himself in a column on his first address to the Diocesan Convention as diocesan bishop. It is interesting to read that and to see whether the last twenty years have shown this to be a vision of what the diocese would become under Jack Spong's leadership. Having just attended the Lambeth Conference as a bishop's spouse, I find the two columns on the 1988 and 1998 conferences almost overwhelming, the first so positive and uplifting; the second reflecting the strong turn to the right which we have also seen in American politics and religion. There is no separate column on Lambeth 1978, but it is alluded to in the essay "A Doughty, Delightful Figure" in part 1, which describes the impact of Desmond Tutu on that conference. I remember our amazement at the spiritual hunger in Australia and New Zealand during our first visit "Down Under," which was not being met in the churches of those countries. I can still feel the tension and excitement that was present in Christ Cathedral in Vancouver in 1992 at the "Face-Off" between the Right Reverend John S. Spong and the Reverend Dr. John Stott. We knew this was being videotaped, and I was sitting in the front row already aware that as Jack Spong's wife I needed to present a picture of calmness and not react too strongly when "goals" were scored or personal attacks were made on my husband.

In part 4 I have included two interfaith essays, not only because they are fascinating, but because this kind of dialogue must be the way of the future.

Part 5 contains essays on moral and justice issues. The first, "Does the Episcopal Church Welcome You?" is one of the most powerful indictments of prejudice I have ever read. The other essays address great moral issues of our day. They all address the particular issue with the theme of inclusiveness and the love of God. The essay on apartheid seems prescient when we remember it was written in 1985 and talks of a "period of grace" and the leadership skills offered by Nelson Mandela and Desmond Tutu. The essays on abortion and assisted suicide reflect powerfully the complexity of the moral issues that we face in our day. While these issues have subtle shadings, a clear consensus has developed that racism is wrong and cannot be countenanced under any circumstances, whether its expression is the terrible incident of a man dragged behind a truck in Texas or the racist jokes of a secretary of the interior or a sports manager. That same consensus is still emerging over equal rights for women and for gay and lesbian people. Both will soon be included in our revulsion against prejudice in every form.

Part 6 looks at faith and spirituality issues and explores how Christianity will look in the twenty-first century. It was on that theme that my husband wrote his most provocative book at the end of his career, for which he received both the greatest applause from this searching world, but also the most scathing hostility from a threatened ecclesiastical hierarchy. He is now writing his autobiography, but these essays capture the passion at the moment in a way a reflective autobiography never will.

•

The first time I met the Right Reverend John S. Spong officially was at a retreat for the newly reconstituted Christian Education Commission of the Diocese of Newark. (I had met him briefly before in a receiving line at a confirmation service at St. Peter's Church, Morristown.) Little did I know at that time that this was the beginning of what was to become the most important relationship of my life.

I was baptized, attended Sunday school, and was confirmed in the Church of England at St. Mary's Church, Sompting, Sussex, in the United Kingdom. This church dates back to about 906 C.E. and thus has been a continuously active faith community for almost eleven hundred years. That sense of continuity has been an undergirding presence in my life. I was confirmed at age thirteen by a very elderly bishop with white hair and shaking hands. In my thirteen-year-old eyes he seemed almost as old as the church — but not quite. My stereotype of a bishop was formed in that moment. Bishops must be very old, bald with a white fringe of hair, tall, slow, and shaky. I had some readjusting to do later in my life.

In my adolescence and early adulthood I continued to attend church, although less and less often, and so I became something of an Easter and Christmas Christian. When I was twenty-three I set off on what was to be a two-year trip around the world, landing in New York in 1962. My father had a heart attack in late 1962 and I decided to stay in the New York area, where in time I met my first husband. After marriage we moved to New Jersey, finally settling in Morris Plains in 1970. When our son, Brian, was born in 1968, I discovered my Anglican roots were still strong enough that I needed to have him baptized. By the time our daughter, Rachel, arrived in 1972, I was regularly attending St. Peter's Church, Morristown, and that was where she was baptized.

My status as simply a member of that church was disturbed when the Reverend Phillip Cato, the associate rector at St. Peter's, invited me to teach the seventh grade confirmation class. It was a challenge I both accepted and enjoyed. I must have done it well, for the next year I was appointed to membership on the Christian Education Committee and quickly became the chair. My new responsibilities included restructuring the whole Christian education program. The new ideas that we introduced eventually caught hold, and in 1976 I was elected to the vestry of St. Peter's. There were still very few women in that role, and little did I understand that I was beginning my training in church politics.

In that same year John S. Spong was elected bishop co-adjutor of the Diocese of Newark. Born in Charlotte, N.C., in 1931, he had grown up in the segregated South and had spent his years in ministry prior to coming to Newark helping to overcome the prejudice of white against black in various towns in North Carolina and Virginia. In Richmond, as he watched his daughters grow into their teens and saw the prejudice against women that they faced, he became a strong advocate for women's rights. By this time he was also a highly regarded author and had written five books, including *This Hebrew Lord,* which is still in print today.

The Reverend Phillip Cato had been a choirboy with the new bishop when they were growing up in Charlotte. He had actively campaigned in the diocese for his old friend to be elected. After the election was over, he campaigned for the bishop and his wife, Joan, to live in Morristown. In 1977 Jack and Joan Spong moved to 43 Ogden Place, Morristown, and as a consequence became parishioners at St. Peter's Church.

Shortly thereafter Phillip Cato suggested I call on Joan Spong and welcome her into community life at St. Peter's. He alluded to the fact that Joan was very shy and that he thought I would be a good person to spend time with her. I sensed there was more to the situation than what he was saying. However, she welcomed my visit, and so we began a very special friendship that eventually included both our husbands. As time went by I came to understand how fragile her mental health was, but in a small way I believe I was able to help her enjoy more of life given the boundaries of her world. She adored my young children, Brian and Rachel, and was always comfortable in their company. She made them cookies, played games with them, and just loved them. I included her in my life at luncheons and other events. When she met my husband, Dick, she liked him and did not find him threatening; perhaps that was in part because he was not "churchy" at all. As time went by we would have dinner at each other's homes. We spent Christmas together on one occasion; on another, Thanksgiving. I helped Jack and his daughters, Ellen, Kathy, and Jaquelin, plan a fiftieth birthday party for Joan. We got to know his daughters, and in 1983 I hosted a shower for Kathy before her wedding, which my family attended.

In 1981 Joan received a cancer diagnosis, and a long period of major uncertainty entered her life. She refused all chemotherapy and decided to fight the cancer by sheer will power.

Meanwhile my marriage was experiencing difficulty. It came to a head when my husband decided to move the family to Pittsburgh. When I refused to go, the end of our marriage came quickly. We separated in 1984.

Now I needed to go back to work in my new status as a single parent. It was Judy Hegg, the wife of the rector at St. Peter's, who suggested I apply for the newly open position of administrative officer for the Diocese of Newark. Judy helped me organize my resume, emphasizing all I had learned while running the Christian education program at St. Peter's and Christian education conferences for the diocese. The Personnel Committee of the diocese was concerned that I was a personal friend of both the bishop and his family, but in the end decided that my particular skills still made me the best candidate for the job. On March 4, 1984, I joined the core staff of the diocese and now became a professional associate of the bishop.

The next six years were challenging and exciting for me as the diocese grappled with life in the 1980s and I grappled with being a single parent and having a professional career for the first time in my life. In this position I organized the annual two-day Diocesan Convention. I was staff to those groups which provided support services to the clergy and churches of the diocese. I worked with diocesan committees and task forces, designed to examine a variety of issues alive in our society. The cutting edge of the diocese was to be found in these task forces whose subjects ranged from changing patterns of family life to the morality of assisted suicide. It was out of the task force report on Changing Patterns of Family Life that the diocese came to a new understanding and acceptance of homosexual persons. Our integrity as a faith community demanded that we act on what we believed so the bishop moved to ordain to the priesthood the Reverend Robert W. Williams, an openly homosexual man living in a public committed relationship with his partner. This ordination raised the issue of justice for gay and lesbian people to the front burner in the Anglican Communion, and it has been there ever since. The Diocese of Newark faces the real world and engages it. We have learned to live in the eye of the storm. My job put me at the center of these controversies. It was exciting, but not without stress and anxiety.

In 1988 the cancer finally overcame Joan's resistance, and she died in August of that year. The core staff provided the bishop with his primary support as he walked through that period. We also discovered during that following year that our relationship was growing from that of friends and colleagues to that of close companions. It was a slow process, which was accelerated when I had a health scare in the summer of 1989 that forced us to face the fact that we had become important to each other. On January 1, 1990, in St. Peter's Church, Morristown, with all our family and some five hundred members of the diocese present, we were married. Although neither of us has ever regretted that decision, I must confess that it was with deep grief that I resigned my position on the diocesan staff because of conflict of interest. Over the years, however, I have turned my skills and my ministry to helping and affirming the work of my husband to the point where we are now a total team and I am comfortable standing in for him on occasion. These past nine years have been rich and rewarding, magical and exciting as we both have grown as people and in our love for each other.

•

I would like to thank Lyn Conrad, the bishop's executive secretary; Lucy Sprague, the bishop's assistant secretary; Johanna Young, production manager for *The Voice;* and the Reverend Larry Falkowski, special assistant to the bishop, without whose practical help in providing all the 220 or more columns this book could not have been compiled. I would also like to remember and thank the mentors in my life: the Reverend Dr. Phillip Cato, former associate at St. Peter's Church, Morristown; Charles Trillich, friend and former vestry person at St. Peter's Church, Morristown; the Right Reverend Richard Shimpfky, former co-chair of the Christian Education Commission of the Diocese of Newark and now bishop of the Diocese of El Camino Real in California. Last but not least I salute with gratitude and pride the women in my life who have in a real sense become my current mentors: Ellen Spong, bank vice president; Katharine Spong, lawyer and lecturer; Jaquelin Spong, physicist; and Rachel Barney, U.S. Marine Corps pilot. Their journeys as young women in professional careers amaze and astound me. Their ability to support me in my current "career" with their love and strength moves me profoundly, and the value I place on their friendship is beyond words.

There is one other person in my life whose care and affection I would not be without: my son, Brian Barney, whose friendship, love, and understanding have been there for me in the bad times as well as the good.

Finally there is my husband. He challenges me, stretches me, loves me, and affirms me in ways I would never have believed possible. His time as bishop of the Diocese of Newark is drawing to a close. We look forward to living into retirement in this diocese with the many friends with whom we have struggled, fought, mourned, laughed, and rejoiced as described in the essays in this book.

CHRISTINE M. SPONG

Morristown, New Jersey
January 1999

PART ONE

The Human Face of a Public Figure

– 1 –

A Most Remarkable Lady

October 1993

She is eighty-six years old and weighs only seventy-three pounds. Her hair is still a natural brown with very few gray threads running through it. Arthritis has stooped her back and snarled her fingers. Her eyesight is failing, and occasionally she expresses a boredom with life itself. But her mind is clear; her love for her children, grandchildren, and great-grandchildren is intense; and her devotion to the policies of the Democratic party from Woodrow Wilson through Franklin Roosevelt to Bill Clinton is still intact.

She lives in a private apartment inside a retirement community in Charlotte, North Carolina, surrounded by family pictures and other personal memorabilia. She still fixes her breakfast and lunch but dines, as she says, "with the girls" each evening. All of "the girls" are in their eighties, and the primary thing they seem to discuss is the quality of food they are served. I see this lady no more than twice a year, but I talk to her by phone once each week. This lady who stands today no more than four feet ten inches tall is my mother.

She was born on the seventh day of July 1907, to people of Scottish (Wilson) and Welsh (Griffith) ancestry. Her baptized name was Doolie Boyce Griffith. Her father was a farmer who dreamed of bettering his life by a wide variety of entrepreneurial activities, most of which did not work out successfully. After investing in a cotton gin that failed, he moved into the city where his wife could run a boarding house and he could take a job in a cotton mill. He rose ultimately to a foreman's position but continued to endure difficult financial days for a long while. These misguided adventures cost my mother rather dearly, for the education of girls in those days was considered a luxury, not a necessity, in this family. So it was that six weeks into her ninth grade of school she was forced to quit to assist the family's fortunes. Aged fourteen she worked days in a five-and-ten-cent store selling sheet music, which she would play for prospective customers. She had a keen intelligence and an exceptional musical ability, but neither gift was to be developed because of the lack of funds.

The religion of this family was a fierce and harsh fundamentalism of the Calvinist Protestant variety. Card playing, dancing, alcohol, and motion pictures were the places where the devil lay in wait to snatch the souls of the faithful from the paths of righteousness. The preacher at the family church, Chalmers Associated Reformed Presbyterian Church, was Eli Griffith, brother of my mother's father and hence my mother's uncle. He pounded the pulpit and told vivid stories of the flames of hell. My mother's family did not leave the church, nor were they expelled, but they made it clear that Uncle Eli was a "bit too strict" to suit them. When her parents were out, my mother and some of her friends, including Eli's daughters, were known to roll up the rug, put rather primitive records on the Victrola, and dance to such tunes as "Red Lips, Kiss My Blues Away," and "Side by Side." Uncle Eli never knew.

Despite this rebellion my mother's religious background shaped her life in powerful and lasting ways. Sunday was "the Sabbath," and we did not violate that day with either work or vigorous play. Profane words like "gosh" and "darn" were strictly forbidden. The family Bible was always visible on the coffee table and was to be treated with the utmost respect.

There is something nice about having the great moral issues of the day reduced to this level. Right and wrong were clearly defined. Gray areas for decision-making were all but nonexistent. All of us knew the rules and the values by which we lived. We also knew what would happen when the boundaries of propriety were violated. Children must be disciplined and the devil within them curbed or else a parent had failed in his or her God-given responsibility. My mother had no intention of being such a failure.

But beyond the rules there was a sweetness in my mother's soul that must have come from her mother, who was small, delicate, and deeply pious. My grandmother said "thee" and "thou" when she spoke of God. She was given the honor and privilege of baking the communion bread for her church's quarterly celebration of the Lord's Supper. She was president of her county's chapter of the Women's Christian Temperance Union. She cooked and served for her family, doing everything from wringing the chicken's neck to making all the children's clothes by hand. But above all, my grandmother invested her love deeply in her three children. My mother was the recipient of that constant stream of love.

My mother was married at age twenty to a man thirty-eight years old with a propensity toward both alcohol abuse and obesity. She lived out the role of wife in an old-fashioned sense. She cleaned the house, cooked the food, birthed, nursed, and raised the children, and was available to her husband for his every need. He was king of the house. She was his loyal servant. She raised her children with her combination of strict rules and deep affection. By example, she instilled in us the virtues of honesty, truthfulness, and the worship of God. She was widowed at age thirty-five with her children of fourteen, twelve, and nine years of age. She was in a state of almost total poverty. Her husband's alcoholism and long sickness exhausted all financial resources, and the burial expenses exhausted the small life insurance policy.

So this uneducated and quite unprepared woman ventured back into the job market to keep her family together. The only work available to her was to be a clerk in the baby department of a major store. Her salary was eighteen dollars a week in return for forty-eight hours of work. To her credit she did not force her oldest child and only daughter to quit school to help support the family in this crisis. Somehow she endured. She sold our modest house and bought another in a much poorer neighborhood, and she managed to make her deceased husband's 1941 Ford last until 1952. Bill collectors rang the doorbell frequently. No coal was delivered one winter until she had managed to pay down the coal bill from the previous winter. The anxiety of approaching the cold weather without heat is still remembered. But she survived and so did we, though I often wonder how she did it.

By the time I entered the University of North Carolina, I had saved over $1,000 from my *Charlotte Observer* paper route. It was that pocket of money that enabled me to dream of a college education, a dream my mother had instilled in me. No member of my family on either side had ever gone beyond high school. As I ventured into the world of knowledge that my upbringing had not prepared me even to imagine, my mother's response was one of only pride. When I tried to tell her what I was learning in zoology or philosophy classes, her only words of caution were for me not to forget the truth of God's word in all my new learning. It was not always easy for me to share with her my journeys out of the prejudices of my upbringing.

Those journeys were destined not to be made in private, since, as a priest and bishop, I had become a public person. When I marched for the civil rights of black Americans and escorted a black child through a cursing, spitting crowd of white protestors into the segregated public schools of an eastern North Carolina town of seventy-five hundred people, my mother read about it in the press. When I advocated the ordination of women to the priesthood in our church and in 1974 cheered the irregular ordinations of those women who became known as the "Philadelphia Eleven," and when I labored publicly for the equal rights amendment, my mother was aware of it. When I advocated equality for gay and lesbian people and ordained to the priesthood an open and honest gay male, and when I rode as a bishop of the church accompanied by my wife in the New York City Gay Pride Parade, it came via the press to my mother's attention.

In each episode deeply ingrained attitudes and a moral system with right and wrong clearly defined collided inside her mind with the love she had for her son whom she trusted. She knew that she had instilled integrity in him. In the ensuing struggle to grow, it was always her love and trust that won out over her prejudices, and grow she did. In time, with great pride, she worked for and supported with her vote an unsuccessful black male candidate running for governor of North Carolina. She welcomed female priests of her church and beamed with pride over the professional success of my three daughters in their heretofore exclusively male occupations of banking, law, and science. She began to recognize that she had known gay and lesbian people who had befriended her and therefore concluded that they must be good people.

With the advantages of education and travel, I nonetheless had to spend a lifetime purging myself of the prejudices of my youth. My mother, without those same advantages, has made a similar journey that even to this moment humbles me. I admire her as deeply as I love her.

Her world today has shrunk to a rather narrow orbit. Her oldest child, my sister, is her primary link to the wider world that exists beyond her retirement community. But inside that community she is loved and wanted by a wide variety of friends whom she visits or who visit her. She brags about her children in a way that embarrasses us all. It doesn't embarrass her one bit.

She is without question the most devoted fan I have. In her eyes I can do almost no wrong. Of course even I do not agree with that assessment, but I suppose every life needs at least one person who feels that way about him or her. For my sake I hope this remarkable lady lives beyond my retirement in the year 2000, for I am not sure that without her constant and unswerving devotion I could endure the ups and downs of my wonderfully exciting but not always easy episcopal career.

– 2 –

Meditation on a Dateline

June 1987

Whether the idea was alive in my subconscious mind or was created by a chance glance at the dateline of the morning newspaper, I do not know. What I do know is that when my eyes fell upon that date, a flood of memories was released and a number of responses were created. That date was my father's birthday. It was a date I had not observed in any official way since his death forty-three years ago. I had to stop to calculate that this would have been his ninety-seventh birthday. To imagine him at ninety-seven was not possible. When he died at age fifty-four, he had gray temples in an otherwise black head of hair. He was five feet nine inches tall, and his 220 pounds created the impression of obesity, with double chins and a hanging midsection.

He had been a short but powerful presence in my life during my first twelve years. He was the source of conflicting emotions which included joy and sadness, hope and despair. In some ways he had twisted and warped me. In other ways, he had given me the drive to achieve, equipped me with a standard of excellence, and helped shape for good or ill my moral values. I wonder both what I would have become if I had never had him, and what I might have become if he had continued to be a presence in my life after age twelve.

My father was a complicated man. He had been a traveling salesman, in fact working for the same company that employed his father and in time taking his father's former position. He appears to have had a relationship with his mother that was marked by elements of neurotic dependency. He lived at home until he was thirty-eight years old. He was his mother's keeper. He clearly needed her approval and the services she provided, and she clearly needed his emotional and financial support. In more ways than one he had taken his father's place. It was only when she died that he was motivated to enter marriage. His wife, my mother, was eighteen years his junior but nonetheless he called her mother throughout their brief fifteen-year marriage. Because he was a traveling salesman, we grew up accustomed both to his absences and to an exhilarated sense of anticipation when we prepared for his return home. He never came empty handed. There would be something wonderful to eat, like fresh crisp fall apples from the Shenandoah Valley of Virginia, or a keg of salt mackerel from the Carolina coast. I adored that salty briny gift from the sea before I learned of salt's danger to my health. It was for our family a breakfast delicacy with scrambled eggs and the inevitable grits.

We were insatiable baseball fans, and Dad's return frequently meant a trip to Griffith Park to watch our beloved Charlotte Hornets play in the Class B Piedmont League. The hated rival was the Norfolk Tars, who, in 1938, edged us out of the pennant by one game. The Tars were the Yankees farm team, and they were led that year by the keystone combination of George Sternweiss at shortstop and Gerry Priddy at second base. The leading pitcher for the Hornets, a Washington Senators farm club, was Early Wynn. Even my sister was addicted to the baseball bug and cheered mightily. We worked with her in our vacant lot games, too, despite her grip on the bat that separated her two hands by six to eight inches. Perhaps once in those years at the ball park we actually caught a foul ball for a souvenir, but every time we went hope burned eternal and we never failed to wear our baseball gloves in anticipation. Occasionally my father would play baseball with us. It was more batting/fielding practice, or catching, than an actual game. His weight made his mobility somewhat difficult. I don't recall ever seeing him run the bases.

In the evenings in that distant history, there was no television to watch, but our minds made the radio programs we did hear quite vivid in the imagination. My children find it hard to believe that a family could gather around a large radio cabinet in the living room, which was in fact a piece of living room furniture, to listen to a radio program. Our family favorites were *Lux Presents Hollywood, Amos and Andy, Jack Benny,* and *The Lone Ranger.* The William Tell Overture will be for me forever associated with that masked champion of frontier justice who rode off into the sunset with his faithful Indian companion, Tonto.

When no family event was planned for the evening my dad played solitaire. My mother was all but convinced that playing cards was the creation of the devil, but there was no gambling in solitaire and my father clearly enjoyed it, so it was a part of our household. I would sit by the hour across the piano bench, which he regularly used for a card table, to watch him play. My task was to turn over what we called the peep cards. He wanted to win, but never dishonestly. It is incredible to me now how caught up I could get in the competition between my father and those cards. I absolutely felt elated when he would win. I was a loyal cheerleader.

Sundays were unusual days in our household. The kids were dressed and delivered to Sunday school at the Church of the Holy Comforter. My mother and father never went, and no one of us ever stayed for church. It was an Episcopal Sunday school, with many incentives such as perfect attendance medals, various contests, and regular opportunities for the children to perform. I regarded it as a pleasant experience to which I looked forward but from which I recall no content whatsoever. I was impressed, however, with the adults who gave enormous amounts of time and energy to that activity. It clearly had value for them and that value was communicated to me in powerful ways. My teachers, the superintendent, and the music teacher are still distinctly defined personalities in my memory. I sensed the dichotomy that my parents seemed to think Sunday school was important, but they did not attend and did not help. The church was itself not an important institution in our life.

There were also painful episodes that centered around my father that have not yet had their seemingly indelible marks removed. My father was a heavy smoker and an episodic alcoholic. He would remain sober for weeks, even months, but once he took his first drink he did not seem to stop until he was hospitalized. His alcoholism was a dark cloud that hung as an aura of fearful apprehensiveness over us all the time. Even in the good times we always wondered when the next episode would occur. He was emotionally abusive, irritable, and impatient when drinking. He threatened my mother physically, effectively terrorizing the children. But I do not know of any threat he ever carried out. He was more deeply into his alcoholic problem the last four year of his life, and since these were my years of ages eight through eleven, they constitute my primary memories and distort, I am certain, my lasting image of this powerful man. I am also quite certain that the combination of drinking, heavy smoking, lack of exercise, and obesity were each contributing factors in his heart disease, which resulted in a heart attack at age fifty-two and death at age fifty-four.

I suppose that I sensed his impending death, but somehow, at age twelve, death is not comprehensible. However, his family gathered, the mood was grim, lots of prayers were offered, neighbors were solicitous, and doctors were frequent visitors in our home. I met this crisis with religious resources that came from I know not where. I had memorized the offices of instruction from the 1928 Episcopal Book of Common Prayer. Somehow I found in those words some strength and some meaning that even today is beyond my power to articulate. I am sure I dabbled in magic, and my view of God was highly superstitious. I struck many a bargain with God during my father's illness and somehow believed that my prayers had a salutary effect in keeping my father alive. When they failed to achieve that goal I had great difficulty, for somehow I felt blameworthy, responsible for his death, and bore emotional guilt so heavy that at times I thought I had killed him personally. I now know I was deeply ambivalent about whether he lived or died. I did not know that consciously, but the signs were apparent both then and later. The alcoholic person can hardly expect to be loved by those who feel victimized by his drinking.

My father's low opinion of himself got expressed in his low opinion of me. I was his namesake and his junior, which made the negative transfer of his emotions and definitions quite simple. He told me time and again that I was inadequate, incompetent, ignorant, or worse. "You can't do anything right!" was his most remembered refrain. I had to live with that parental definition. From some place I received the ability not to accept his judgment and, therefore, not to wallow in it. Instead it represented for me a kind of battle cry, calling me to a motivation to achieve that has dominated my life. It forced me to exercise my intellectual capacities, to meet expectations placed upon me, to harness my energy, to utilize creatively my time, and to become an overachiever. That has not always been an asset in my interpersonal relations, but it has caused me to find outlets for my creativity and to enter those outlets with vigor.

I owe that part of my life in a strange and perverse way to my father. But I often wonder if that would have been my response had he continued to live and had his life continued in the task of eroding my self-confidence and my sense of worth. I do not know. I am glad he was my father. I think I am glad he was my father for only twelve years.

I have many memories of my father to celebrate and many others that even forty-three years after his death cry out to be healed. I do not pretend to know what heaven means, but if it presents an opportunity for me to know this man anew, I would count it a privilege of a lifetime. I would want to know the source of the pain that he felt that needed alcohol to anesthetize it and the meaning of that dreadful sense of inadequacy that he inevitably passed on to me. I would also want to know what his dreams were for his life, his marriage, his children, and most especially for his firstborn son. I would want to observe him freed of those distortions that bound him in obesity and alcoholism. Finally, I would like to feel his love and to offer him mine, and just once more, in a childlike fashion, I would like to be in his embrace and feel the security of his hug. It seems like such a small request but it is enormously big in the secret recesses of my heart. Strange that all of this can pour forth just upon the conscious notice of the dateline in a morning newspaper.

– 3 –

An Annual American Celebration: Graduation

June 1984

Pomp and circumstance; caps and gowns; multicolored academicians acting out the liturgical rites of spring; happy parents, relieved parents; students embracing one another in anticipation of separation that may be final; aging alumnae greeting associates of former years, as memories bring the past once more into the present. It is graduation day, the annual American celebration of passage.

Graduation time this spring found me in the parent role as I watched my daughter receive her doctor of jurisprudence degree, walking through that necessary doorway into the practice of law. It was a transition moment for her — and for me as well. I saw my daughter that day in a radically different way. She looked very mature in her doctoral gown with the colors of her alma mater as she peeped out from her academic hood. Her fiance was there acting as proud as either of her parents. Sisters, cousins, roommates, friends all gathered to reminisce, to celebrate, to ponder, and to savor that moment of time.

As I watched this daughter enter the great hall at her university, a whole lifetime passed before my eyes: a snowy February Sunday morning twenty-five years ago when at 3:30 a.m. the labor pains signaling her imminent arrival started her parents on the seventeen-mile journey to the hospital. A long, slow freight train blocked our path on that trip for what felt like eternity. Her birth came in time to allow me to return to give thanks at the 8:00 a.m. Eucharist at Calvary Church in Tarboro, North Carolina. We named her Katharine, to which we added Mary, for she came into our lives on the Feast of the Purification.

As the graduation procession marched past me, I remembered the day of her baptism, and especially her godparents. Thelma and Jack Denson were an older, childless couple who taught me what godparents can be. Kathy would bring to them a glow and a warmth that was irrepressible. To my daughter they were surrogate parents and grandparents as well as best friends. She shared their home for many a day and night until she was well into her twenties, and their deaths she mourned with an intensity that those who stood outside that relationship could never understand.

Other vignettes surfaced — some fun, others not quite so pleasant. I remembered adenoids, tonsils, breathing difficulties, playmates, birthday parties, kindergarten, children's choirs, Girl Scouts, and the inevitable Girl Scout cookies. A budding feminism caused her to join with her sisters to create a game called "A Woman from A.U.N.T." There were football games and basketball games which instilled in all of us a sense of community identity. I recalled watching the trauma a child experiences when moving from those roots to a new city. Other fleeting images focused on confirmation, youth group activities, the first love, the first date, the first job, watching habits develop, seeing sensitivity grow, facing pain together, experiencing death together. Vacations always spawned their own folklore. Our most famous episode involved making soup in the only pot we had at the beach, which was a diaper pail. The tasty final product we gleefully named "diaper pail soup." In time there was the choosing of a major field of study, college, serious love, taking law boards, anxiously awaiting the law school selection process, the elation of being chosen, the pressure of the first year of graduate study, summer clerkships, preparing to take the bar examination, engagement, and finally graduation. These were the unselected episodes that passed before my mind's eye as I watched that graduation ceremony. Some lingered to be enjoyed anew, some vanished in a twinkling as quickly as they appeared. All pointed to the experience of that moment: the realization that life is transition.

To see a child well launched is the special and peculiar pleasure of parenthood. This daughter, once so helpless and dependent, is now so competent, so independent. In her infancy and childhood she ministered to my needs to be needed. Now she meets me on the adult level of a friend, a close friend, an understanding friend, a long-time friend, even an uncomfortable friend, for she knows me too well. As I observed her transition into professional life, I became strangely aware of my own transition into the world of what is euphemistically and perhaps hopefully called "The Middle Years." Through her eyes I look anew at my life from the perspective that emerges on the far side of parenthood.

Before me lie the remaining years of my career. In that time I will be seeking to do better the same things that I now do. The emphasis may change from time to time, but the context of my life is set. This creates in me both security and a sense of entrapment, which then leads me to speculate about my future goals. They seem rather modest when compared to the goals that marked my youth. There may be some new things that I cannot now foresee, but that is not likely. Perhaps I will become a grandfather and be able to view life from still another angle. Perhaps I will encourage, challenge, push, or prod the next generation of our clergy into using the excellence they possess to give the church the vitality it will need in the future. Perhaps I will in some way assist this church of ours to embrace the twenty-first century with integrity and power, celebrating knowledge breakthroughs and theological pluralism as well as the contributions of various ethnic groups that, if embraced, will manifest a unity in the church that is both catholic and breathtaking. Perhaps I will continue to assist the breakdown of sexual stereotyping so that we will all see one another as people first, male or female second, and that God may be experienced beyond the limits of all human sexual symbols. Perhaps I will grow to be more receptive and hospitable to those parts of the religious experience which I cannot easily understand or appreciate today. In time I will retire, leaving it to others to measure the impact of my days and to continue the chain of witness.

My daughter's life passed before me in review on the day of her graduation. Then my own life propelled me forward in thought, hope, and fantasy. The two experiences are interlocking. Because graduation is a special moment of transition, we celebrate it with pageantry. We freeze it in time with cameras; we store it forever in our memories. But there is also the inevitable realization that transition is found not just in the big events; it is our daily bread, the truth of our every moment. We are powerless to stop the process of change and transition. Coming to terms with the inexorable nature of time elicits our response.

Because we are creatures caught in an eternal flow of time, we sink our roots to discover a place where we belong. We attempt to develop relationships that are deep, that endure, that are trustworthy. We pledge ourselves to be a part of other lives — to be dependable for them as well as dependent on them. But finally we are invited to see that it is this transient quality of life that compels human beings to the activity of divine worship. We are drawn to seek that Rock of Ages on which we can stand, that truth beyond the flux of life which abides forever. We probe our world for meaning that lasts, for a sense of worth that will not fade, for an affirmation that will transcend change. In each of these ways we are looking ultimately, I believe, for God. If we do not find this God, our life will take on a frenetic quality destined finally only to pass away, carrying each of us with it. However, if we do find and commune with this God as a living presence, we will be enabled to stare at the passing sands of time with peace and equanimity rather than in pain and despair. We can connect ourselves to eternity when it breaks into our human fragility. We can lose our frantic grip on life, on each other, on things, on yesterday and be carried into what will be, not as passive victims, but as willing explorers who have encountered the Holy and who know that God is real.

It takes a celebrated moment of transition to startle us into seeing that all life is movement, that every day is a new graduation. This very transitory existence invites us finally to be open to the holy God who is met in the process of change, to rejoice in our union with this God who produces in us that unique particularity we call personal existence. Then we can dare to embrace the changes and chances that are ours and walk into every new day convinced that nothing can finally separate us from God.

Graduation presses me to review the past and to contemplate the future. Finally, however, it calls me to worship and to participate in the prayer of the hymn writer who said, "O Thou Who Changest Not — Abide with Me."

– 4 –

It's a Girl

June 1988

Yes, I know it has happened millions of times before, but this is the first time it has happened to me. Yes, I understand that people who experience this new status act giddy, are talkative, and show endless photographs. But how else does one communicate the holiness of life in vital stages of transition when there are no obvious signs that compel others to rush up and inquire? This new status has to be, and is, announced, imposed, broadcast, and bragged about while pictorial proof is produced.

So, allow me to shout from the rooftops to my diocesan family that on April 6, 1988, Katharine Shelby Catlett, my first grandchild, was born. You certainly need to know that she weighed seven pounds nine and one-half ounces (yes, that half ounce is important), that she measured twenty-one inches and that mother and grandfather are both doing well, as indeed are all the other principals — like the father, the other three grandparents, the aunts, uncles, great-aunts and two great-grandmothers. Their only problem is that they do not write a column. Surely you want to ask what she looks like. Well, if she had a cigar and a martini, she would resemble Winston Churchill in miniature! She is a baby girl, lovely to behold, gentle, soft to the touch, and precious. She also has a loud speaker on one end and no sense of responsibility on the other.

One week after her birth, my episcopal schedule was bent just a bit to allow a brief visit to Richmond. I held her, cradled her, burped her, and kissed her for about three hours, just as I had done to her mother some thirty years before. It was a touching moment for me, calling out of my depths some sense of the elemental mystery of life itself and making me aware of the privileges and opportunities that life has sent my way. My father died when I was only twelve. He never knew the meaning of being a grandfather. He could not participate in that moment when life leaped another barrier and entered another generation. He did not live long enough to experience the aging process and to know what it means when the great expanses of a seemingly limitless future begin to narrow, the doors of opportunity begin to close, and the power of life begins to flow to another generation. He could not look into the face of his grandchild and experience at once the intimations of immortality that he saw in that tiny face and the specter of human finitude that he saw in himself. These joyful insights have now been granted to me and I have relished them. For the first time I now can grasp emotionally and recognize clearly what my own father missed.

Just being a father was my life's greatest thrill and, I still believe, my life's greatest accomplishment. I loved every moment of that experience. My three daughters, born in 1955, 1958, and 1959, have given to me my deepest sense of affirmation as a human being. When they were just little creatures they would wait for my arrival home in the evening or after a trip, with a gleeful anticipation that had to have been primed by my wife, to whom I am ever grateful. I would see their faces in the windows, noses pressed flat against the panes. I would hear their screams of excitement as I fiddled at the door with the key. Upon entering the house, I would be besieged by their clamoring attempts to attach themselves to me, hugging my legs, arms, and neck until the ecstasy of the greeting ritual was concluded, usually by rolling over and over on the floor. Touching was important to them and to me. Nothing felt quite like their little arms around my neck, their soft faces against mine, their kisses upon my cheeks. Of course they outgrew that and became kissless, distant teenagers. Yet, with a twinkle that allowed all of us to know that love was real even when space was required, we knew that we had the kind of relationships that would survive adolescence and grow into the mutuality of adult respect. The joyful memories of childhood were related to such things as play night on Thursdays, while their mother went to choir rehearsal, and play day on Saturdays, which involved three girls in one wagon being pulled to the park to swing and slide and then to the candy store for that once-a-week exotic delicacy.

Other images of those days centered around pillow fights, birthday parties, football games, basketball games, baseball games, and sliding down the stairs in a heavy quilt that never was quite the same again. Perhaps our favorite game was built on the joy of anticipating Christmas. "Blue light play night," we called it. It consisted of putting Christmas records on the record player in October while we strung Christmas lights all over the furniture and carpet in the living room and entered joyfully into the fantasy and magic of that wondrous season. It was a wonderful game until the lights burned the synthetic carpet in an exciting new pattern with scorch marks every twelve inches or so!

These are the moments that build enduring relationships that link parent to child, then parent to adolescent, then parent to adult child, and, finally, grandparent to grandchild. The ties are deep, the bonding is real when life is deeply shared. I will not see my granddaughter, Shelby, with much regularity. Her mother and father are attorneys in Richmond and I am a bishop in New Jersey, so 350 miles separate us. Three visits a year will be the average and the norm. I will be known to her primarily through her mother who will pass on to her the folklore of the family, the tales of her own childhood embellished, perhaps, by that childlike imagination that never quite separates reality from the world of make-believe. Grandparents act as if the birth of the first grandchild is only a time of joy. Perhaps our talking about it so exuberantly is but a vain attempt to hide its darker shadows. But the birth of a grandchild also brings with it the shock of mortality. This little bundle of flesh and blankets represents the future in a way I can no longer represent it. My life is locked into its own past. I know all the wildernesses of yesterday. She will dwell in the promised land of tomorrow, though in fact, in retrospect, it will become wilderness to her. The promised land always exists only for the next generation. In her face I am forced to see my own aging process.

I will be sixty-two years old when she enters the first grade and seventy-eight when she finishes college. I tell myself that there are some advantages in this. I repeat the cultural wisdom of grandparents that suggests that I can always leave the baby and return home, an option no parent has. I remind myself that her birth does not doom me to twelve more years in the PTA. I will not have to be bound to the time requirements of chauffeuring her to dancing classes, cotillions, piano lessons, soccer games, or youth group activities. I will not have to endure the process of helping her get her driver's license or wait anxiously until she returns home at some ungodly hour from the senior prom, I will not have to live frugally in order to pay for her college education. But, as I contemplate these "advantages," I feel no joy, for, complain as I may, those were the things that gave me life, that convinced me of my primary value, that drew out of me the gifts of nurture that made my parenting years glow with pleasure and pride. Those gifts are now the gifts that my daughter and my son-in-law have to give. They will bear the primary responsibility and experience the primary fulfillment. I am a grandparent, which is something like being the cherry on top of the whipped cream — not essential but very pleasant. Well, if my future is to be the cherry, then bright, red, and tasty I will try to be.

I have touched more than once in my fifty-six years the wellsprings of life, those holy moments where the human and the divine meet. I know on existential levels that they are real. These moments have sustained me in the years of struggle and toil, of passion and creativity. I trust they will sustain me now as age increases and power declines. So I face my finitude reflected in the face of a tiny one who now bears my name and whose eyes have not yet focused. I give thanks to the God who has been my help in ages past and who will be my hope and Shelby's hope for years to come. That's the agony underneath the ecstasy of grandparenthood. I embrace both emotions, for they are part of life and I want to drink deeply of everything that life offers. Welcome, Shelby, for you have already helped me do just that.

– 5 –

My Cousin Bill

March 1998

He won the primary by 611 votes. There were almost 800,000 cast. We called him "Landslide Spong."

In Virginia in 1966 to win the Democratic primary was tantamount to winning the election. Republican opponents in the general election were like walk-ons in a play. No one noticed them and only their families could recall their names. So William Belser Spong Jr. prepared to enter the United States Senate. His defeated opponent was a two-term Democrat seeking a third six years in the Senate. His name was A. Willis Robertson. He was seventy-eight years old. Had he been reelected in 1966, he would have been eighty-four when he completed that third term. It was the age factor that surely led to his defeat.

Senator Robertson was an old-line conservative southern Democrat aligned with what was then called the Byrd Machine. Senator Harry Byrd Sr. controlled Virginia politics for more than a quarter of a century. So effective was his organization that he could gather on the porch at his family home in Berryville, Virginia, with a few of his closest associates and pick the next governor, lieutenant governor, and attorney general of the state. Their power had never been seriously challenged until the election of 1966. The old Senator Byrd had retired with ill health and his son, Harry Byrd Jr., had been appointed to fill his father's seat. One commentator referred to "Little

Harry," as the new Senator Byrd was called, as possessing everything his father had possessed except "wit, humor, personality, and intelligence." Senator Robertson had no son ready to step into his spot. He did have a son named Pat who would someday be a well-known televangelist who would dabble in presidential politics as the choice of the religious right. But in 1966 Pat Robertson was still sowing his wild oats. So Senator Robertson chose to defy the odds and to run once more.

That is what opened the door of opportunity to the state senator from Portsmouth. Bill Spong was called a "young Turk" in political circles in Virginia. He was able to bring on board a whole new generation while not alienating his seniors, which enabled him to eke out the narrow victory that sent him to the Senate.

Bill and I were not just first cousins, we were close friends. His father and my father were the middle two boys in a family of seven children. They were close in age, close enough in looks to be frequently mistaken for each other, and were bonded brothers. They both loved baseball and even considered professional careers in the sport. Bill's father, my Uncle Belser, did become sports editor of the *Portsmouth Star.* My father, Bill's Uncle Shelby, became a traveling salesman living in Charlotte, North Carolina. Death separated the two brothers in 1940 when Belser Spong died at age forty-nine of a heart attack. My father, hearing the news, drove to Hampden Sydney College to inform his nephew and take him home for the funeral. In the days following my father became Bill's surrogate father. During World War II Bill was in the army at Fort Bragg, North Carolina. Every time he had a weekend pass he spent it with us in Charlotte. He was eleven years older than I so he was a special war hero to me. My own father died in 1943 when I was twelve. Bill came to the funeral, and he became for me something of what my father had been to him in similar circumstances just three years before. During the war Bill was in Europe, and so several years passed before I saw him again. He returned after VE day, entered law school at the University of Virginia, became a Rhodes Scholar, passed the bar, got married, and began to practice law in Portsmouth. I was now a teenager, as lost and immature as any fatherless teenager one has ever known, but I would spend a week each summer with Bill and his wife, Virginia, and he became for me a guiding spirit.

In 1949 I entered the University of North Carolina and in 1952 the Virginia Theological Seminary. During those years I saw my cousin very little, but he did come to my ordination, both as deacon and priest, and we stayed in touch.

When I lived in Tarboro, North Carolina, about a hundred miles from Portsmouth, we would often go to the North Carolina–Virginia football game. When Bill entered Virginia politics, becoming a member of the State Assembly and later a state senator, he managed to get annual tickets to the Atlantic Coast Conference Basketball Tournament. He included me in his party of political associates, some of whom would later become federal judges and candidates for governor of Virginia. Attending this tournament became my "Lenten discipline" and continued during my years in Lynchburg and Richmond.

Meanwhile Bill's political career was soaring. The quality of public education was to be his major theme. This was in the days when Virginia, ordered by the courts to desegregate its schools, responded with a policy of massive resistance to the law of the land. In some counties Virginia went to the absurd extent of closing public schools and opening white private academies. The quality of education for all children declined in those dreadful days. When the State of Virginia began to emerge from this dark chapter, a statewide commission, designed to seek ways to restore quality public education to all of the children in Virginia, was appointed by the governor. State Senator William B. Spong Jr. was picked to chair this commission. It won for him a statewide reputation as a reformer, a moderate, and a politician not wedded to the dying patterns of the old South.

It was on the basis of this reputation that he defeated Senator Robertson. Entering the strange world of Washington politics, he was invited with other freshmen senators to address the National Press Club. Fearful that someone in the media would call him Senator Sponge, he used his five-minute introductory speech to secure proper name identification. His first act as a senator, he announced in his southern drawl, would be to introduce a bill to protect the rights of songwriters in Hong Kong. He would be joined in this effort by the senior senator from Louisiana, Russell Long, and the junior senator from Hawaii, Hiram Fong, and they would present the Long Fong Spong Hong Kong Song Bill. His name was never mispronounced by members of the media.

Bill was a thoughtful senator, independent and issue-oriented. He did not know how to attack his opponents' character. His two most strategic votes were on the confirmation of Nixon appointees to the Supreme Court. He supported Clement Haynesworth, whom the

Senate failed to confirm. He opposed Harold Carswell whom the Senate also failed to confirm. Both were conservative judges. Bill's opposition to Carswell was based on his conviction that the man was not qualified. Senator Hruska of Nebraska had defended this appointment on the basis that the common people of this country needed to be represented on the Supreme Court by a common person, rather than an outstanding judge. It was a strange argument. Bill's vote, however, was one that neither conservative Virginia nor Richard Nixon would forget.

When Bill ran for a second term a sea change had occurred in Virginia politics. The word "Democrat" had become identified with anti–Vietnam war protest, riot-torn urban areas, and the burning of the American flag. The Democratic Party nominated George McGovern, who lost Virginia to Richard Nixon by a 70–30 margin. Bill's seat was targeted as vulnerable. On the night before the election, Vice President Spiro Agnew flew to Richmond to address a giant rally in which he castigated the McGovern-Spong wing of the Democratic Party. Right-wing money poured into Virginia in the last two weeks of that campaign, which bought a media blitz portraying Bill as a radical Democrat, supportive of every left-wing cause imaginable. Bill felt these charges were so absurd that he would not defend himself against them. When the votes were tallied he had lost the Senate seat by a 51–49 percent vote. The man who defeated him, William C. Scott, was later voted by the Washington press corps "the dumbest man in the U.S. Congress." It was small consolation.

His defeat devastated me. Bill was remarkably calm. We spent the night after the election together. I was so offended by the way he had been misrepresented that I vowed never again to be silent on justice issues. I would publicly take on the right-wing political and religious lobbies on the issues of race, human rights, and the immorality of war.

Bill left the public glare and became dean of the law school at the College of William and Mary until his retirement. My life became more and more public and even political as I spoke frequently to public issues in Virginia from my pulpit in the heart of Richmond and from my position on the Richmond Human Rights Commission. The public nature of my life was enhanced when I was elected bishop in 1976.

Bill Spong attended the consecration and read the Epistle at that service. I became his family's chaplain. Over the years I performed the weddings of his daughter and his son. I baptized his grandchildren. I buried his mother, my Aunt Emily. Three years ago I buried his wife, Virginia. While I was on sabbatical in New Zealand, Bill died very suddenly of an aneurysm. I grieved that I could not conduct his funeral. I should not have worried. His will stated that I was to conduct that service at a time convenient to me and to his two children. So a public memorial service was held at William and Mary shortly after his death, but his funeral was postponed until my return.

On December 27 Chris and I went to Charlottesville, Virginia, where the surviving members of his family gathered with my family. Between the two of us there were seven grandchildren present. It was in that setting that I buried my cousin. His wife's cremated remains I also interred. It was the final act of love in a relationship that had been lifelong.

The essence of life is that we give to others what someone else has given to us. My father gave to Bill what he could when Bill's father died. Bill gave to me what he could when my father died. I have now given to his children what I could when he died. Someone will give to my children what they can when I die. That is what the Communion of Saints is all about. One always lives in debt to someone else. That debt never can be paid to the one to whom it is due. It is always given to someone else. Jesus said "freely you have received, so freely give." I think I understand what that means.

– 6 –

Making a House a Home

December 1989

In August of 1988, my wife died after a long illness of both mind and body. Many, many times in my priestly ministry I have been involved as a pastor with death and bereavement. In preparation for that role, I studied the psychology of grief, identifying in that study the elements of loss, anger, guilt, and, not infrequently, even a sense of relief that are a part of human grieving. In grief situations I practiced these learnings in my efforts to assist those who mourn to walk through that valley and to find a way back into creative life and healing.

As a pastor I sought during the period from death through the funeral itself simply to listen and to be helpful in arranging details.

The real grief work begins some two weeks later after family and friends return to the routines of their own lives and the bereaved begins the task of adjusting to new loneliness and new circumstances. My assumption was that the grieving persons had to do the major work of healing for themselves. The pastor's task was only to assist that process. I still think that to be the case.

The missing component in my pastoral knowledge in those years was some first-hand understanding of how grief looked from the inside of the bereaved person. If the pastor's task was to assist in the healing process, what were the steps through which the bereaved had to walk, or the tasks that only the bereaved could accomplish for himself or herself? Those things I had not experienced, for I had never lived on that end of pastoral ministry. This is not to say that I had not known bereavement. In my childhood I had lost a grandfather and a grandmother. But these persons, while loved, were not central people in my everyday world. Even when my own father died when I was twelve, it still did not grip my life in a primary way. My father traveled extensively in his job so most of my boyhood was lived without his being at home. So except for the effect of his death on my mother and upon the economic reality of our family, my life was changed little by that bereavement. I certainly had no comprehension of what occurred in the life of a partner when one's mate died.

Now, for almost sixteen months, I have known the meaning of that reality and I have learned many things, both profound and mundane. Because it is easier to discuss the mundane let me start there, for grief is shaped by the many ways in which the routines of life are affected. It is also determined in large measure by the personhood of the bereaved.

I am a man who was raised in a very traditional family where sexual stereotypes were both clear and accepted. In the world of my upbringing, the man did not cook or do domestic chores. Men might carry out the garbage and take care of the yard, but the kitchen was not a male sphere. Hence, when I became a widower I knew almost nothing about housekeeping, cooking, grocery shopping, or what goes into entertaining. I knew that salt and pepper were spices, but beyond those two, my ignorance was limitless. I had never heard of rosemary, oregano, or cumin, nor did I have the slightest idea of what each spice did or was supposed to do to each culinary item.

I also came to recognize that never in my life had I had any say in what I ate except on those occasions when I scanned the menu at a restaurant. My role as a child was to come to the table when the meal was ready. That was also my role as an adult and a husband. I ate whatever my mother prepared for me in my childhood and whatever my wife prepared for me in my adult life. Both were exquisite cooks. I had no reason to complain, and yet it never occurred to me that I had never had a choice in this area of my life.

When one lives alone, however, choice becomes a reality. I discovered that I had likes and dislikes. Grocery shopping became an adventure. As a widower I have yet to buy canned vegetables, except for corn and tomatoes that I use in the making of soup. I have yet to purchase frozen vegetables. The fresh vegetable counters are the places over which I linger and the varieties of vegetarian delicacies fascinate me. I did not know that lettuce came in numerous forms. What I now recognize as iceberg lettuce was the only lettuce I once thought existed. Endive, red leaf lettuce, and romaine have now enriched my life. So have the wide variety of "greens" — kale, mustard, spinach, turnip greens, and even dandelion greens have now graced my table. Brussel sprouts have become a favorite, competing on equal terms with the more familiar broccoli, green beans, asparagus, and zucchini. I have reveled in fresh beets, though by the time they have been cooked everything in the kitchen is "beet red." Potatoes have also found in my kitchen a place of honor, lending themselves as they do to a wide variety of uses.

As my fascination with vegetables rose, my dependence on meat declined. Pork is not something that I care to eat beyond a spicy country sausage that marks a festive breakfast celebration. My beef consumption cannot equal ten pounds a year. I adore lamb, but have not yet learned to cook it adequately, so I eat it only when a restaurant offers it. Fish and fowl have become the protein staples of my diet, and fish has expanded tremendously in its potential. Fresh tuna, prepared with Beaujolais wine, garlic, mushrooms, and spring onions, is an unforgettable taste treat. So are the various shellfish when cooked with lemon, butter, and a good Chardonnay.

Baking breads has also added to my palate delight, with buttermilk biscuits and corn muffins topping the list and reflecting my southern lineage. I still subscribe to that southern chef's theory that the Civil War was actually fought because the Yankees insisted on putting sugar into the cornbread.

Beyond the delight of discovering my own food tastes, I've learned about keeping house. I knew how to load and turn on the clothes drier, but no one had ever told me that one has to clean the lint tray regularly. So for one year I used the drier without emptying the lint tray. The drier first became less efficient and then began to struggle mightily. Still, I never noticed a problem. One night, in a death strain, the drier caught fire, fused the wires, scorched my clothes, and almost burned down the house. When the repairman came he showed me the lint tray, caked with the deposits of a year and spilling over and clogging the ventilating pipes. I'm sure he thought I must be the dumbest adult he had ever confronted. A new drier cost $400. It was a cheap lesson. It might have taken a new house for me to learn. Today, I keep a very clean lint filter!

In other household responsibilities I find that my tolerance for disorder in my living space is very low. A clean kitchen, a made-up bed, a living room that welcomes me and any visitor who might enter, without the offense of clutter, are essential to my sense of well-being. I have come to appreciate my home with a new intensity. It is sanctuary and warmth to me. The open fireplace, the stereo with a rack of CDs, my favorite chair, a good book, and perhaps a glass of vintage Merlot constitute a rare and deeply pleasurable evening.

Entertaining has also grown in me as a desirable activity. I have now presided over numerous dinner parties in my home, most of which I have prepared and served myself. Again, the learnings have been genuine. I did not know that tablecloths needed to be ironed. I thought they came ironed. I had never in my life seen one being ironed, and I still cannot understand exactly how they fit the typical ironing board. But iron them I now do and cringe ever so slightly when a guest spills coffee or red wine on that newly pressed surface.

I have never been particularly observant and have had no sense of beauty until now, when I am responsible for creating that beauty. I take great pride in an elegant table, set with delicate china, crystal wine glasses, and gleaming silver place settings. Polishing silver has also become an art form for me. The centerpiece is something I do not believe I have ever noticed before in my life. Now, however, flowers have become important, and although I do not understand about flower arranging, I do like a low centerpiece set off by candlesticks that is accentuated by dimming the dining room lights.

I also never noticed that the way in which the food was presented — the elegance of its presentation — added to the pleasure of the evening. A sprig of parsley is not something to be removed before eating. It needs to be appreciated as part of the ambiance of the platter.

It had been easy for me to be unaware of all that went into entertaining when my wife was alive, and I wish now a thousand times that I had recognized and affirmed this gift that she gave to me so graciously and so generously.

Loneliness is the other, and more profound, side of grieving, and its reality also created for me new learning processes. As I moved into areas that were vacated by my wife's death that loneliness was intensified. I began to see life as it might have looked to her and became cognizant of the not always creative ways in which I interacted with her world. I also recognized that the times we had together were not all that they might have been for either of us, because neither of us understood what the other was doing when we were apart. She looked to me for access to a wider world of issues and excitement. I looked to her for the peace and tranquility that were missing in my public persona. When I return home today, it is a return to an empty house, to the companionship of television, to a conversation with my own thoughts.

Not to have a life partner is to be locked almost exclusively into a professional role. It is never to escape being "the bishop." It is to be but half of a person. I have learned the wisdom of the ancient insight recorded in the book of Genesis that quotes God as saying, "It is not good for a man (or woman) to be alone." But being a widower has given me a joy and a new appreciation for certain roles that once my culture taught me were roles only women could play. It has enhanced my awareness of the potential depth that is present in a peer relationship where sexual stereotypes are broken and where sensitivities are allowed to flow freely over once set role models. One guest, rising from my table after dinner, voiced this truth when he said, "Bishop, you're going to make someone a good wife." The comment was greeted by laughter at the ironic twist of gender and stereotype. I responded that I would never marry any woman who insisted on doing all of the cooking, cleaning and entertaining. I will demand a share in each of these.

All of this is to say that bereavement can also be an occasion for growth. The person I am today is different from the person I was sixteen months ago, when my wife died. That person is less sexist, more appreciative of a wide variety of gifts, and, hopefully, capable of being a better, more interesting, and more sensitive husband.

I hope that is true because over the New Year's Day weekend I will take the vows of holy matrimony and will once again become a husband. The one who will become my wife is Christine Mary Barney. We ask your prayers and your good wishes. I trust that for us all, it will be a happy New Year.

– 7 –

Christine

January 1999

She stands only five feet six inches tall. Her hair has become beautifully gray. She has a brilliant mind that is combined with a rare sensitivity and an incredible kind of human wisdom. I marvel at her capacity to be insightful, appropriate, and loving simultaneously. I also stand in awe of her courage, her ability to confront distortions, her willingness to engage evil, and her intense and uncompromising personal integrity.

Who is this incredible person? I know her as Chrissy. Others know her as Christine. On January 1, 2000, most of the world will celebrate the arrival of the third millennium, but Christine and I will celebrate something that is to us even more spectacular. It will be our tenth wedding anniversary.

Never before have I known what it means to share life so totally with another person, but in the years of our marriage that kind of deep trust and ultimate commitment has done nothing but grow. Those who knew me in what I call my B.C. (Before Christine) days understand just how deeply she has enhanced first my humanity and second my ministry. She is not just a sustaining and loving wife, she is my editor, the organizer of my life and my outside commitments, my confidant, my partner in dreams and visions, my alter ego, and my most appreciated personal advisor. She is also much loved and valued by each of my daughters.

She is my capable stand-in. At funerals that I am not able to attend of people deeply involved in the life of this diocese, she is present to read, on my behalf, words of condolence and appreciation. In British Columbia in the summer of 1996 I was doing a series of lectures when an influenza bug felled me, reducing my voice to a whisper with laryngitis. Christine replaced me and delivered my lectures for the next three days until I was able to return. The conference did not seem to lose a thing. When I was laid up this fall with viral meningitis, she delivered a lecture for me in Houston and two lectures in Little Rock. It was, I am told, a remarkable performance.

Increasingly the church at large has recognized us as an inseparable, interchangeable partnership. In 1995, the Kanuga Conference Center invited the two of us to lead a conference that they advertised as "Conversations with Christine and Jack Spong." The conference was sold out in no time, and Christine's contributions were greeted with standing ovations. She was later invited to repeat those lectures in Mississippi, and this fall the two of us led the clergy conference for the Diocese of North Carolina in which, once again, the advertisement listed as "keynoters" Christine and Jack Spong.

Long before she became my wife she was an active Christian and devoted member of her church. She was twice elected member of the vestry of St. Peter's Church in Morristown. While a member of that same congregation, she undertook to revive the educational program for those whose ages fell between one and ninety-nine. She organized and directed that program as a full-time, unpaid volunteer until the life of St. Peter's was revived and strong enough to expand its staff significantly. She then became co-chair with Richard Shimpfky of the Christian Education Commission of the diocese. The Diocesan Education Conference was born under their joint auspices. In 1984 she was chosen for the position of diocesan administrative officer and served with distinction in that office for six years. She was asked to consider running for the position of warden of St. Peter's at about the same time we decided to get married. David Hegg, then her rector and always my close friend, was, however, not eager to have as his warden the wife of the bishop. I did not blame him. Besides, as my full-time partner, she would have time for little else.

That commitment to do ministry together has transformed my episcopacy. Christine is not only welcomed, she is now expected everywhere I go. When family responsibilities have prevented her from going with me on a Sunday confirmation visit, which has occurred less than half a dozen times in our lives together, the disappointment in the congregation is so great that we have to plan another visit to that church just so that she can be present. I have the sense that if she went instead of me, it would create no disruption at all — if she could only confirm.

The two of us have also been committed to what we call a "ministry of hospitality" in this diocese. During an average year, we will entertain about three hundred people in our home for a meal, and we will welcome about thirty overnight guests. Our home has functioned like a diocesan hotel and social center. Both of us enjoy cooking, and we do it together. We avoid getting into each other's way by a simple division of labor. I will, for example, be responsible for the first course and the dessert, and she will prepare the main meal on one occasion; for the next, we will simply reverse the roles. She is the professional chef with extraordinary skill. I am the rank amateur. However, I have been a quick learner, and now I do all of the pies and most of the soups, and I have certain dishes that are uniquely my own. We collect recipes from restaurants around the world and add them to our repertoire. At the famous Pump Room in Chicago we ran into a whipped potato dish that was unusual and memorable. When we enquired about it with much delight, the chef came to our table and shared with us its elegant simplicity. One starts with Red Bliss potatoes, which cream beautifully. With the skins left on, flecks of red adorn the final dish. To this is added chopped chives to provide flavor as well as flecks of green. Then with milk, butter, and salt to taste we cream them into a smooth, delicious dish. At the last moment we add enough horseradish to perk the dish up, but not sufficiently to reveal that horseradish has been added. It has been a hit every time. That recipe is one of our staples and one of our favorites. Our usual dinner party is a group of eight. We try to entertain our new clergy and their spouses soon after they arrive in the diocese. We also like to bring together our clergy and lay leaders with the exciting guests who grace the life of our diocese as speakers at convention or at the New Dimensions diocesan lectures held three times a year. Neither Christine nor I will ever forget a dinner party at which Bob and Terry Lahita of St. Elizabeth's in Ridgewood joined Wanda and Dick Hollenbeck (my former secretary and her husband) to help us entertain Fred and Ruth Westheimer. She is, of course, better known as "Dr. Ruth." Memories of the conversations that marked that evening still double us up with laughter.

Among our favorite social occasions is the spring luncheon we have hosted for a number of years for all our retired clergy, their spouses, and any clergy widows who are able to come. Between thirty and fifty folks who carry in their minds the oral history of this diocese arrive before noon and seldom depart before four. It is a rich and wonderful day for both of us.

Christine also has a private party for clergy spouses or partners about once a year, to which I, like all the other clergy, am specifically not invited. It is a group in which both male spouses and gay and lesbian partners of our clergy now feel quite comfortable and welcome. This has been Christine's way of saying that the spouse or partner of an ordained person has a unique life experience that needs to be both shared and celebrated. I am allowed to help prepare that meal and set up the tables and chairs, and I can also help to clean up, but I cannot be present. All of the conversations from those evenings are held by Christine to be in the sanctity of the confessional. Frequently I will become aware, from the spouse but never from Christine, that she has become pastor to a clergy spouse or partner and that she knows that person far better than I.

When I am away on a lecture series, Christine becomes a second pair of eyes and ears and interprets my audience to me as we move through the event. When we are in a hostile environment, she is almost like a bodyguard. She watches for strange behavior and any threatening presence. On two occasions she has been apprehensive of actual physical violence in a nonwelcoming group and on both occasions she has moved quietly, but effectively, to defuse the situation or to take necessary security precautions. She has walked with me through a shouting mob of fundamentalist protesters in San Diego, endured with me a bomb threat at Catholic University in Brisbane, Australia, and sat silently while I was being verbally abused in audiences in various places around the world. She has held my hand at General Convention when we walked past Fred Phelps and his anti-abortion campaigners from Wichita, Kansas, who were carrying placards proclaiming "Spong and Tutu are fag lovers." She has my trust and my love so totally that it is fair to say that I no longer know how to function as an individual apart from her. We are a team and she has called me into a whole new realm of being.

How can one speak of this kind of relationship without sounding maudlin, soupy, and sentimental? I do not know. I do know that I love her so deeply and that I live in her as she lives in me. I do know that I would give her anything I possessed, including my life if that were to be required. I also know that when our date of retirement comes on February 1 of the year 2000, the people of this diocese will feel her loss, I suspect, far more profoundly than they will feel mine. Honesty compels me to say these things publicly before that date arrives.

So thank you, my beloved and wonderful Christine, for being the person you are and for enabling me to be the person your love has created.

– 8 –

A Doughty, Delightful Figure

December 1984

On Tuesday, October 23, I was one of four hundred people who crowded into St. Peter's Church, Essex Fells, New Jersey, to listen to the 1984 Nobel Peace Prize recipient, the Right Reverend Desmond Tutu, the general secretary of the South African Council of Churches, newly elected bishop of Johannesburg, and the world's best-known Anglican bishop. Surrounded by microphones and cameras from national networks and from a host of local television and radio outlets, along with journalists from every major New York and New Jersey newspaper, this doughty and delightful figure shared with us his faith, his hope, his love, and his Lord. It was a remarkable day.

Desmond Tutu is not a large man. He controls no army and has no bodyguard. He acts from no economic power base. He has no political ambitions. He stands alone before his oppressors, armed only with personal integrity and the righteousness of his cause; yet people of every opinion, friend and foe alike, regard him as powerful. In some ways he is larger than life. He is clearly the spiritual heir of Mahatma Gandhi and Martin Luther King Jr. With the awarding of the Nobel Peace Prize, he has now broken more visibly onto the international scene and has become a near legendary force in the perpetual struggle for human justice. The fact that his roots are squarely in the Christian faith and that he carries the ordination and consecration credentials of a bishop in our Anglican Communion makes him a source of great pride to Episcopalians. There is a special joy to us in the Diocese of Newark, because Desmond Tutu is our longtime friend. He has been a visiting bishop in our diocese. He has confirmed members of our churches. He has met with the trustees of our Diocesan Investment Trust to discuss the question of social responsibility in our investments. He has spoken at our Diocesan Convention. He has lived for a month in the rectory of Trinity Cathedral. His infectious laughter has brightened the halls of our diocesan office building. The people of this diocese have prayed daily for him in his struggle against apartheid. When his passport was confiscated by the South African government and when he was arrested by South African police, our people poured out their protests in letters. They wrote to the prime minister of South Africa, to the South African ambassador to the United States, to the president and secretary of state of this country, and to the senators from New Jersey. Bishop Tutu is part of our life and we are clearly part of his. Upon being awarded the Nobel Peace Prize, he flew to South Africa to share this award with his people. But in just four days he returned to honor his long-standing commitment to be a guest lecturer in the Diocese of Newark.

I first met Desmond Tutu in July 1976. He was dean of St. Mary's Cathedral in Johannesburg, the first black priest to hold that position. I had been a bishop for only three weeks and was therefore the newest bishop in the Anglican Communion. As part of my preparation for my new episcopal duties, I was traveling first to Geneva to meet with leaders of the World Council of Churches and then to Rome to meet with Vatican leaders before representing my church in three mission consultations in the Anglican provinces of Kenya, the Indian Ocean (held on the Island of Mauritius), and South Africa. I landed in Johannesburg two days after the bloody and notorious Soweto riots. Almost three hundred black teenagers had been killed by trigger-happy South African policemen. The atmosphere was tense with fear in the white community and with grief and rage in the black community.

Dean Tutu was the voice of Soweto. He gave expression to the feelings of both grief and rage. Two weeks prior to the riots he had been the voice of prophetic warning. In an open letter to the South African prime minister, he had sought to make the government aware of the escalating tension and anger that was about to erupt among the young black people who felt white oppression so heavily and who saw no way to redress their grievances in a peaceful or political manner. These young people, Dean Tutu stated, had reached the point where they would rather die than continue to live under the pain of apartheid.

The *London Times* ran Dean Tutu's open letter as a front-page story. The government of South Africa predictably ignored the warning and the plea. The explosion came, and young black people armed with sticks and rocks offered their bodies to the murderous rain of police bullets. The South African leaders and the press blamed the "lawless youths" and hailed the police as heroes of law and order. The black South Africans found themselves outpowered and reduced to hopeless impotence; yet the tragedy brought to the nation's attention the voice, the spirit, and the courageous leadership of the indomitable Dean Tutu, whose forum would grow from Soweto to Johannesburg to South Africa to the world.

While I was in South Africa, I assisted in the consecration of Dean Tutu as bishop of Lesotho. He was the first bishop on whose head I laid my hands in consecration. At that moment the newest Anglican bishop in the world ceased to be Spong of Newark and became Tutu of Lesotho.

We met again at Canterbury, England, in 1978 during the Lambeth Conference. At this gathering of Anglican bishops from around the world, Bishop Tutu emerged as a world leader. A major issue before the bishops was the question of ordaining women to the priesthood. Many people wondered how the African bishops would vote on this issue, since the status of African women was generally quite low. Bishop Tutu, who has opposed oppression of every form, led the battle for sexual wholeness in the ordained ministry of the church. The African bishops followed his lead, and they became the crucial votes that legitimized the priesthood of women in the provinces of the Anglican Communion. It was one of Desmond Tutu's finest hours.

In 1979 Bishop Tutu moved back to Johannesburg to accept the position of general secretary of the South African Council of Churches, an ecumenical position that elevated him to the status of the leading Christian voice of his nation. In May 1979 he was the featured speaker at the Special Convention of the Diocese of Newark that voted to raise $6 million for the national Episcopal Church ACTS/VIM (A Committee to Serve/Venture in Mission) capital campaign.

In the intervening years we have stayed in close correspondence. In 1981 Bishop Tutu accepted an invitation to return to Newark as a speaker for the New Dimensions lecture series. The South African government revoked his passport and prevented him from leaving his country. On his behalf I flew to Washington for an hour-long audience with the South African ambassador. It did not result in a new passport, but I did write an article about that conversation, which was published in a national magazine and which added, I hope, to the awareness the American people have of the evil of apartheid. It also exposed, I trust, the pathological reasoning of those who seek to justify the attempt to build a nation on that evil premise.

Bishop Tutu has worked tirelessly for his people. He has not scored impressive victories. Apartheid is tenacious. But he will win. Freedom will come to the black people of South Africa. That is not in doubt. The only thing in doubt is whether that freedom will come through peace and goodwill or after violence and bloodshed. Desmond Tutu may be South Africa's last and best hope. By awarding the Nobel Peace Prize to this man, the world is expressing a yearning that nonviolence will in fact topple systems of oppression, that humanity will prevail over inhumanity, that the unarmed and powerless Desmond Tutu will achieve a victory over the armed and powerful South African government and thus strike a blow for liberty everywhere. To many that may seem a crazy dream. To those who know Desmond Tutu, it is a compelling and winning vision. I for one bet on this man.

– 9 –

Farewell, My Treasured Friend

March 1997

I flew to Austin, Texas, to tell him goodbye, to thank him for all that he has given me: friendship, advice, inspiration, courage, a role model of leadership and commitment. This man also had a vision of what the church could be that was enormous. A radically dedicated faith community could change the world, he said. It was the task of that church, in his mind, to be an outpost of God's Kingdom and a sign of God's presence among us.

For more than thirty years this man has been my father in God, my mentor, my benchmark in what it means to be a bishop in the church of God. His name is John Elbridge Hines. From 1964 to 1973 he was the presiding bishop of our church.

In the years of our friendship hardly a week went by that we did not talk by telephone. For the last two months that contact has been impossible. His body has deteriorated. He lives in his own interior world. He does not even read his mail. His death is imminent. So significant has this man been to me that I could not let him or our friendship simply fade away into nothingness. So I flew to Austin, I entered his room, engaged his eyes, watched the faintest trace of a twinkle that once brightened his face as we would talk. I told him what he has meant to me. I rehearsed those moments when he had stood at my side in difficult decisions. I expressed my appreciation for those parts of my episcopal career that he had inspired. I also wanted him to know that his ability to accept without bitterness the slings and arrows of those enraged by his witness had made it possible for me to do the same as part of my witness.

John Hines was born in Seneca, South Carolina, the son of a Presbyterian country doctor and a brilliant Episcopalian mother. From his father he learned to identify with the poor and the dispossessed and to discern the times so accurately that he could act today on that which was inevitable tomorrow. From his mother he received his devotion to the church, his keen intelligence, and his quick, engaging wit.

From the time he entered school at age five, he was always a leader in his world. He led his class academically, captained the football, basketball, and tennis teams, and was president of the student body. Entering the University of the South at the ripe old age of sixteen, he debated whether or not to seek a career in medicine, which was his father's passion, or in the church, which was his mother's passion. No matter how big or complicated his world became, he had the ability to rise to the top. In order he was president of the student body at his university and then at his seminary. He was elected bishop of Texas at age thirty-five and presiding bishop of the Episcopal Church at age fifty-four. He shaped the life of this church more dramatically than any single person in this century. He led us all beyond the limits of our fears into countless new frontiers. He called into being a whole generation of new leaders who are today in key positions throughout the church. He made us proud to be Christians and Episcopalians and proud that we had chosen to follow our callings into the priesthood.

In 1964, when the General Convention of our church met in St. Louis to choose a new presiding bishop, the common wisdom was that the choice would be the Right Reverend Stephen Bayne, the Anglican executive officer and former bishop of Olympia. He was by far the best known of the three nominees. The others, Emrich of Michigan and Hines of Texas, had no national reputation. There were two nominations from the floor — Louttit of South Florida and Wright of East Carolina. Bishop Bayne led on every ballot but the final one. Despite his enormous ability, he was perceived as a bit imperial, a bit pompous, a bit distant. He appeared to enjoy the trappings of ecclesiastical power a little too much. It was a fatal flaw. John Hines was third in the first four ballots, second on the fifth, and elected on the sixth. The church was stunned by the choosing of this relatively unknown new leader, but the process of getting to know Doc Hines began in earnest.

I met this man first in 1966 on a tennis court in Lynchburg, Virginia. He was visiting our little Diocese of Southwestern Virginia and my bishop, William Marmion, had asked me to arrange a tennis match. I did, and my bishop and I lost to John Hines and a layman named Billy Fix. It was not deliberate. This presiding bishop was very competitive.

Those were difficult days in the life of this nation. Racial tensions were high. John Kennedy had been assassinated. The disillusioning war in Vietnam was sapping the nation's strength. The cities of this land were exploding in racially tinged violence. It was not a time for business as usual. As one city after another went up in flames, John Hines turned this church to a new mission field. With a member of his staff named Leon Modeste, he walked the streets of Bedford-Stuyvesant and other urban centers of this nation to confront personally the reality of urban and racial pain. In his mind a church that did not engage these issues would die of irrelevance. So at his first General Convention in Seattle in 1967 he called this church to take its place "humbly and obediently at the side of the poor and the dispossessed." The prepared budget of the national church was scrapped. The General Convention Special Program was born to invest the church's resources, not in structures of the church, but in indigenous community groups designed to bring dignity and power to the people they represented. It became the church's operative theological principle that an empowered person could never be a dehumanized, marginalized, or oppressed person. Empowering the powerless became the very shape of the church's ministry. It was a breathtaking moment in church history.

The crescendo of this movement grew through the South Bend Special Convention of 1969, where the church faced its role in sustaining the corporate power of racism. This was a time when black people were demanding reparations, and the church first used its shareholder power to force corporate America to face its own racism. The move to have American business divest itself of its role in supporting apartheid in South Africa was, for example, a John Hines initiative.

Across this land, as the implications of their church's stand for justice began to be felt, the people in the pews recoiled. John Hines was the symbol of this dramatic shift in direction, and the vilification he received was unbelievable. Editorials throughout America, but especially across the South, excoriated him as a communist, a destroyer not just of the church, but of "society's values." The hatred flowed so freely from those "pew-sitting Christians" that bodyguards were hired for this presiding bishop and a bulletproof vest was worn by him at the General Convention in Houston in 1970.

In Virginia, where the *Richmond Times Dispatch* was one of the most vicious editorial critics of the church's ministry to the poor and the church's challenge to the racist patterns of the past, I found myself called to defend my church and my presiding bishop in a very public way, including running a full-page paid ad in that same newspaper.

At the Louisville General Convention in 1973 John Hines tendered his resignation as presiding bishop. It was to be effective in 1974. At that same convention, I was elected to the Executive Council of our church. I would have six months to serve with John Hines on the church's national "vestry" before his successor, chosen in reaction to his dramatic and stretching leadership, would return our church to its path of risking nothing while claiming a new and benign piety. In some sense I would become a part of the Hines voice that would remain at the national level of our church's life when his leadership departed.

Far more than his successor realized the church traveled for years on the energy of the Hines years. The new leadership fought a constant rearguard action to slow it down. They failed. Women were ordained irregularly in 1974 and canonically in 1977. The Prayer Book was revised in 1976. The debate about the place of gay and lesbian people in the life of the church began in 1979. John Hines led this church for at least another decade beyond his actual retirement.

Our friendship developed significantly during those years. My writing career had become established, and I approached him about the possibility of being designated his biographer. I wanted to show how effective leadership could transform an institution. He finally agreed. For the next two years I studied his life. I listened to him tell his own story for countless hours. I was given access to all but his confidential mail. I interviewed his friends and his enemies. I traveled to Seneca to speak with his teachers and neighbors. I followed the trail of his priesthood from St. Louis and Hannibal, Missouri, to Augusta, Georgia, and Houston, Texas. To understand his episcopacy I devoured the journals of the Diocese of Texas from 1945 to 1964. I had probably another year of research to do when Newark elected me to be its bishop in 1976. With great sadness I stored my seventy hours of taped interviews and stacks of notes and printed matter until I could find the time to return to this project. I never did. I gave my research to a Texas priest named Ken Kesselus, and he wrote the powerful story of the Hines years published in 1995 under the title *Granite on Fire*. I did, however, have John Hines as the guest of our diocese at nine consecutive conventions, and he advised me on every issue of my career, from homosexuality to physician-assisted suicide. In retrospect I now know that my study of his life prepared me for the role of leadership that being bishop of Newark required. I have indeed been a bishop in the style of John Hines, perhaps even his heir. He has remained to this day my closest friend.

I talk to young clergy and lay people today who have never heard the name of John Hines. That is inevitable. Fame is so fleeting, so transitory. But those of us who shared his time know that he was a moment of grace, and we are proud to be part of a church that could produce John Elbridge Hines.

Farewell, my treasured friend.

– 10 –

John A. T. Robinson Remembered

September 1995

One of the great mentors of my life was an English bishop and New Testament scholar named John Albert Thomas Robinson. He burst into public awareness in the late fifties when he testified before a commission seeking to ban the novel *Lady Chatterley's Lover.* For a bishop to favor *Lady Chatterley's Lover* titillated the English media, who love juxtaposing religion with sexual exposé. People were not aware at this time that this bishop of Woolwich was also a serious student and a prolific, if not yet well known, writer.

In 1962 a back ailment required that John Robinson be confined to bed for a number of months. His fertile and imaginative mind was freed from other distractions, and he wrote a little book called *Honest to God,* which appeared on the bookstands in 1963. It made the controversy about *Lady Chatterley's Lover* look pale by comparison. This book forced people to recognize that the language of traditional religion was not a language that people believed today whether they continued to use it or not.

An advance story in London's *Sunday Observer* trumpeted the headline, "Bishop says the God up there or out there will have to go." Thus, the church was launched into what came to be known as the "Honest to God Debate," and John A. T. Robinson became a household word in the English-speaking world.

That little book sold more copies than any religious book since

Pilgrim's Progress. It was translated into dozens of languages. It was discussed, not just in religious circles, but in pubs, on golf courses, and over bridge tables. It brought religion out of the churches and planted it firmly on Main Street.

One would think that the leaders of the churches would have welcomed such an initiative, but that would be to misunderstand the nature of institutional religion. The religious establishment, instead, recoiled defensively. Every would-be theologian rushed into print to denounce this book. Calls were issued for Bishop Robinson's resignation or for him to be deposed for heresy. A book of reactions to *Honest to God* was published to keep the waves rolling. It revealed just how deeply John Robinson had touched the hot buttons of religious fear that the traditional defenders of the faith struggle to conceal.

The echoes of this debate reached my ears in my small town parish in Tarboro, North Carolina. I did not rush to read the book. Reviews indicated that it quoted extensively from Rudolf Bultmann, Dietrich Bonhoeffer, and Paul Tillich. I was quite familiar with these thinkers and so I dismissed the book as a popularizing effort of no great significance. Nonetheless I placed the book on my reading schedule, and finally got to it in 1965.

I remember the day I first opened this book. Vacationing on the Outer Banks of North Carolina, I sat on the beach one afternoon with *Honest to God.* I did not put it down until I had read it through three times. I knew from that moment that my life would never be the same.

John Robinson made me aware that my childhood understanding of God would not live in my world. He forced me to face the fact that the words of both the Bible and the Creeds sound strange to postmodern people and that my faith had to grow or it had to be abandoned. I began on that day the long, tortuous, and, to this moment, not yet completed process of rethinking all of the symbols of my religious past so that I could continue to claim them with integrity. I also pledged myself never again to use pious claims that I clearly no longer believed.

This book drove me first back to the Bible. I knew that the Noah story, or the splitting of the Red Sea story, could not be literally true, to say nothing of the stories of Jesus turning water into wine, walking on water, and ascending to the heaven of a Ptolemaic universe that had ceased to exist with Copernicus. My church had prepared me poorly, I discovered, to live as a believer in a post-Copernican world, to say nothing of a world shaped by such giants as Newton, Darwin, Freud, and Einstein. The church still lived in a world of miracle and magic, where reward and punishment were meted out by God according to human deserving.

Seven years later, in 1972, this internal struggle emerged externally in the form of my first book, which was deeply shaped by the "Worldly Holiness" chapter in *Honest to God.* My publisher entitled my book *Honest Prayer* hoping, I am sure, that it would be pulled into the *Honest to God* energy that was still abroad.

In 1973 I first met John Robinson. This larger-than-life man came to speak in Richmond on the tenth anniversary of the publication of *Honest to God.* He was very British, displaying little emotion. After the session I was introduced to him. I thanked him for what his writing had meant to me. I presented him with a copy of *Honest Prayer.* We talked for a while, and then we each returned to our respective lives.

Five years later in 1978 John and I met again at the Lambeth Conference of the Anglican bishops of the world. I was now one of those bishops, and John, who had returned to Cambridge to teach New Testament, was present as a consultant. Both of us, bored by the speeches, decided to leave early and walked through the woods of Kent to discuss the New Testament. We came across a country pub and stopped to share a "pint." We even engaged in the pub game of "bowls," but all the while discussing the New Testament. It was such a pleasant experience that we decided to repeat it each day. So while the bishops were debating, John and I probed the Gospel tradition and I learned from his incisive mind.

In those years John and I both continued to write books which addressed the theme of bringing the church into dialogue with today's reality. I read everything he wrote. John Robinson's echoes were heard in me every time I spoke and certainly every time I wrote. When one reviewer referred to me as the American Bishop Robinson, I was deeply touched. After Lambeth John and I began to correspond. I yearned to bring him to lecture to our diocesan family, and finally he agreed. Six months before his scheduled appearance, however, John wrote that he had received a cancer diagnosis and had only a few months to live. He sent me a copy of the sermon he preached at Clare College, Cambridge, the Sunday after he received the diagnosis. I was deeply touched by it, though it made me aware of how lonely I would be without this kindred spirit. John died in the early months of 1983. In my grief I was pleased to be asked to write the American tribute to him published in *The Christian Century*. Someone else had recognized how important he was to me.

I did not have either John's intellectual training or his Cambridge Ph.D. Yet after his death, in a real sense, I was the only other bishop who was addressing publicly the issues he had raised. That fall of 1983 I published a book entitled *Into the Whirlwind: The Future of the Church*. It marked a watershed moment for me from which there was no turning back. It was not that it was a great book, but reading it today I discover that the seeds of every book I have written since were present in its pages.

In 1988 *Living in Sin?* came out. That book was for me the kind of birth to the wider public that the debate on *Lady Chatterley's Lover* had been for John Robinson. Because of that book and the controversy it sparked, I increasingly found myself occupying the space in which John Robinson once stood and bearing the hostility he received. Now I was the most controversial bishop in the Anglican Communion. My vocation clearly was to transform Christianity so that it could be lived out appropriately today. Each new book fueled this growing flame. Invitations to lecture began to come in from across America, as well as from Australia, Canada, New Zealand, and the United Kingdom. To be a bishop leading this debate became the heart of my vocation. Hence, I worked long hours lest I violate either the integrity of my office or of my scholarship. I could not walk away from the role for which everything in life had equipped me. I have lived this role with vigor, yearning more than once to have had John's counsel.

This past summer I returned once again to the United Kingdom on a lecture tour. I had speaking engagements in Yorkshire, Aberystwyth, Cardiff, Sheffield, Leeds, Milton Keynes, London, and Leicester. There were also breaks to allow us to visit family and friends. In one of those down times I came face to face with John Robinson once again.

We went to visit two friends, formerly members of St. Peter's Church, Morristown, who now live in a tiny, secluded village in Herefordshire. To our amazement their next-door neighbor was John Robinson's only brother, Edward. We spent an evening with him reminiscing about John's career and his influence.

My tour ended at a conference in Leicester for an organization called "The Sea of Faith," where I debated the radical English theologian Don Cupitt. To my joy a member of this conference was Ruth Robinson, John's widow. Once again we spent an evening remembering John Robinson. It was as if grace had touched me twice. The theological child of John A. T. Robinson had been welcomed home.

I have now lived and worked twelve years beyond the life span of my mentor. I have picked up and addressed some issues that never surfaced for him. It has sometimes been a lonely journey. Today I can see the horizon of my career and wonder who the next John Robinson will be.

There will always be the "John Robinson" role present in the life of the church. It will be welcomed by some, feared and hated by others. But that role is always the means by which growth and the renewal of the church is accomplished. I have been privileged to walk, however ineptly, in these footsteps.

– 11 –

I'm Just Wild about Harry!

June 1989

Some years ago the *Reader's Digest* ran a regular feature entitled "My Most Unforgettable Character." If that series were still extant, I would submit this column for their consideration. It would, however, be entitled "My Most Unforgettable Priest." My candidate for that designation would be Harry Ellsworth Smith.

Harry Smith is red-haired, rotund, and regal. He reminds me of a comic strip figure from my childhood, the Toy King. He dominates the scene in which he is present. He has strong convictions about which he is not bashful. He speaks with a voice that pierces the silence, commands attention, and demands response. He has an integrity that is awesome. He places the church that he loves and serves so far above his personal agenda that it is as refreshing as it is unusual.

In his active ministry Harry Smith never served a prestigious, socially prominent church. He entered the Episcopal priesthood when he was in his early thirties. His first two assignments were as vicar and rector of two small Illinois congregations. Both were too weak to support a full-time priest. He supplemented his income by becoming the director of a Cook County Head Start program, where he developed effective administrative skills. From there he entered the field of education, serving first as the dean of students at the Hunter

School in Princeton and later as chairman of the English department and assistant principal of the Fieldston School in New York City.

Despite his secular employment Harry still had the heart of a priest and worked that vocation out, first as part-time assistant at Christ Church, Hackensack, and later as the rector of St. Paul's, Wood-Ridge. St. Paul's was a strange rectorship. Harry received no salary save for the use of the rectory, and he served St. Paul's only on weekends and in the evenings. "A little of Harry is worth more than a lot of some people," one member of his congregation stated. The facts reveal that St. Paul's grew, thrived, and prospered under this arrangement, and when Harry departed from Wood-Ridge this church returned to a full-time, paid rectorship.

In a high-risk vocational decision Harry resigned in 1980 from both his position at St. Paul's and at the Fieldston School to become rector of St. Mark's in West Orange. No tougher assignment was ever given a priest. The former rector of St. Mark's had become schismatic over the changes in the new Prayer Book and the ordination of women. He decided to leave the Episcopal Church for a splinter church, and he sought to take St. Mark's with him. The Diocese of Newark sued to recover our property. After years of litigation, carried by this now deposed priest to the New Jersey Supreme Court, the diocese won the case and the property was restored.

On Sunday morning, September 30, 1979, I reclaimed that space for the worship of the Episcopal Church. Less than five members of the former congregation were there to receive me. We had to rebuild the Mother Church of the Oranges almost from scratch. St. Mark's had been a rather traditional Anglo-Catholic parish. That tradition needed to be affirmed, but this congregation also needed to learn to live in the present rather than in the past. It also had to learn to anticipate the future. The new rector must be a person of vision, courage, and raw strength. We had no margin for error. I knew only one man who could give it even a fifty-fifty chance of succeeding. His name was Harry Ellsworth Smith.

I went to Harry Smith. I offered him the challenge and the risk. I pledged to him that the diocese would be behind him with all the support we could muster. I assured him that if we failed to revive that church with him as the rector, I would be content with the realization that it simply couldn't be revived. My confidence in Harry Smith was complete. Harry accepted. On January 6, 1980, joined by three hundred members of this diocese, I installed Harry Smith as the rector of St. Mark's. It was a moving service displaying a corporate diocesan strength. That service remains for me today one of the highlights of my episcopal career.

Harry met this congregation in many ways. He was at heart an old-fashioned high churchman. He never wore anything but a black suit. There was never any doubt about who "the Father" was. He received communion on his tongue. I was never certain whether or not this was a liturgical excuse that he found convenient for sticking out his tongue at me in complete innocence.

He was also a powerful preacher. When Harry mounted the pulpit, people responded as if a prophet of old had proclaimed "thus saith the Lord!" He coupled this homiletical gift with pastoral sensitivity and creative management. Slowly but surely, almost brick by brick, the congregation of St. Mark's began to emerge into a new vitality. Today the average Sunday attendance is just under one hundred. It is a still small, still fragile church, but in Harry's nine years as rector the growth rate has averaged more than 30 percent a year.

Harry believed that his diocese and his parish were inextricably bound together. Parish and diocese did not, in his mind, have separate destinies nor did they live in opposition to one another. So as his gifts enriched St. Mark's so were they also freely given to this diocese. Few priests have ever shared as deeply as Harry in the leadership of a diocese. Through the Diocesan Council, the Department of Missions, and the Strategy Committee Harry has shaped our common life. Through the Stewardship Commission, the ACTS/Venture in Mission campaign and the Capital Structures campaign, Harry has helped to place this diocese on a sound financial footing. He is one of only four persons, and at this moment the only priest, to receive the Bishop's Cross, the highest award this diocese can confer upon its leaders.

Through his strength, commitment, and leadership, Harry has been to this bishop a friend and a challenge, an ally and a protagonist, a supporter and a critic. He has also been my pastor and confidant. I admire him as I have admired few people. He approaches the pantheon in which my heroes like John Hines, William Marmion, and Desmond Tutu reside.

William Shakespeare had Hamlet observe about his father to Horatio, "He was a man, take him for all in all, I shall not look upon his like again." Those words could be just as easily applied to Harry Smith.

On June 30, 1989, Harry Smith will retire as rector of St. Mark's

Church, West Orange. For one year he and his wife, Alberta, will work as missionaries in Chapala, Mexico, with their close friends Catherine and Melchior Saucedo. Then, in 1990, retirement from the active priesthood will be accomplished.

I could never have been the bishop of Newark without Harry Smith as one of our outstanding priests. I have a sense that there will be an aching void when he leaves and a vacuum where once his leadership has been. I call upon our clergy to recognize that in the retirement of Harry Smith a major priest leader of our diocese is departing, and I invite them individually and corporately to respond to the vocation of rising up and stepping forward to take his place.

To Harry I say, well done, my brother. You have been strength to me. You have, time after time, shown me the Christ refracted through your being. I thank you for that. You have inspired me and many others to see the sacrifices of ministry and the way of the cross to be nothing less than the source of life and the pathway to God. You have given so freely of your gifts to your church, your diocese, your bishop, your parish, and your people. This diocese and this bishop will always be in your debt. You will remain for us unforgettable. We pray that the God you have served so faithfully will now sustain you in the days of your retirement. We shall not soon look upon the like of you.

– 12 –

His Name Was Ray Roberts

May 1990

His name was Ray Roberts. He was forty-eight years old. He was a priest. He graduated from the Episcopal Divinity School in Cambridge, Massachusetts. He had been both married and divorced. He was the father of a twenty-year-old son.

He came to this diocese in 1981 to be the founding vicar of the newly reopened St. Thomas' Church in Vernon. He had an exquisite artistic sense that is visible even today in the way St. Thomas' has been restored and beautified. He was a culinary expert. Dinner in his home was a memorable dining experience both for taste and ambiance. In 1986, he became the rector of St. Peter's Church in Livingston. He had a quiet pastoral manner that created confidence. He also had the ability to calm troubled waters.

In 1987, in a routine naval reserve physical, he was diagnosed as HIV positive. He died of AIDS on April 16, 1990. He was a homosexual person. His final request to me was direct and intense. "Bishop, when I die please tell my congregation that I died of AIDS and that I was a gay man. I want to be honest in my death in a way that I could not ever be honest in my life." I promised Ray that I would be true to that request.

Ray Roberts was a private person. He did not move in broad social circles. He preferred solitude. In many ways he was quite self-sufficient. When he separated from his wife, he told her that he was gay. Marriage was for him a closet in which to hide from himself and from a hostile world. It did not work for him. But being a divorced father served as an even better closet and stopped whispers in their tracks. Inside that closet he hid successfully.

Ray also shared his sexual orientation with his father, now deceased, but he swore him to secrecy. He did not tell his mother, his brothers, or his sister. He felt there would be hurt or that they would not understand. The religious tradition in which the family lived tended to view homosexuality as depraved and sinful. He did not tell his son. Ray felt that he was too young and would not comprehend.

He did not tell his bishop. The price was simply too high. The church has always been willing to receive the gifts of its gay priests, but it has seldom been willing to acknowledge with honesty their presence or to affirm their being. The church that Ray knew would rather participate in a cruel denial. That denial goes on today. The church's word to homosexual people is forthright. You cannot be who you are. You must, therefore, pretend to be who you are not. That is the price of survival in this institution.

Such has been the message of the church for years to gay and lesbian persons. It has been delivered in shrill and judgmental terms. Ordination to the priesthood is open only to those gay and lesbian people who are willing to be dishonest and hide. If one is honest, then ordination is forbidden, lest the wrath of the disturbed hierarchy descends in rage. Included in that disturbed hierarchy are both gay bishops and bishops who have quietly and secretly ordained "practicing" homosexual persons.

Ours is a strange church, issuing double messages and exhibiting little moral character on this issue. This duplicity is recognized widely both inside and outside the church, and it does not issue in respect for either the church or the hierarchy. Still, this dishonest ecclesiastical game is played and in the face of this game those who wish to survive learn to lie. Ray Roberts learned to do just that, so he never told his bishop about his homosexuality.

When Ray moved to the Diocese of Newark he continued to play that game with me, his new bishop. He and I were friends, but it was not a close or a deep friendship. I enjoyed my visits to his church and to his home, but they were largely polite pro forma occasions. Ray's loneliness seemed exaggerated in Vernon. It was an isolated community. There are very few single people in that part of our state. I often wondered how appropriate that assignment was for a single man.

When he moved to Livingston, I was pleased for him. That move brought him nearer the population center of this diocese and in some ways broke his isolation. Yet, in his typical manner, he maintained his private nature and began in a pastorally sensitive way to lower the tensions that existed in St. Peter's parish and to build a trust that had been lacking in that church. He preached with apparent sincerity. His business training enabled him to administer the affairs of his parish with skill. He was generally appreciated by his congregation. When he became ill, this appreciation was acted out with obvious caring. When his illnesses lingered, people wondered. When his illnesses reoccurred again and again there was a lively concern with perhaps a few haunting questions that began to circulate. But the primary response was still one of tenderness and caring in which most of the people of his congregation shared.

About one week before Ray's death, I met with the vestry of St. Peter's Church and shared with them the medical opinion that Ray would not survive. I also made them aware of the nature of the disease and, following Ray's instructions, I told them the fact that Ray had so closely guarded as the secret of this life. On the night after his death, I met and talked with the entire congregation of St. Peter's — again sharing both the medical facts and the truth that Ray had wanted to be known.

The emotions and feelings that greeted this revelation ran the gamut of possibilities. There was pain, grief, fear, love, concern, anger, and continued attempts at denial. For some members of his church Ray's gentle, loving life succeeded in putting a different face on such words as "homosexual" and "AIDS." For others, Ray was a person who had been invited deeply into the secret places of their lives. They had trusted him, and out of that trust had grown a genuine fondness. This experience now collided with the realization that they had not really known this man at all. For many an intense inner dialogue began in which this new and intensely personal knowledge began to interact with the prejudiced stereotype that had dwelt in them as long as they could remember.

My grief for Ray Roberts is on two levels. First, I grieve for the human being who was my friend and one of my clergy whose creative energies were terminated before he had entered the fiftieth year of his life. Secondly, I grieve over the realization that the prejudice and fear in which I too have shared had killed Ray Roberts long before the moment of his death.

I am now convinced by both my academic study and my pastoral experiences that homosexuality in perhaps 95 percent of its expression is not a matter of choice. It is rather a given in life over which no one has any control. It results from a combination of prenatal forces that are both random and constant. Statistics consistently seem to demonstrate that some 10 percent of the population of human beings in the entirety of human history have been gay and lesbian persons and that it will forever be so. Recent studies reveal that homosexuality is also present in about the same proportions among the higher mammals. It appears to be a minority expression of sexuality that must be considered normal in the sense that the figure of 10 percent appears to be the norm for all Homo sapiens, in all times and places.

Yet, historically, the presence of this phenomenon has elicited fear, prejudice, and explanations that cast irrational blame in many different directions. These negative emotions have resulted in violence and murder as well as loss of jobs, homes and family for gay and lesbian people. The homosexual person has had to live with public and private condemnation. He or she has been defined as sick, depraved, subhuman, distorted, demon possessed, and evil. The Bible has regularly been quoted to justify this hatred and judgment. Living with these intense levels of negativity is never easy. The collective weight of judgment in both church and society is so heavy that many a homosexual life is broken, distorted, and even in some sense forced out of life by the judgment. Homosexual persons commit suicide in far higher percentages than do heterosexual persons. Alcoholism is 300 percent higher among gay males than among the whole population.

Another way of dealing with this rejecting presence is seen in the development of ghettoized subcultures where gay and lesbian people can snub their noses at the straight world that ostracized them. These countercultures sometimes exhibit behavior patterns consciously designed to offend their rejectors. For many people this subculture and the behavior patterns they confront in the publicity stemming from this lifestyle is all they know of homosexuality, and this feeds both their distorted stereotypes and their fears.

Other gay and lesbian people prefer to hide in the midst of the straight world. Some hide inside marriage. Some hide inside a religious tradition that requires an unmarried status. Some hide in quiet dishonesty. If they have an intimate relationship, it is secret, furtive, and hidden. It should surprise no one that permanency in relationships is hard to achieve in a world of hiding. It is also difficult to develop stability in intimate relationships when the two people involved have their egos and their self-respect shredded daily by a hostile and ignorant world. Lives thus broken by these pressures in turn also feed the negative stereotype that enables homophobic people to assume with confidence that all homosexual persons are promiscuous or sick.

For a tiny segment of the gay and lesbian population there is the dawning possibility of accommodation inside the accepted life of the social order. They have "come out" in an honest way to a small number of special friends. As acceptance grows that number expands and with it wholeness grows where fear and ignorance once reigned supreme.

In his forty-eight years of life Ray Roberts never achieved this breakthrough. Neither his church nor his world seemed to him capable of accepting him as he was. The sad truth is that he was probably right in that judgment. "I have lived a lie," Ray stated to me less than a month before his death. "No one has known the real Ray Roberts," he continued. "Now I am dying, and in a real sense I have never been allowed to live." There was no bitterness in these words or in this man. There was simply resignation and the realization that perhaps in his death he could find the forum for his long repressed yearning to be honest. Time had run out for him. Perhaps, however, Ray's honesty would succeed in pushing back the barriers of prejudice just a little bit, and others who were caught by the same forces that had encircled Ray's life might have a different opportunity and because of that a different ending for their lives.

That was Ray's hope, and that hope fueled his dying wish that I say these things. You and I need to be aware that we are members of a society and a church that by our words and deeds, our denial and rejection, our dishonesty and violence, kill our gay and lesbian brothers and sisters. We kill them every day. Among those vivisectioned victims are those whom we have, in hiding, ordained to serve us as priests.

It is my hope and my prayer that by following Ray's final request of me to make public the disease of which he died and the reality of the person he was, that I have given voice to him anew and in some small way I have given back to him the honesty that the church required him to sacrifice as the price of his ordination and his career.

We commit Ray Roberts to the care and keeping of the God we worship, a God to whom there are no outcasts and a God to whom none are judged to be unloved. We Christians assert that we see the human face of this God in a Christ who reigns with outstretched arms and welcome from a cross to which the cruelty of humanity has nailed him. From that painful throne this Christ issues an invitation: "Come to me all who travail and are heavy laden. I will give you rest." It is a scandalous outrage that the church that claims to be the body of Christ cannot make good the inclusiveness of this invitation.

May God grant to Ray Roberts the divine gift of life and peace and may God call this church of ours out of our blatant hypocrisy and into the honesty of both truth and integrity.

– 13 –
Wanda
December 1993

I shall never forget the first time she came into my office. A committee of our core staff that had done the preliminary screening for the position of executive secretary to the bishop presented me with three finalists. It was now my turn after personal interviews to make the decision. I had read the resumes of each candidate. One stood out for a variety of experiences that ranged from raising chickens to building totem poles. This candidate also possessed exceptional office skills and managerial ability. Her name was Wanda. She entered my office with what I came later to recognize as her characteristic level of energy. She was small and wiry, but she was a commanding presence. The time went by quickly and pleasantly. When the interview concluded, I was sure that this was the person whom I would choose. Our interviewing committee, I soon discovered, had also ranked her number one. On March 9, 1984, Wanda Hollenbeck became the bishop's executive secretary, and for ten years she has put her personal stamp on the life of the Diocese of Newark and upon my entire career. On January 1, 1994, she will join her husband in his retirement, and together they will move to Pennsylvania. An incredible era in my personal life will on that date come to an end.

Wanda has been my public face to churches, to the press, to a wide variety of callers expressing every emotion from tearful gratitude to angry outrage. She has worked patiently to schedule my busy life for everyone's convenience, and no matter where I go in the diocese, the nation, or the world people speak of Wanda with deep appreciation and ask to be remembered to her.

She has shared with me the joys and sorrows, the ups and downs, the excitement and pain of many moments. Wanda understood the long illness that preceded my first wife's death and the bereavement that followed. She and her husband were also in my home with four other close friends in November of 1989 when I uncorked a bottle of champagne and proposed a toast to Christine Barney, who had agreed to become my wife. Beyond our respective children these six people were the first to know of this impending marriage. This indicates better than anything I can relate how very close Wanda had become to me and indeed to Chris.

In the decade that she has directed the bishop's office this diocese has moved from relative anonymity into being perhaps the best-known diocese in the Anglican Communion. She lived through both the destruction heaped upon this diocese by irresponsible priests and the joy of seeing three of our diocesan clergy elected to the office of bishop and five others become official nominees for that office. She watched three of our clergy become deans of cathedrals and others move to crucial positions of parochial leadership in such dioceses as Southern Virginia, New Jersey, Western Massachusetts, Western Michigan, Connecticut, and Delaware. She saw ordained women being elected to key positions, including the rectorship of our third largest parish. She was in place to see our diocesan task forces bring in reports that challenged the whole church on such subjects as human sexuality, the environment, what it means to call the Bible the Word of God, the future shape of the church, the church's ministry to seniors and children, and finally our corporate efforts to define the unique claim of the Christ in a pluralistic world. Each report stretched the emotional boundaries of our diocese and forced the church at large to engage these issues openly and honestly. Wanda rode with us the tide of congratulation and anger that accompanied the ordination of an openly gay man to the priesthood. That ordination became a moment of defining truth for this diocese. Though it spoke an incredible word of welcome to many in the metropolitan New York area, it also caused the House of Bishops to honor this bishop by narrowly voting to disassociate its membership from him. But less than a year later the General Convention vindicated this diocese by refusing to write these prohibitive prejudices into canon law. The telephone calls and letters that accompanied these events would have overwhelmed anyone other than Wanda.

Internally Wanda rejoiced in the election of Petero Sabune as dean of our cathedral. He was a man who had always been one of her favorites. She was not embarrassed to have favorites. She grieved when Harry Smith retired to Mexico. He was always a welcome visitor in her office, as were Elizabeth Kaeton and many others.

Wanda was the glue that kept the Cathedral House staff together. She got to know every person who worked there personally. People turned to her instinctively with both work-related problems and personal stories.

Each month Wanda and I had to produce a column like this one for *The Voice*. The subject matter always presents itself out of our common life. Sometimes I explore a burning contemporary issue like health care or quality public education; on other occasions I seek to interpret an event that occurs in the church at large. Sometimes I write a personal profile on a priest or even on my mother. On still other occasions I will chronicle a personal experience that engages my attention like my visit to a Buddhist Temple in China or the time I was mugged. The first draft of this column is one that only Wanda could decipher. It is almost always one or two pages longer than the space available. Authors are not good editors of their own material, but Wanda has become a good remover of excess words and phrases. She began this task with tender sensitivity but has graduated to eager editorial surgery.

She also worked with me on my books. Every book I've written as a bishop has first been part of our diocesan lecture series. Frequently they followed the subject of our study task forces. *Living in Sin?* was my contribution to our diocesan debate on changing patterns in sexual ethics. *Rescuing the Bible from Fundamentalism* was my contribution to our diocesan study on how the Bible can be the Word of God in the twentieth century. *Born of a Woman* and the book that will be out early next spring, entitled *Resurrection: Myth or Reality?* are both further amplifications of that biblical theme. Because of the addition of our able suffragan bishop I have found time to add diocesan Advent and Lenten lectures to my schedule so that these biblical themes can be shared first with the clergy and people of this diocese before they are shared with the world at large through my books. Wanda worked on all the presentations as they grew from individual lectures into an integrated manuscript.

In every book on which we have worked together I have tried to acknowledge my debt to Wanda in the book's preface. When my next book comes out in March that acknowledgment will move from the preface to the dedicatory page. The dedication will read: "For Wanda Corwin Hollenbeck, without whom my professional life would not be complete, either as a bishop or as an author, and for whom my gratitude is overwhelming, my respect genuine, and my affection real." This is my way of saluting a unique person who has shared my episcopal career more deeply than anyone else, and in whose debt I will always live. No one has ever filled her position with such integrity, such competence, and such sheer joy.

Wanda warned me two years ago that she would not be here to the end of my career, unless I died young! When her husband retired they would want the freedom to travel. I treated that news by refusing to think about it or even to consider it. But the warnings grew more and more frequent until that fateful September day when she came into my office and said: "Jack, there is something I need to tell you." I had become deeply dependent on this lady for the very structure of my life. I have balanced an enormous work load both in the diocese and beyond because Wanda has kept the various pieces together. My briefcase is packed by Wanda with files I need, the sermon or lecture notes required, and the pertinent correspondence for every engagement I have. Wanda has brought a special grace to her job, and to my life. It will never be quite the same. Yet time moves on, and a new adventure now lies before both Wanda and me.

Transitional moments in life always have a bit of death connected to them. Of course I grieve to lose this great human being. But my primary emotion at this moment is deep gratitude that I have had the pleasure of being associated in work and of having the chance to know and to love Wanda Hollenbeck. That will always be one of the greatest privileges of my life.

PART TWO

Religion and Politics

– 14 –

English Fiscal Decisions and U.S. Policies

September 1981

England was very much in the news this summer. All of the romanticism of the ages was celebrated at St. Paul's Cathedral, London, when the heir apparent to the English throne and his queen-to-be pledged their love and exchanged their vows before the archbishop of Canterbury. The accoutrements of wealth, social position, and power were in clear evidence. The titled lords and ladies, appropriately attired, took precedence over such heads of state as Margaret Thatcher, François Mitterand, and Helmut Schmidt, to say nothing of the wife of our chief executive who was seated far below the salt.

It was a gorgeous pageant, a fairy tale come to life, filled with horsedrawn carriages, plumed attendants, and the original beefeaters. Castles were in style, and even American Express decided to rerun its "dukes commercial" inviting us not to leave our castles without our credit cards.

The honeymoon continued the pattern. The queen's royal yacht, *Brittania,* awaited the royal couple in Gibraltar for a Mediterranean cruise. Abroad the yacht was a staff of 254 people to serve the slightest wish or whim of either the prince or princess of Wales, the only two passengers.

It was for all the world a moment of fantasy, a cloistered bit of unreality that carried all the aura of romantic make-believe. Yet it really happened, as 750 million people around the world who saw it via television can attest.

There was another England in the world's attention this summer. It was an England of street rioting and burning cities. It was Liverpool, Birmingham, Manchester, and London caught in pitched battles between hordes of angry and forlorn young people and the British police. Staid old England rocked under the embarrassing impact of seeing tear gas and plastic bullets used for the first time in her domestic history against her own people. The youthful mobs had all the marks of America in the sixties, save for two things.

First, these riots were not primarily rooted in racial discord. Yes, Asians and Africans were a part of the angry crowds, but native-born white English youths were in the majority. These riots reflected economic problems far more than racial problems, and all of the pent-up frustrations of inflation, unemployment, and powerlessness in a system that had ceased to be personal broke forth in destructive frenzy.

The second difference was that the government in the United States in the 1960s was liberal and open to hear the voices of despair. The government in England at this moment is conservative and responded to this crisis with calls for law and order and with the suggestion that parents exercise stricter discipline over the rioting young people.

The present government of England has been in power for two years. It was elected by a swing to the right that America is also witnessing with a mandate to slash government spending in an attempt to solve economic woes. In the process the safety net of support for the poor has been dramatically weakened. The budget cuts fell heavily on the backs of the lowest 25 percent on the socioeconomic ladder. Once more a Western nation has discovered the fact of the radical interdependence of all human life and the incompetence of doctrinaire rhetoric or doctrinaire economic policies to solve the problems of the whole body politic.

The finery of Buckingham Palace and the wedding of the century stand on one side of England. The riots in the streets by the poor, the unemployed, and the frustrated stand on the other side of England. It is a striking contrast.

I know of no American who does not hope that the Reagan economic policy of cuts in the federal social services budget on one hand and a tax cut weighted toward the wealthy on the other will succeed in halting inflation, stimulating industry, creating jobs, and restoring hope and prosperity among all the people of America. But we cannot watch England two years after similar policies have been enacted with a sense of confidence that we are on the right path. No nation will survive when part of its population is dieting and another part is hungry.

The vision of the enormous gap between the affairs of British royalty and the affairs of British cities in the summer of 1981 is chilling, to say the least. I hope the Christians of this country are ready and willing to inform the corporate conscience of our nation so that the poor never feel that they have to stand alone.

– 15 –
Religion and the Election
October 1984

Religion is in the news in the political campaign of 1984. It has been an issue growing in importance for some time.

In 1952 the religious issue was dim and distant. The major presidential candidates were Unitarian Adlai E. Stevenson and unbaptized Dwight D. Eisenhower. (Both later became Presbyterians.) Yet, despite no explicit connection to the mainline religious heritage of this nation, no voice of concern was raised. Religion was a private matter, not a public matter; hence, no religious issue entered the campaign.

By 1960 that had changed, and the religious issue surfaced when Roman Catholic John F. Kennedy opposed Quaker Richard M. Nixon. Interestingly, the passion of the issue was focused on Kennedy's Roman Catholicism, not Nixon's Quakerism; and yet the Quaker commitment to pacifism, if followed by Nixon, would have had profound political ramifications on this nation and this world. Kennedy met his detractors by assuring them that he would not let his religious beliefs determine his public policy. The position seemed completely satisfactory to Protestants and Catholics alike in 1960.

In 1963 when John Kennedy was killed, in 1968 when Martin Luther King Jr. was killed, and in 1969 when Dwight Eisenhower died, this country was present for the church funeral services through the technology of television. We became Roman Catholics with Kennedy's family, missionary baptists with King's family, and Midwestern Protestants with Eisenhower's family. Many recovered the nostalgia for their religious past.

As this nation endured the violence of our cities, the agony of

Vietnam, and the disillusionment of Watergate, there arose a deep hunger for something else.

That hunger found expression in 1976 in Jimmy Carter, a self-confessed born-again Christian. At least part of his appeal lay in the familiar religious values he espoused with such honesty. A president who regularly taught an adult Bible class at his local church was something new in American politics.

In time others recognized the power of religious feelings in the body politic and began to position themselves to tap that pool of potential voters. In the 1980 presidential campaign, all three major candidates — Jimmy Carter, Ronald Reagan, and John Anderson — claimed to be born-again Christians. That was not an accident, for a crowded field is attracted to any issue only if its political value is clearly evident.

With Reagan's victory religion became actively politicized as he incorporated explicit religious goals into his program. To the evangelical Protestants he endorsed legislation that affirmed what were vaguely called "family values." This included vigorous support for restoring prayer to public schools and for notifying parents when teenagers sought birth control assistance from public clinics (the "squeal" rule, as it was called). Reagan openly and constantly sought the advice of such evangelists as Jerry Falwell and Jimmy Swaggart, who in turn publicly pledged their support to the Republican party.

To the Roman Catholic part of his constituency Reagan offered outspoken support for the anti-abortion amendment and went so far as to withdraw American money from international agencies working on family planning in underdeveloped nations when any of that money was used for abortion. He asked for tax credits for parents whose children were in parochial schools, and he established full diplomatic relations with the Vatican. The pope, cardinals, and archbishops were photographed with him and came to the very edge of endorsing his reelection bid publicly.

When Senator Paul Laxalt of Nevada sent a letter to evangelical ministers urging them to use their churches as registration centers for new voters, he claimed that Ronald Reagan was God's instrument chosen to recover the values of the past. The implication was that to oppose Ronald Reagan was to oppose God. The president himself encouraged this attitude when he suggested that those who opposed prayer in the public schools were in fact opposed to religion. In these instances many believed the line between cultivating a voting constituency and sinking into demagoguery was, in fact, crossed. But there was no doubt that the religious issue had power.

Nonetheless, polls show that Reagan's position on these issues met with wide approval. Voters in significant numbers, who would normally vote Democratic because of economic issues, in this election year are voting Republican because of religious issues. Through religion Reagan has made inroads with the ethnic Catholic vote of the Northeast and with the working classes of the South and West, where the evangelical movement finds its primary support. Through religion, then, workers vote with owners, labor with business. It is a bold campaign strategy — and a successful one.

The Democrats, recognizing their opponents' success with this issue, have not been hesitant to show off their own religious credentials. In the Jackson campaign, for instance, the candidate never failed to identify himself as "the Reverend" and to make sure that people saw him as an ordained minister who became a politician. Jackson built his campaign on the support of black clergy and black congregations. His campaign stops had the flavor of a religious revival, complete with invocation, Gospel music, and benediction. His speech at the Democratic convention was evangelical black preaching at its best, deeply moving to all; and to those who had never experienced southern black worship, it was fascinating, as well as a little frightening.

Senator Gary Hart, the foremost challenger to Mondale, was once enrolled as a ministerial student in the Yale Divinity School. Despite his appeal to the young, upwardly mobile professional segment of our population, he revealed in his speeches a deep familiarity with religious concepts and issues.

Democratic nominee Walter Mondale made much of his status as the son of a Methodist preacher and appropriated the religious issue by attacking Reagan and forcing him to "clarify his remarks," which is the political code phrase for correcting political mistakes.

As the 1984 campaign heated up, the Kennedy solution of 1960 no longer satisfied the Catholic hierarchy. The Roman Catholic archbishop of New York suggested that he could not understand how any Catholic could support a candidate who would allow abortion. When vice presidential candidate Geraldine Ferraro stated that she accepted the position of her church on abortion but would not force those views on her non-Catholic constituency, the archbishop pronounced this position inadequate.

The religious issue has been growing. In 1984 it has become intense. What does it mean? We live in a time of rapid change. That change sweeps over us constantly, challenging our identity at crucial points. Values are in flux, not because morality is dying, but because technology is opening new choices that defy old alternatives and stereotypes. The moral authority of religious institutions has been dissipated by the scientific revolution, which has relativized truth and reduced religious infallibility claims, either scriptural or papal, to impotence. Instant communications and supersonic travel have shrunk the globe to tiny dimensions, and in the process they have shrunk our tribal security systems into insignificance. We are scared, cut adrift, without anchor or shared values, lonely and lost. Having no future security to embrace, we have turned to the golden era of yesterday and looked for the religious security of the past. We naively hope that prayer in public schools will stop crime and juvenile delinquency, that a ban on abortion will put an end to sexual indiscretions, and that a father figure president who plays his role with expertise will restore our security.

The common wisdom is that Reagan will probably win in 1984. He certainly has gained the popular ground on the religious issues. But the problems we face as a nation and as a world do not lend themselves to simple solutions; and they will not go away, no matter who is president. Those who dare to hope that the answers are at hand in this election will be disillusioned.

In time a new religious consciousness will emerge, and we will then find the ability to let our old consciousness die, not because it is wrong, but because it is no longer appropriate. It has happened before. It is always fearful. It is rarely fatal. In 1988 there will be another presidential campaign. I look for the religious fervor to fade. I hope we are not so rash as to pour into the concrete of legislation or constitutional amendment the passion and foolishness that infuse the religious issues of 1984.

– 16 –

Lunch at the White House

September 1987

It began with a telegram signed by George P. Shultz, secretary of state. He invited me to join a group of religious leaders in Washington to discuss the crises precipitated by proposed congressional budget cuts in the area of foreign aid. His letter suggested that serious moral issues were at stake in these cuts and that the administration had to marshal a constituency that would fight against these cuts. Leadership people in various segments of life were being invited to hear the administration's point of view. This particular day was to be set aside to talk with the nation's religious leaders.

There was no question that the administration took that day seriously. Thirty people representing Protestant, Catholic, and Jewish traditions gathered at 10:30 a.m. in the Roosevelt Room of the White House, where we were welcomed by Jay Morris, the acting head of the Agency for International Development (AID), who then introduced Vice President George Bush. The vice president talked for about fifteen minutes and then proceeded to answer our questions. Questions and answers alike revealed the administration's problem. Foreign aid is involved in humanitarian efforts to deal with hunger, economic development, and disease eradication, all of which have traditionally had the support of the religious community. But foreign aid is also an arm of the foreign policy of the government and includes military aid and the building of national security. Indeed, some 60 percent of all foreign aid falls into this latter category. Therefore, a vote for increased foreign aid is also a vote for the Nicaraguan Contras and a vote for the anti-terrorist activity that has Mr. Bush involving this nation in the scandals of Iranscam. Mr. Bush defended his policies as best he could but the questions did not let up. He was on the defensive from start to finish. When the vice president departed we were introduced to the second-in-command of the newly restructured National Security Council, Lt. Gen. Colin Powell, a very impressive and articulate black general who had recently come to Washington from Germany to be the first deputy to Frank Carlucci, the director of the NSC. Vacancies were created in the council by the resignation of John Poindexter and the dismissal of Lt. Col. Oliver North. General Powell focused on the need for security before any humanitarian effort could achieve success. But he still seemed to be infected with President Reagan's "evil empire" concept that assumes that Americans are the good guys and Russians are the bad guys. In a nice and quite sincere way he hinted that the religious leaders present and religious leadership in general are naive in their failure to understand the nature of evil and the necessity for strong deterrence. This nation is committed, he stated, to the support of democracy around the world.

My mind flashed back to Vietnam. Was democracy what America

was undergirding there? Was that the goal for which fifty thousand American lives were sacrificed? Were President Thieu and Vice President Ky the champions of democracy? Why then did they never seem to have popular support? Is it not generally agreed today that Ho Chi Minh would have won any free election? Now that this nation is no longer bleeding in that war, what happened to all those dire predictions of things that would occur if we lost or withdrew? Vietnam seems to be at peace. The Vietnamese people are busy rebuilding their nation. Their government appears to be remarkably free from both Russia and China. The domino theory has been proved false, and this nation has actually begun a trade relationship with Vietnam. The major casualty of the colonial foreign policy that produced Vietnam, other than the lives of those killed and wounded, was the despair created in the very soul of America. The loss of pride and the disillusioned generation are still present in our midst. After the further insults of Watergate, of bribes in exchange for hostages, of illegal behavior in the basement of the White House, of sex and corruption among television evangelists, and of the escapades of presidential candidates, idealism in this country is struggling to survive. The questions the religious leaders asked General Powell revealed that the rhetoric of our government was thin and no longer believable — perhaps an inevitable result of the abuse of trust!

General Powell was followed by Charles Redman, the assistant secretary of state for public affairs, a man well known to the American public as the spokesperson to the press for the State Department. He is a bright, articulate person who handles himself well in dialogue. It was his task to make us aware of what would be lost if the proposed cuts in foreign aid were to become law. It was fascinating to note that in none of his examples was humanitarian aid mentioned. What would be lost was rather our ability to secure our embassies around the world, our ability to counter communist propaganda through such things as the United States Information Agency and the Voice of America, our ability to continue our war on terrorism and to stop the flow of drugs into this nation. None of these are unworthy goals of this nation's foreign policy, but they do not represent humanitarian aid. When the identity of the five nations that receive the lion's share of America's foreign aid turned out to be Israel, Egypt, Turkey, Pakistan, and El Salvador, the questions became even more pointed. The aid to Israel and Egypt is in compliance with the Camp David Accord. Turkey and Pakistan are important to us militarily — we give them aid, they provide us with bases with which to encircle the Soviet Union. El Salvador is the primary conduit through which aid flows to the Contras. By way of contrast, any aid given to the starving masses of the sub-Sahara, Ethiopia, and drought-afflicted Mozambique is minuscule.

When the priorities revealed in the Foreign Aid Appropriations Bill were pointed out, the undersecretary responded by noting the importance of security to this nation. No one had disputed that. Yet this was hardly the proper basis on which to appeal to the religious leaders for political assistance under the guise of being humanitarian.

Mr. Redman added one further gratuitous comment. The United States has done more than any other nation in the world to dismantle apartheid in South Africa, he stated. I sat there wondering why the black leadership of South Africa was so totally unaware of this great assistance. Why would Archbishop Desmond Tutu in desperation say after Mr. Reagan refused to back economic sanctions, "The West can go to hell?"

At the conclusion of the morning's agenda, we moved to the State Department for a lovely luncheon. My dining partner was Alan Keyes, assistant secretary, International Organizations Bureau of the Department of State. Keyes, a native of Sacramento, California, and a Harvard Ph.D. in political science, is a brilliant and articulate young Reaganite. He is also black. I referred to the comment on South Africa made by Assistant Secretary Redman that morning. It was like throwing a victim to a hungry lion. Mr. Keyes leapt to the defense of South Africa and excoriated Archbishop Tutu, proclaiming that he represented no one. He argued vigorously that sanctions and divestment were wrong, and that the blacks of South Africa had been making enormous progress, which has now been set back by do-gooders like the church leaders and liberal white politicians. I asked which American black politician might share his point of view. This precipitated a vigorous attack on Jesse Jackson, though I had not mentioned his name. I had in mind people like Leonard Coleman, secretary of community affairs in the administration of Thomas Kean, Republican governor of New Jersey, Sharpe James, the outstanding black mayor of Newark, Andrew Young, mayor of Atlanta, William Gray, congressman from Philadelphia, or any member of the black congressional caucus. All of these Mr. Keyes quickly dismissed as uninformed. They were people who played on the apartheid issue to gain political power in this country, he suggested. I asked why the South African government was so violent in its opposition to sanctions and divestment if all it did was to make the Afrikaners wealthy, as he had stated. He did not answer. He seemed quite content, rather, to blame the movement to impose sanctions for the violence that he predicted would soon overwhelm South Africa. His voice rose, his passions erupted. He interrupted me constantly and he filibustered me from soup to fruit. Aware that Mr. Reagan had searched for a black American to appoint as ambassador to South Africa I inquired why Mr. Reagan had not appointed him. He certainly held with vigor the Reagan point of view. Mr. Keyes responded that he had been offered the position and had turned it down. I shuddered to think of the disillusionment he would have brought to the hopes of black South Africans had such an appointment been made. I also cannot believe that Mr. Keyes would have been confirmed by the Senate. He was a fascinating man. At last I had met a brilliant, articulate black Reaganite.

Before we adjourned, Secretary George Shultz addressed the gathered group and responded to our questions. He is a man of generous spirit, conspicuous integrity, and a clear set of values. He made his case well, but at its heart it fell into the same "evil empire" pattern. We are an open, gregarious people who like to mix with our neighbors, he argued. The Soviets are a closed society, he continued. They are untrusting people who are skilled at spying because they do it to each other all the time. This difference, he suggested, explains why this nation builds embassies in the center of the action while the Soviets prefer to build fortress-like embassies in the outlying districts of foreign capitals. Inside those fortresses they set up their own community life and venture forth to mingle with other people only for sinister purposes. The secretary clearly believed his own message and was surprised when it was questioned. The great need for foreign aid to be sustained at present levels, he suggested, was to make our open embassies in the center of life safe from terrorist attacks. It was a revealing comment.

My mind journeyed back to 1967, when I had been a guest of the American embassy in Quito, Ecuador. That embassy was surrounded with barbed wire and had jagged broken glass embedded in the concrete that covered the top of its very thick walls. It hardly looked like an open embassy out of which great mingling with the people occurred. That was twenty years ago, long before terrorist attacks on embassies became a popular foreign sport.

The day adjourned at 2:30 p.m. and I took a cab to the airport. I had seen the Reagan administration at work — the vice president, the secretary of state, the undersecretary of state for public affairs, the first deputy in the National Security Council, and a black State Department undersecretary who had been offered a sensitive ambassadorship. These leaders were all decent men, well educated, and, I am sure, well meaning. But the day confirmed my worst fears about this administration, and it enabled me to understand why the Iran/Contra scandal was almost inevitable. There is a myopia among our nation's leaders that rises from a distorted vision of reality. The leaders of this administration are so convinced of the sinister evil present in the Soviets in particular, and in the communist system in general, that they are incapable of seeing their own weaknesses. The defeat of communism in their minds is so virtuous a goal that it makes any tactic acceptable and even righteous, including the tactic that led to the illegal sale of arms to the Nicaraguan Contras. Yet, the lesson of history is that communism is rarely defeated on a military basis alone. Has this administration not yet recognized the fact that even with all of America's military and economic power this nation was still not able to impose its way of life upon the Vietnamese? The government we sought to undergird in that tragic land never had popular support. Even in a dictatorship some consent of the governed, some sense that the needs of the people are being addressed, must be present. We fail to remember that Adolf Hitler had a powerful base of popular support when he came to power in Germany. So indeed did Castro in Cuba, Lenin in Russia, and Mao in China. The conditions upon which they fed, the circumstances from which they drew power made them viable options in a civil struggle. The Soviets will not be defeated in the developing countries of this world by the infusion of American military aid to those forces who oppose the communists. They will be defeated when the cesspools of injustice and exploitation are removed, when ruling oligarchies are convinced that a new balance must be struck between personal wealth and corporate good, and when the little people are empowered to control or share in the creation of their own national destinies.

Senator Joseph McCarthy has been dead since 1957. His spirit, his fear, and his paranoia about communism, however, are still heard in the echoes and assumptions of Washington's most powerful people. The post–World War II mentality that sees the East-West struggle in terms of Armageddon, that consigns the Eastern bloc of nations to the "evil empire," that assumes that our competition with communism is a fight between good and evil, virtue and demons, freedom and slavery, represents the vestiges of a still potent McCarthyism.

In economic competition virtue cannot be claimed by anyone.

Each side uses the weapons available to win the struggle, and each side tries to make its cause reasonable, plausible, and ethical. So America invades Grenada, bombs Libya, and funnels arms illegally to the Contras while Russia invades Afghanistan, supports Castro, bugs our embassy, and continues its relentless historic push into the Middle East.

National security is not to be ignored, but it also cannot with any credibility be romanticized and called humanitarian aid. Foreign aid will inevitably support the foreign policy goals of the United States. We are not a uniquely generous nation. Other countries in the world give a higher percentage of their gross national proceeds to foreign aid than does the United States. If the aid we do give is predicated on the assumption that evil is incarnate only in the Soviet Union, that assumption is delusional. How surprising it would be to discover that the same delusion motivates the Soviet Union in its policies toward the West. Is it not time to set such delusions aside? But can that ever be done so long as either side holds a bifurcated view of reality?

It is apparent to me that the military establishments of both power centers have been created by the same irrationality. Both sides stand in this tiny world with mighty armaments aimed at the heart of those perceived to be their enemies. Both are dedicated to protecting their virtuous way of life from being infiltrated by the sinister forces that oppose them. Each side believes that its opponent alone is the source of the world's evil. Accompanying this distortion is the strange assumption that a cherished way of life can somehow be protected by the stockpiling of atomic arsenals. That is sheer insanity. If either combatant goes to war to protect its system both system and humanity will die. Yet we have been so trapped in this tribal way of thinking that it remains the operative assumption of both major powers. To many people, it does not even yet appear ludicrous. Those who do see are frequently dismissed by the power brokers in both governments as naive, irrelevant dreamers.

Thirty years have passed since the McCarthy era ended. The world has changed dramatically in those thirty years. It is time that the influence of his point of view be excised from the body politic of this nation. This administration will surely be the last one to operate out of the McCarthy assumptions. No matter who wins the next election the mantle of leadership will fall on a new generation shaped by the new consciousness of a radically interdependent world. The rhetoric of the cold war will fade, the limited worldview of tribal thinking will die, and the threadbare and distorted images that East and West hold about each other will finally be surrendered. Only then will hope be born, and peace can begin to grow. This nation must survive a weak and discredited administration for two more years to be able to watch the emergence of a new vision, a new consciousness, and a new consensus. The Soviet Union must make the same journey. In many ways its transition appears already to have begun under the leadership of Mikhail Gorbachev.

A single day in Washington listening to five representatives of this administration sing variations of the same song hardly qualifies one to be an expert, yet the similarity of the basic theme present in each spokesperson convinced me that this administration will never escape its own flawed view of reality. The day was sad in many ways, but there will be a new dawn if we can outlast this debilitating mentality. I doubt if my conclusions represent the desired goals of the secretary of state when he decided to consult with thirty of America's mainline religious leaders.

– 17 –

Diagnosis: Spiritual Vacuum and Moral Decay

May 1991

Lee Atwater was not my favorite politician. He had a capacity to go for the jugular and seemed not to care that the reputations of human beings were violated in the process. In a congressional campaign in South Carolina he exposed the fact that the Democratic candidate he opposed had once undergone shock therapy for depression. Atwater ridiculed this medical procedure by saying at every possible point in the campaign, "I'm not going to respond to allegations made by someone who was hooked up to jumper cables."

The Bush campaign against Governor Dukakis was also run by Lee Atwater and, in my opinion, descended to a new low in American politics. Atwater said of Dukakis, "I will strip the bark off the little bastard and make Willie Horton his running mate." It was a line filled with half-truths and deliberately designed to play upon the racist fears of white America. The Atwater-engineered campaign made Bush's promise of a "kinder and gentler" presidency somewhat hard to take seriously.

But when this man reached the pinnacle of being appointed to head the Republican Party, tragedy in the form of a malignant brain tumor struck. The not-yet forty-year-old Lee Atwater listened to his death sentence. Before he died, steroids and other drugs had given his face an excessively bloated look and even his motor functions were beyond his power to control.

Yet, in the two years he lived with this sickness, Lee Atwater had time to think about the ultimate issues and real values. The result of that thought process was salutary. In his death he may well have given this nation and this world a legacy that will far exceed the legacy of his short but meteoric political career.

Cynics will dismiss Atwater's thoughts and actions in those closing days of his life as a deathbed conversion. I prefer to think of it as an opportunity rarely given to younger adults to do their aging and maturing rapidly and under pressure from their own finitude. With all of us the aging process brings a wisdom, a less combative stance, a grace and new value system born of a longer-range view of life.

As a sign of this newfound wisdom, Lee Atwater apologized to his political enemies for his character assassinating rhetoric. He also reflected on who he was and on the way he had lived his life. These insights were won at the price of his life, but they were insights nonetheless that need to be heard.

Listen to his words: "Long before I was struck with cancer, I felt something stirring in American society. It was a sense among the people of the country — Republican and Democrats alike — that something was missing from their lives, something crucial. I was trying to position the Republican Party to take advantage of it. But I wasn't exactly sure what "it" was. My illness helped me to see that what was missing in society is what was missing in me: a little heart, a lot of brotherhood.

"The '80s were about acquiring — acquiring wealth, power, prestige. I know. I acquired more wealth, power, and prestige than most. But you can acquire all you want and still feel empty. What power wouldn't I trade for a little more time with my family? What price wouldn't I pay for an evening with friends? It took a deadly illness to put me eye to eye with that truth, but it is a truth that the country, caught up in its ruthless ambitions and moral decay, can learn on my dime. I don't know who will lead us through the '90s, but they must be made to speak to this spiritual vacuum at the heart of American society, the cancer of the soul."

Lee Atwater died on Friday, March 29, 1991. He was buried from Trinity Episcopal Cathedral in Columbia, South Carolina.

Mr. Atwater not only named the American sickness, he also exemplified it prior to the onset of his cancer. The 1980s were in fact years of incredible greed and the lust for power. A "me first" mentality was present in this nation and found expression in our politics, our foreign policy, our arms sales to Iran, our priorities, and even our organized religious life. It was a decade in which the wealth of the wealthiest Americans increased dramatically while the poverty of the poorest Americans became painfully and embarrassingly apparent. Our corporate life today contains vast numbers of homeless people, constant street corner begging, and crowded soup kitchens. They are the immoral legacy of what is proudly called "the longest bull market in history." Sufficient resources to serve this segment of our population are not in short supply, but the willingness to care for the victims of our system is.

To protect our oil interests we entered a war against Iraq that was masqueraded as a war to free Kuwait from Iraqi aggression. It was a clever propaganda ploy built on a germ of truth. In one week of that war we spent more money than it would take to rebuild the core cities of this land and to rescue our own American poor from hopelessness. Flag-waving triumphalism became the mark of this nation, but our hypocrisy was revealed when the Kurds, who do not possess oil fields, became the next victims of Iraqi aggression. This hostile action was met with our national piety and the pledge not to get involved in the internal affairs of Iraq, as if that were an option that the victor in a war could avoid.

Everywhere one looks at our national life the lack of a shared value system is seen. There is clearly a yearning for the "it" that Lee Atwater sensed but could not finally describe. There surely is something missing at the heart of this nation. Atwater called it "the spiritual vacuum and the cancer of the soul." The search for meaning has not been found in the pursuit of wealth and power that has marked our national life. The role models of the eighties — Michael Milken, Donald Trump, and Ivan Boesky — are hardly heroic figures today. Atwater was a part of that quest for wealth and power, and he had it. But the tragedy of his life enabled him to see how pitifully empty a quest it was.

Other movements born in that age of greed also sought to fill the vacuum and speak to the same perceived emptiness. One was the rise of evangelical fundamentalistic religion. When one views the future as empty and devoid of meaning, one clings nostalgically to those symbols that promised meaning in the past. If there is nothing better on the horizon, people will cling irrationally to what used to be. Yet that also failed us. For the television evangelists, old-time religion simply joined itself to the same American greed and choked on its excesses. The result was an even deeper disillusionment.

Still others opted for the more modern version of salvation that they perceived to be present in the New Age movement. New Age literature flooded college campuses, and its books bounded to the top of best-seller lists. It was religion with a modern thrust, but New Age thinking became so thin and amorphous that few were finally sustained by it.

Even the use of drugs that destroy life and wreck our social structures is now revealed as just another aspect of the human quest for meaning. Drugs are not a modern invention. They have been around and known for centuries. What is new is the widespread sense of hopelessness and despair that makes escape desirable. It is indeed a desperate life that escapes its present pain by destroying both its present and its future. But that is the legacy of modern drug use.

There are others who have used the physical pleasure of sex as their escape from meaninglessness. Life for them has been reduced to the fleeting and transitory moments of sexual pleasure. Love and sex have been separated, and the quest for thrills has been inserted into the empty places of the human soul.

As a Christian leader I survey this world and I feel its emptiness. I look at my church and yearn to see and to hear it address the Atwater concern, to speak with power to the vacuum that lies open at the heart of life. I am not always encouraged. Some of our church leadership is content to waste our energy in a vain attempt to revive yet again the old-time religion in something called "the decade of evangelism." Others seek to still their anxiety by a blind and foolish attempt to restore something euphemistically called "biblical morality." Upon careful scrutiny, however, "biblical morality" becomes a code word for perpetuating the prejudices of the past against women and homosexual persons. Still others seek meaning by lapsing into traditional ecclesiastical power games attempting to perpetuate such dead causes as papal infallibility or biblical inerrancy. It is ever so revealing that churches that claim to have all the answers do not allow any questions to be raised.

My vision for the future of the Christian church involves a faith community that can speak to the "cancer of our soul." It is a vision that will be realized only when the church becomes honest. Honesty will be revealed when the church confronts its world as an institution that admits it does not have all the answers and demonstrates thereby a desire to be both a humble listener and a humble learner. The church's invitation to the world does not come with the phoney promise of the past that somehow the church can deliver certainty. We have never done that. We have only delivered the illusion of certainty. Our invitation to the people of our generation is to become a fellow pilgrim with us, seekers after God and seekers after God's truth.

Pilgrim people are a people on a journey. For that journey we must travel light. We will take with us our Bible, not as the inerrant word of God but as a rich and treasured chronicle of our ancestors in faith who were on this journey long before our time. We will observe in that text the integrity with which our spiritual parents wrestled with their God and with their world. We will learn from their record how we might be in dialogue with God in our moment in time with an equal integrity. The Bible cannot be for us a blueprint. It cannot take the answers that came to people who lived at another time and make them a straitjacket that people in our time might be forced, or even encouraged, to wear. It is a guidebook that we cannot abandon.

Along with that Bible we must also take some water with which to baptize and bread and wine with which to feed each other as we walk on our way. Add honesty, integrity, and the willingness to walk together in real community, and this journey will take us far beyond the ecclesiastical protestations of the past that work to hold us back. A pilgrim people that journeys together toward God must be in touch with the issues of our day, allowing our deepest prejudices to be challenged, loving ourselves and others into an expanded life, willing to be opened to a new emerging consciousness. We must also keep the vision of God before us as we walk into every new frontier.

This is the task of Christ's church in the age that Lee Atwater called an age of moral decay and spiritual vacuum. The church that can speak to this moment with power and relevance will be the church that will succeed in reviving Christianity in the next decade. I pray that the people of this diocese can be a part of that life-giving remnant.

– 18 –

Mr. Clinton: It's Time to Name the Demon

November 1994

The midterm elections for the Senate and Congress are now upon us. The common political wisdom is that the Democrats will either lose their congressional majorities or have them diminished significantly. This is attributed to the perceived unpopularity of the president of the United States, Bill Clinton, which seems to be focused primarily on his character and his perceived values.

It is not my purpose here to defend the presidency of Bill Clinton, but I do find the viciousness of his opponents to be so obsessive as to drive me to seek some understanding of its source.

This president is the first chief executive to address the budget deficit effectively since Harry Truman. The budget deficit received great lip service from our presidents from Mr. Eisenhower to Mr. Bush, but no effective action accompanied the rhetoric. Mr. Clinton also took on the powerful lobbying efforts of the National Rifle Association on two occasions. He secured passage of the Brady Bill, which neither Mr. Reagan nor Mr. Bush had been able to achieve, and he also got through Congress the first ever comprehensive crime bill, which included a ban on assault weapons.

Mr. Clinton got the NAFTA agreement passed despite the predictions of an economic disaster, which has never materialized. I submit that those three achievements represent no small accomplishment for a not yet two-year-old presidency.

Mr. Clinton also took on the issue of universal health care. No president has done that before, though every president since Franklin D. Roosevelt has talked about it. His bill was battered by lobbying groups representing the medical profession, the hospital association, the legal profession, the insurance industry, and even such industrial giants as IBM. In the midst of the battle, incredible misstatements of truth were uttered. American health care was praised as the finest in the world. It is, but only for the wealthiest 20 percent of our population. That claim would be visually inoperative if its proponents would visit urban medical centers where untold numbers of the poor are forced to use hospital emergency rooms as their primary care physician. They receive low quality care with no preventive health measures and at a cost five to ten times higher than a public clinic or a private physician. These costs are hidden in the escalating premiums of our health care insurance and in the Medicare and Medicaid portion of our federal budget that drives the national deficit year after year. Yet to listen to Washington's political oratory, you would think that today's system is free and the Clinton attempt to reform health care would bankrupt the nation with bureaucratic costs. In fact, there is in this country a frantic lobbying attempt to protect the vested interests of those who now make incredible fortunes out of the present health care inefficiency. Deliberate lies and smear campaigns are part of the effort.

Mr. Clinton's attempt to reform health care failed. The vested interests won. This will mean bankruptcy for those who lose their insurance, and for the least affluent it will mean that poor health, poor life expectancy, and only expensive emergency room care will continue to be their fate.

In foreign affairs Mr. Clinton has extricated the nation from Somalia, into which an already defeated lame duck president, claiming humanitarian and not national security motives, had placed this nation. He has been criticized for not invading Bosnia in the face of drastic human rights violations. Then he was criticized for invading Haiti in response to drastic human rights violations in our own hemisphere. When entrance into Haiti turned out to be a peaceful negotiated program for American military personnel, the criticism did not cease.

Amid these struggles there has been a constant and concerted effort to denigrate the character of the president. Ancient stories of Whitewater and lurid tales of long past sexual indiscretions are trotted out regularly, first in the gutter press and then in the legitimate press. No charges are ever proved, but the investigations are endless, with new charges or new versions of old charges chipping away daily at the integrity of both the man and the office. No president in our history has had his personal life scrutinized quite so vigorously. Becoming wealthy while in public office has been standard operating procedure for a number of our recent presidents from Johnson to Reagan. Marital indiscretions have marked the lives of even revered presidents like Franklin Roosevelt and Dwight Eisenhower. The Clintons, on the other hand, remain relatively poor and they have held their marriage together, living through the bumps and pressures of a career family, in our explicitly sexual society, that older chief executives would not even understand. But to hear his critics, he is the most immoral man ever to sit in the oval office, and he presides over a nation of sexual puritans.

What is the source of this religious sounding but blatantly political criticism? My own experience offers me a clue. In the last several years, because of my writing and lecturing career, I have been the recipient of some amazingly negative activity at the hands of evangelical, fundamentalistic, and conservative religious groups in this country and around the world. This activity has included character assassination, the attributing to me of base motives, and even the threat of physical violence and death.

When I have met representatives of the religious right in public debate, I have found them not only hostile, but their conduct has with regularity lacked personal integrity. For example, an evangelical bishop, who debated with me at one of our seminaries, went home and doctored the tape recordings of that debate for public sale in order that his performance seem superior to what it was in fact. An English evangelical priest with whom I debated in Canada wrote an addition to his conclusion when the "text" of the debate was published by his evangelical friends so that he could cover points he felt he had left uncovered. Conservative members of the Roman Catholic hierarchy have attacked my integrity whenever I have dared to disagree with the position of their church on birth control, mandatory celibacy, the role of women, or their drive to make abortion illegal. Australian evangelical sources described me as "an atheist in purple," among other things, as they picketed with hostile posters and defaming literature at almost every lecture I gave in that country. In New Zealand a concerted effort was made by ecclesiastical figures in high places to demonstrate that I was an ill-informed Christian, with no scholarly credentials at all. So dishonest and vicious were these attacks that I began to study the relationship between right-wing religion and this killing and pathological anger.

It was only then that I began to understand the treatment that President Clinton receives, for I think it roots in the same place. The hot button issues of the religious right are abortion and homosexuality. Both underlie the deceptive and pious campaign for "family values." Mr. Clinton has infuriated this mentality by moving to treat homosexuals with dignity in the military and by making discrimination based on one's being homosexual illegal. He has moved by executive order and by the appointment of moderate Supreme Court justices to make abortion legal, safe, and a matter of legitimate choice for all women in this country and throughout the world. For this he was publicly embarrassed by Pope John Paul II in Denver and the integrity of his vice president was attacked by Vatican representatives in Cairo.

The change of special prosecutors in the Whitewater affair was engineered in part by the Republican senators of North Carolina who have deep ties to the religious right of Robertson, Falwell, and Buchanan. The group in Arkansas that seems to produce a sex story a month is also closely identified with the religious right. Into the bloodstream of American politics this religious mentality pumps its visceral emotional hostility against the president, attached as it is again and again to the twin issues of homosexuality and abortion.

In time, the legitimate Republican leadership of Robert Dole and Newt Gingrich picks up the tone of these attacks without the content and decides that this president is so weak and so hated that nothing he proposes should be passed. So the obstructionist politics of the past year become dominant on the Washington scene, and the people's distrust of anyone who is a politician increases.

Mr. Clinton has been a better than average president. He is an intelligent, able man who has managed this nation well in his first two years on the watch. Yet despite increasing prosperity at home and peace abroad, we have a president whose ratings continue to scrape bottom.

I think the time has come to name the demonic forces that permeate American political life today. It is the right, seeking to impose its narrow agenda on this nation, that seems willing to destroy the credibility of those who oppose them.

I encourage our president to confront this mentality head on. It is risky politics, because opposing someone's religious convictions is thought to be to be inappropriate for a political leader.

But I for one am a religious man who deeply resents the fact that the word "Christian" has today become identified politically with a right-wing fundamentalistic, anti-female, homophobic, anti-abortion, conservative mentality.

I think that if Mr. Clinton named this demon, he would discover that a considerable number of those of us who constitute Christian America would support a campaign that would expose the hatred, hostility, and thinly veiled violence that masquerades today under the banner of religion.

I commend this course of action to him in the next two years as he runs for reelection.

Update — November 1998

This column was written in 1994. It describes the bitterness that members of the political and religious right wing felt for President Clinton. He has been the most investigated president in American history. That investigation was begun over a Whitewater land deal in Arkansas while Mr. Clinton was the governor. In this ill-founded business venture on which Mr. Clinton actually lost money personally it was alleged that money from this deal paid off some of his political indebtedness. Yet four years of investigation turned up no inappropriate behavior. Nonetheless the investigation continued to be expanded to what was called Travelgate and Filegate. Still nothing that led to the supposition of illegal or improper behavior. The investigation became like a bone that the dog could not stop chewing. The connection between this ongoing investigatory process and the increasingly shrill hostility of the religious right were clearly documented. The Republican majority dismissed the first independent prosecutor and, driven by the recommendation by Senators Lauch Faircloth and Jesse Helms of North Carolina, both dependent on the support of the religious right, named Kenneth Starr to this post. Starr's own religious and moralistic background as well as his ties with the religious right made him ideal to pursue their purposes.

The Achilles heel for this president was his weakness for women and sex. His history in this area was clearly compromised. Mr. Starr played off of a law suit filed by Ms. Paula Jones charging Mr. Clinton with sexual harassment to expand his investigation into the arena of Clinton's sexual behavior. Having found nothing to justify his four-year $40 million investigation of other presidential activities Mr. Starr practiced entrapment politics and discovered Mr. Clinton guilty of sexual improprieties, not with Paula Jones but with Monica Lewinsky, and seeking to cover that up with lies under oath. Finally Mr. Starr has hit paydirt. His venom then poured out as he released volumes of salacious sexual testimony. The design was to weaken this president to the point of resignation or removal.

This president had stood for equality for blacks more than any previous president in American history. He and his wife, Hillary, have helped to lift women into the mainstream of American life with not only their example but with the appointment of Janet Reno to be the first female attorney general in history and Madeleine Albright to be the first female secretary of state. He refused to allow Congress to compromise a woman's right to choose an abortion and even vetoed the proposed ban on the partial birth abortion procedure. He has been liberal on gay rights issues and even nominated a homosexual man to be ambassador to Luxembourg. Thus he continued to press the emotional buttons that infuriate the religious right.

When they trapped him in his lies about sexual improprieties, the Republican Congress led by Speaker Newt Gingrich and a host of southern-accented congressmen who owe their seats to the support of the religious right moved to impeach Mr. Clinton. He was clearly guilty of improper behavior and seeking to cover it up. The question is whether that part of his life should ever have been investigated by an independent prosecutor in the first place. While not admirable, this conduct on the part of the president did not constitute treason or high crimes and misdemeanors.

The nation to its credit reacted negatively to this impeachment initiative and supported the president they felt was being mistreated. The elections in November of 1998 brought this issue to a head and the Republicans hoping to ride this presidential scandal to great congressional majorities woke up to find themselves badly battered. When the smoke of the election battle cleared, the Democrats had gained five house seats and had held even in the Senate. This compared with predictions of a ten to forty seat Republican gain in the House and a projected gain in the Senate of six seats to give them a filibuster-proof majority. The boil of religious hatred that had been building for at least six years was lanced. The sanity of the American electorate reemerged. The nation said in the election "No More." Mr. Clinton paid a price for his weakness. There is no doubt about that. His legacy in history will be forever tainted. But he also revealed the demon that was infecting this nation, and the voters purged it or at least rendered it politically ineffective.

In the presidential election of 2000 we will have kinder and gentler candidates who will appeal to a kinder and gentler electorate.

– 19 –

Where Is the Christ in the "Christian" Agenda

November 1995

There is no question that religion is an active force in American politics today. The organization known as the Christian Coalition claims that up to 35 percent of the votes that created the sea change in the

Congress last November came from the religious right. Names like Pat Robertson, Ralph Reed, and Jerry Falwell are as well known in political circles today as they are in religious circles. So powerful is this influence that candidates for the presidency, from the incumbent Democrat to the challenging Republicans, seem increasingly willing to dance to the tune of the religious right. So we hear much talk today about "family values" and other themes which appear to be of great importance to this major bloc in the electorate.

The appeal of the religious right rises, I believe, out of deep levels of frustration, anger, and fear that are present in the body politic of this land today. Family life is, in fact, under stress. The divorce rate is rising. So is the out-of-wedlock pregnancy rate. The consumption of alcohol and the use of drugs also reveal an upward statistical chart among young Americans. All of these are symptoms of an underlying dis-ease present in this society. Beyond those symptoms other economic realities press in upon us, creating national anxiety. The wealth of America is expanding, but that expansion does not seem to embrace many middle-class citizens. Middle-income families have not experienced a significant increase in their buying power in more than a decade. At the same time the costs of such things as education for their children, especially at the university level, and of medical care for the entire family have skyrocketed. Families that feel they cannot provide for their children the necessary preparation for life or are one medical crisis away from bankruptcy live with high levels of stress. Two incomes are frequently required to keep a family at the same level that one income provided a generation ago.

The specter of job insecurity also haunts most middle-class Americans. The rally in the stock market has been fueled by corporate downsizing, creating what Wall Street loves to call "lean and mean" industries with great bottom line expectations. The incredible rise in the value of technology stocks in particular reflects the fact that high tech equipment can do the work today that large numbers of human beings once did. The machines can do it better, more cheaply, and without expensive benefits.

World trade agreements and the existence of multinational corporations also fuel this sense of job insecurity. In today's world of instant communications and global manufacturing, facilities can be transported with amazing swiftness to Korea, Mexico, Singapore, or Brazil, where labor costs are significantly reduced. The combination of technology and the threatened mobility of whole plants are major depressants on middle-class wages, and together they create the fear that lingers just below the level of consciousness in the life of the working American.

When stress is high and fear is rampant, people look for someone to blame. Targets are readily identified. Anger usually focuses on those movements which are presumed to have created the problems that the angry one is experiencing. Over the decades since the Second World War, there has been a challenge to the status quo, first from racial minorities, then from women, and now from gay and lesbian people. Each challenge has disturbed the complacent security of yesterday. There is also a perceived sense of corruption that permeates the national psyche. We hear it articulated when politicians speak of "welfare cheats who live like kings while working Americans pay high taxes to support them." It is effective, if not always honest, campaign oratory. Because "liberals" have historically supported a compassionate society in which the weak and poor are cared for with dignity and since they have also been in the vanguard of those movements which have incorporated heretofore alienated groups into the mainstream of the social order, the "liberals" are regularly identified as the enemy. Calculating political operators know exactly how to manipulate these feelings for their own gain.

A major source of security in yesterday's world was found in the religious values around which the whole society was organized. Those religious values were rooted in and grew out of the dominant religious system of our land which was clearly identified as Christians. To achieve freedom and equality every emerging group, from blacks to women to gays, has had to challenge the stereotypes imposed by that religious system. Liberals and intellectuals tended to support those challenges which destabilize traditional religious convictions. Historically it must be recalled that Christians have quoted the Bible to provide them with a clear conscience and a pious justification for their support of slavery and segregation, their opposition to the full emancipation of women in both church and society, and their continuing oppression and victimization of gay and lesbian people.

As the tides of history have flowed, it is no longer socially acceptable to advocate slavery or segregation, but this latent racism can be and is expressed in opposition to quotas or affirmative action plans. It is not politic to oppose equal rights for women, but this visceral negativity toward the feminist agenda can be and is expressed in the emotional opposition to abortion and in the desire to punish unwed mothers. It is not reasonable to remove basic human rights from gay and lesbian people, but enormous hostility can be and is aroused over the issue of adding sexual orientation to the list of protected minorities. This homophobia is expressed in the irrational cry that such tactics have created "special privileges." In that form this concern has now reached the Supreme Court. So not surprisingly, the political right wing of America has joined forces with the religious right wing of America and around these fears and these issues they have organized themselves in the quest for political power.

Today this coalition threatens to impose its agenda on the whole nation; before our eyes it is flexing its political muscle. The political process is being bent to accommodate these concerns. It is a strange spectacle. I think I understand the issues. I certainly recognize the fears. I do not, however, appreciate the suppression of human freedom and the violation of human dignity that today flow into American politics from the religious right. Above all else I resent the fact that this narrow and ofttimes mean-spirited agenda has caused the word "Christian" to be filled with negative content.

I am embarrassed that the word "Christian," for example, has been applied publicly to that hostile negativity against women that creates the environment in which murder at family planning centers is actually encouraged. I am offended that homosexual people are still abused and even scapegoated by "Christian" groups, including certain bishops, who seek to exacerbate the public ignorance in order to justify their own prejudices. I am angry when all-male gatherings of decoratively dressed ecclesiastics, in the name of an exclusively male deity called "Father," solemnly pronounce moral judgments concerning what a woman can and cannot do with her own body. I resent anyone who defines a woman, in the name of the Christian God, primarily in terms of her reproductive functions. I am angry when Christian words are used to justify violence against the poor and the weak under the euphemistic title of "necessary welfare reform." I am saddened when entities that are called "Christian bookstores" have their shelves filled with material that not only is lacking in intellectual competence, but that also allows and even justifies hostility toward other religious groups. I am despairing when I observe that major themes in the books on the shelves of these stores define homosexual persons and women inside the prejudiced stereotypes of the past and even unwittingly encourage child abuse under the general rubric of justifying corporal punishment. I regret that those same politicians who have identified themselves with this "Christian agenda" have also been a voice raised against this society's willingness to care for young mothers, a voice against immigrants, a voice against health care for the poor, and even a voice against health care for children. I cringe when I see my Christ used this way, and I want to cry out to the public that this is not now, and never has been, an expression of the Christ I know, the Christ I serve, and the Christ I worship.

If the Christ is to be part of today's political debate, then let it be the Christ who invited all to come to him, as the words of the hymn say, "Just as I am, without one plea." Let it be the Christ who reached out to the marginalized of his world — the lepers, the Samaritans, and the women — and enfolded them in his love and restored their human dignity. Let it be the Christ who broke open the barriers that separated the human family into warring factions, called in that time by the names Jews and Gentiles but by a thousand other names throughout history.

If the name of our Christ continues to be misused in the political arenas, then those of us who are disciples of this Christ must be willing to enter those arenas to confront and to challenge that misuse. I, for one, do not intend to be silent should this anti-Christian charade continue. Human evil and human mean-spiritedness must be named for what they are. They can never be justified by an appeal to the name of Jesus.

The time has come to call the sleepy, and frequently uninvolved, mainline Christians of this nation to rise and, for the sake of the Christ we serve as well is in the name of human decency, to say to this narrow right-wing religious agenda, "Enough! Enough!" This nation, with its deep and significant religious roots, must call its citizens to a nobler vision than this. It must no longer be possible for anyone to justify their distress, their hostility, and even their greed for power by covering them over with the sweet name of Jesus.

– 20 –

Election 1998: The Defeat of the Religious Right

December 1998

It was a fascinating election. The pollsters and pundits who like to instruct the electorate on what it is that people are thinking and feeling were almost 100 percent wrong. Preelection prognostications suggested that the Republicans would gain six to twelve seats in the

House of Representatives and perhaps enough seats in the Senate to enable them to shut off debate if they so chose. These estimates were considerably down from those that circulated a month earlier when a Republican blowout was being predicted. Goaded on by a moralistic religious right, this party hoped to exploit the Clinton scandal into a major political bonanza. That agenda dictated a policy that allowed hundreds of pages of salacious testimony to be made public about Mr. Clinton's relationship with Monica Lewinsky. It fueled the Republican calls for impeachment and caused the Congress to authorize, on almost totally partisan lines, an open-ended House of Representatives investigation. The nation was looking at the spectacle of a prolonged one- to two-year television extravaganza that would feature Kenneth Starr, Linda Tripp, Secret Service personnel and advisors to the president, each going over what they knew about the oval office affair. That, in turn, would have given birth to a continued barrage of sex-oriented talk shows on radio and television. They would speak of how degrading and offensive this presidential behavior was, but would delight in wallowing in this material with condescending relish. But the destruction of this president was their passionate desire.

President Clinton has incurred the undying wrath of the religious right by supporting the two issues that have become the twin phobias that motivate this conservative, religious part of our electorate: namely, the quest for justice for our gay and lesbian citizens and a woman's right to choose an abortion. This president had not only sought to liberalize the armed services policy which dismissed homosexual members from the military, but he had actually nominated a gay man to be ambassador to Luxembourg. He had also vetoed every congressional attempt to limit abortions, including the proposed ban on partial birth procedures. The visceral hatred against Mr. Clinton seemed to know no bounds.

The salivating eagerness with which the religious right embraced the sex scandal at the White House, however, seemed to overwhelm their political judgment. It captivated their total attention and presented them with the perfect opportunity to purge this evil man from their world. They set about with single-minded devotion to seek a reversal of the last two presidential elections. In their strange religious way they saw this opportunity as a "gift from God," rewarding them for "their true faith." They were primed for a great political victory.

In the days leading up to the election, however, two events occurred which galvanized the consciousness of this nation in a different direction. In Wyoming a twenty-one-year-old university student named Matthew Shepard was pistol-whipped by two young males, then tied to a remote fence post in sub-freezing weather and left to die. The reason for this inhumane murder was that Matt Shepard was a gay man. Shortly thereafter in Buffalo, New York, a much-loved doctor named Barnett Slepian was murdered in his own kitchen by a sniper. The reason for this act was that this doctor was willing to do legal abortions. The rhetoric of hate marking the religious right had thus translated into the activity of killing. The step from rhetoric to action is far shorter than fanatical religious voices seem to understand. The eyes of the nation began to comprehend the price of intolerance and the kind of behavior that lies at the end of unrestrained religious zeal.

Awakened by the horror of these murders, the citizens of this nation looked anew at the shrill voices of those national leaders who respond to the organized religious right. As that realization of where fanaticism can lead began to rise to awareness, a political reaction set in. The polls began to show the Republican margins shrinking. To counter this declining trend the Republican central committee led by the Speaker of the House, Newt Gingrich of Georgia, decided yet again to seek to exploit the White House scandal in an attempt to rebuild their once imposing lead. So a new national advertising campaign was adopted, which had the effect of turning this election into a referendum on Bill Clinton and impeachment. The official reason stated by those who signed off on this strategy was that it was designed to get out the core vote of the party, which in large measure is the religious right. The results were exactly the opposite of what they anticipated.

When the votes in the election of 1998 were counted, the political shock of the decade had been registered. Al D'Amato, the three-term Republican senator from New York, a strong anti-abortion politician who had presided over the politically inspired anti-Clinton Whitewater hearings, was defeated by a 55 to 45 percent margin. Senator Lauch Faircloth, the North Carolina Republican who was Jesse Helms's hand-picked candidate and who had played a significant role in the appointment of Kenneth Starr as independent counsel, was unseated by a young opponent who had never before run for public office. Representative Michael Pappas in New Jersey, who had composed and sung a flattering song to Kenneth Starr based on the children's rhyme "Twinkle, Twinkle, Little Star," had his ditty used by his opponent in his television ads to the revulsion of the people of his district. Representative Pappas was defeated by freshman Democrat Rush Holt, tipping the scales toward a Democratic majority in New Jersey's congressional delegation.

In South Carolina, Georgia, and Alabama the religious-right-endorsed Republican candidates for governor, two of them incumbents, were defeated. In South Carolina Fritz Hollings, almost the sole Democrat left in the Senate from the deep South, held on to his Senate seat against a heavily financed religious-right-endorsed candidate.

Meanwhile, moderate Republican governors, like George W. Bush in Texas, George Pataki in New York, Jeb Bush in Florida, John Engler in Michigan, and Tommy Thompson in Wisconsin rolled up impressive victories by ignoring both the Clinton scandal and the religious right and began the process of wresting Republican leadership away from the religious mentality that occupies the right wing. Even our fine governor in New Jersey, Christie Whitman, began to appear less as a fringe Republican nationally and more as a mainline Republican.

When the sun rose on the day after the election, the Democrats had gained five seats in the House, had held the Republicans even in the Senate, and had regained a new foothold in the once conservative South, while the pollsters and pundits were eating crow as they tried to explain just how it was that they had been so wrong. As a result of this election, the impeachment of President Clinton has become all but politically impossible and, even if impeachment were voted by the House, any chance of a Senate conviction has disappeared.

Forty-eight hours later Newt Gingrich, the architect of the "Contract with America," the shutting down of the federal government, and the impeachment hearings had announced his intention to withdraw from the race to succeed himself as speaker and to resign from the House of Representatives. In his place a nonideological, pragmatic man of conservative credentials and wide legislative experience, who seemed to sense that an effective politician is ultimately a person who understands the necessity of compromise, was chosen to succeed him. Without actually saying it Republicans were now looking for a face-saving way out of the impeachment process, and even a separation from the albatross of being the party of the religious right.

Thus it can be said that this election brought about a sea change in American politics. The religious right has finally crested. Those voices that claimed to speak for God, but who had spewed forth so much venom and hostility that the American political system had been poisoned, had finally overplayed their hand. The Republican Party was forced to begin an internal assessment which will inevitably bring about change. They will recognize that their continued dependence on the religious right, their willingness to play to the religious fears and prejudices of those motivated by the abortion fight, and a rampant homophobia is not a winning formula. It is rather a prescription for a permanent minority status. The successful Republican governors, who ran quite independently of the religious right, are today clearly the wave of the political future, even in the Grand Old Party.

Four years ago I wrote a column urging Mr. Clinton to name the religious demon that was threatening to destroy this nation's political system, to run the risk of being publicly critical about the distorted religious perspective of his most vehement critics. He did not do so. Then, to complicate matters, his own irresponsible behavior played directly into the hands of his religious enemies. Unable to stand success, however, the excessive zeal on the part of these religious fanatics finally brought them down. That is, perhaps, the only redemptive thing to emerge from the White House scandal.

I suspect that from this time forward the religious right will continue to decline until another major dislocation in our society creates a new wave of rampant insecurity that will enable these religious voices to come roaring forth once more, seeking to impose their particular security system with its narrow-minded, traditional, and moralistic solutions on the whole society. But for now I believe we can bid farewell to the Pat Robertsons, Jerry Falwells, James Dobsons, and Ralph Reeds as political leaders. Their day is over. The era of sexual McCarthyism is at an end. It was a good election in November of 1998.

PART THREE

Religion and Church

– 21 –

New Bishop, New Hopes, New Dreams (Excerpts)

March 1979

. . . A change in leadership is always a time of uncertainty in any institution. We are obviously in that kind of a period. Besides a new diocesan bishop, we have a number of new staff members. In regard to the office of bishop, the person who occupies that position will make a more immediate and more obvious impact, and about that person there will inevitably be higher levels of uncertainty. We have to go through that period during which our theme song seems to be "Getting to Know You, Getting to Know All about You."

I would like to speak to that and to tell you how I hope to function as the bishop of Newark. I have been told that I do not have a shrinking violet personality. In the twenty years of my priesthood I frequently was involved as an advocate in issues before the church. I was an advocate for the Christian education emphasis and the Seabury Sunday School Curriculum in the fifties. I was an advocate of and apologist for the social involvement of the church in the 1960s. I was an advocate for the civil rights movement, for the disengagement of the United States from Vietnam, and for the new thrust of indigenous ministry that would be sensitive to the anti-colonialist tide in our overseas jurisdictions.

In the seventies I have been an advocate for a radical new approach to adult education. I was an advocate for and a participant in the liturgical movement that issued in our new Prayer Book. I was and am an advocate for the full participation of women in every area of life of both the church and the social order, certainly including ordination to priesthood and the episcopacy.

A diocese that elects an advocate person to be its bishop is venturing, I hope, on an exciting course, not always peaceful, but never boring. I assume that you did not elect me to be something I have never been. I assume that you wanted the person I am to serve in this office. Since I have published books, printed articles, appeared regularly on radio and television, my life and point of view have long been a matter of public record. No secret was made of that when I was nominated and elected. But advocacy is not an easy role in the episcopal office, for it is important, also, that the bishop be bishop of all the people — liberals and conservatives; urbanites, suburbanites, and exurbanites; Protestant and Catholic; men and women; those who are pro-women's ordination and those who are anti-women's ordination — and of all those on different sides of all the other issues that are regularly debated among us.

It is also important for the bishop to be a symbol of unity. But unity on what level? Unity at the price of standing for nothing? Unity that assumes that change should be aborted because change always upsets some part of the family? Unity on the level of petty superficiality? Unity that produces a boring inertia? That I cannot be and I will not be. My vision for this diocese is that we will be a people who have a commitment to Christ and to truth that is so deep and so passionately held among us all that we will call, indeed encourage, every person in this diocese to be what he or she is. I hope we will be a people of God willing to struggle in the public arenas of this convention, the Diocesan Council, the Department of Missions, and the Convocations to bear witness to what each of us most deeply believes. I hope to see this diocese reach a level of maturity that will enable it to live creatively with tension, to welcome varying and contending points of view. I hope we will always be open to one another, that we will listen lovingly, that we will never fail to affirm persons even when we cannot affirm positions. I call the congregations of this diocese to a sense of responsibility that is expressed in your financial priorities. We cannot have a family where local units act out their pique at either the national or diocesan church if they disagree with some stand or on some issue. The Canons bind us irrevocably into this diocesan family. I do not believe in divorce or in separation, and I will abide by the Canons to the letter of the law in order to make that witness.

When our convention meets, I hope these gatherings will be dynamic, exciting collections of diverse points of view seeking to speak as the body of Christ to the issues of our day, whether public issues or church issues. I remind this body that only this convention can speak for the Diocese of Newark. As the bishop, I see my role to be that of speaking to the church, or to the diocese, or to the world; I do not see myself as speaking for the church or for the diocese. I will do my advocating for those things about which I have strong convictions when I speak to this convention and in other public arenas. I want to be free to prod your consciences and the consciences of the public about issues and policies, even when I am sure that mine is a minority voice. So one style which I hope to live out is to place into my annual convention address my point of view on the issues before us and my opinion on various matters that affect the life of the church. I do not plan to equivocate. I will attempt to be open and persuasive. I will be speaking as your bishop to the church. Be assured I do not believe in episcopal infallibility, but I do believe in episcopal leadership — I hope strong leadership. Once I return from that address to the chair, however, I intend to be as fair a presiding officer as I know how to be. I shall seek to refrain from comment or questions or even the giving of information. For I will have had my say, and as presiding officer my task will be only to facilitate this convention while you are engaged in the task of speaking for this diocese to the world and the church. My agenda in the chair will be only to enable you to speak your corporate mind. I encourage each of you to be advocates for the truth as you understand truth. I will respect that and encourage that. This will make our diocese dramatic and exciting. We will know that our unity in Christ is deeper than any issue and that unity in Christ will enable us to express our diversity — debate any issue. Some of us will win some of the time; some of us will lose some of the time; but pray God no one will be bored any of the time, and maybe we will encourage more substantive issues to come before us in our various resolutions. It will take commitment and maturity to make this kind of Diocesan Convention and diocesan family work. I believe we have that kind of maturity. . . .

– 22 –

Lambeth 1988: Women Bishops, Polygamy, and the Nature of Prejudice

October 1988

The Lambeth Conference of 1988 might well become known as the gathering of male bishops that opened the episcopal office to women and approved the practice of polygamy for men. Indeed it did both, even though in each instance it tried to limit the occasions on which the practice would occur. Strangely enough, both of these votes represented a rising awareness of the discriminatory plight of women in widely disparate situations throughout the world. The priesthood and the episcopacy of the church are the primary positions of power within institutional Christianity. For most of the years of Christian history these positions have been reserved to men alone. The opening of the priestly level of that male fiefdom to women was approved ever so tentatively by the Lambeth Conference of 1978.

In an equally tentative way the opening of access to the office of bishop, in which the essence of Anglican ecclesiastical power and leadership resides, was approved for women in 1988. In typical Anglican style, the approval was not given easily. The language of the resolution was fearful, hesitant, well nuanced, and clearly compromised. Safeguards were added for the sake of the "delicate male conscience." No word of joy or celebration was heard. However, the resolution was passed, and with its passage the last Lambeth Conference "for men only" became a fixture in history.

There will be no turning back. Those who still think that is not so might meditate on the possibility that the Magna Carta once signed might have been reconsidered, or the Emancipation Proclamation once issued might have been recalled. History does not reverse the movement toward democracy and inclusiveness. Those few bishops who announced after the vote that "they could not be in communion with a woman bishop" should plan to go fishing during Lambeth 1998, for women in episcopal orders will be a significant presence at that conference.

At the same conference and by vote of the same constituency, the condemnation of polygamy was tempered. Polygamy to the Western mind seems to contain a painfully primitive definition of woman. Yet it was affirmed as a legitimate lifestyle for newly converted

Christians in those nations where polygamy is an accepted legalized institution. When one examines the social structure of countries like Sudan, Kenya, and Uganda, a number of issues emerge. First, tribal wars, historically such a part of the cultural ethos of this region of the world, regularly decimate the male population, leaving an imbalance in the ratio of women to men. Secondly, the patriarchal nature of local life in those lands has determined that the educational and economic opportunities open to women are extremely limited. Thirdly, and resulting from the first two facts, marriage is the primary means by which women are able to be sustained. To keep women in these cultures in the state of unmarriedness would be to compromise their ability to survive or to drive them into prostitution as their sole means of support.

Heretofore in these countries, under the pressure of Victorian missionaries, a polygamous family that converted to Christianity was forced, as the price of baptism, to become a monogamous unit by dismissing the additional wives. That presumably will no longer be required. Polygamy must be, at best, only a transitional stage in the evolution of these nations and a temporary way station for these women. In these extreme circumstances, the bishops voted for a system that offers life rather than death. This makes that vote in that context a positive, even a liberal, vote. However, if polygamy is allowed by either church or society to become a permanent solution it will mean that the church in those lands has made peace with symptoms to the neglect of the causes and has become in the process apostate.

We can accept the transitory reality of polygamy only if, in the name of the universal God, the male sexual game we call warfare, whether on a tribal scale or world scale, is challenged and brought to a halt. Also, that discrimination against women which finds expression in limited educational and economic opportunities must be confronted and routed. Marriage must be an option freely chosen, not an economic necessity required for every woman. The dignity of being a woman must be located in creation, not in a relationship with a man, no matter how beautiful that romantic concept might be.

When these two votes — one to allow women to be bishops and the other to recognize polygamy as legitimate — are analyzed deeply, the nature of all prejudice begins to be clear. In both issues the reality is that women who are powerless are defined by men who are powerful. Women are then forced to live with that male-imposed definition.

Those with power always define those without power in terms of the needs of the powerful. So women have been defined by men as subhuman because they are not male, as sex objects who exist to gratify men, as helpmates designed by God to play subservient roles that serve male comfort and male pleasure. When women are not allowed to define themselves, their only recourse is to acquiesce in or to fight against the male imposed stereotypes. That is the nature of prejudice.

Emancipation begins when women refuse to accept the male imposed definition of femaleness. It moves on to rebellion against the stereotype and it concludes with the acquisition by women of power that enables a new vision and an enhanced humanity to be achieved. Then women become bishops, prime ministers, presidents and vice presidents, Supreme Court justices, lawyers, doctors, bankers, senators, scientists, pilots, governors, and attorney generals. In that process women define themselves, their roles, and their nature. They thus demonstrate what power does when it comes to heretofore powerless people. Women alone, in time, must and will define what a woman is. Men will accept that definition, adjust to it, and live with the new realities. Peer relationships will replace the dominant-submissive, male-female models of the past.

From a woman bishop to a polygamous marriage is an enormous stretch, but both are steps along the path to a full humanity. One reaches empowerment, the other simply survives to fight another day. But ultimately for all people, self-definition will replace anyone else's definition of any human being, and when it does a new day for all humanity will dawn.

The same principles underlay three other major Lambeth issues: the social action resolutions, especially as they relate to the racial flash point in parts of the world such as South Africa; the debate so primitive and yet so real on homosexuality; and even the various ecumenical and interfaith resolutions.

Lying behind apartheid and racism is the same, ever-present principle of prejudice. A group of people with power define the powerless ones and then force that definition upon the victims. Black people historically have been defined by white people as nonwhite and therefore as subhuman.

Black people are thus, it has been argued, to be colonized, enslaved, segregated, and reduced to various forms of servitude that help to ease the life and increase the comfort and wealth of those with power. In South Africa the classic struggle has reached the stage where blacks are no longer willing to live within the white world's definition. Yet, the white world steadfastly refuses to adjust its vision and responds by utilizing its massive power to keep the prejudicial system intact. The options for the blacks are reduced to the single strategy of raising the price of prejudice until it is too expensive even for the whites to maintain. Hence, the present confrontation becomes inevitable. No one — white or black — doubts the eventual outcome. The only question is what will the cost be. Lambeth added its voice to the call to end apartheid, to employ economic sanctions to raise the price of apartheid. Lambeth also condemned every other expression where people with power define those without power. It was a consistent witness against prejudice and a consistent call to justice and wholeness.

The debate on homosexuality was fascinating and revealing. The resolution was an innocent one, simply to guarantee the human and civil rights of gay and lesbian people. In the early days of the conference homosexuality was said to be an "American or Western problem." African bishops asserted that "it was unknown in Africa," that it was not an issue for the African church. However, once the issue was debated and amendments were offered to strengthen the resolution, the African bishops were vehement and emotional in their denunciation. Lambeth was treated to African oratory so violent and homophobic that Jerry Falwell would have been embarrassed. What happened, one must wonder, to the "nonproblem that did not exist in Africa"? Here the nature of prejudice was revealed once more. People with power have defined people without power.

Because homosexual persons are not heterosexual people, they are thought to be less than human, heterosexual people assert. Because the majority is heterosexual, those not part of that majority must be abnormal, depraved, debauched. "They cannot exist," said the African leaders. "But they do exist," said the Lambeth Conference. "But they should not exist" said the African leaders, "and if they do exist where they ought not to exist, they are evil and should be repressed, denied, obliterated." Funny how it is that victims of prejudice never quite recognize their own prejudice when they are part of the defining majority. Lambeth barely began to notice that homosexual persons, like blacks and women, are no longer willing to be defined by anyone except themselves. In time, Lambeth will affirm that principle and come down on the side of this oppressed and persecuted group of God's children.

One does not usually think of ecumenical and interfaith resolutions as another manifestation of human prejudice, but I believe the principle of prejudice operates in this arena also. Every religious group starts out with the assumption that in some form it possesses the entire truth, or at least more of the truth than anyone else. Empowered by this assumption they proceed to define other groups as less than truthful and, depending on the level of difference, conclude that their inadequate opponents are worthy recipients of a missionary effort to give them the whole truth or to free them from distorted truth.

The ecumenical movement arises only when various Christian bodies give up their claims to ultimacy. That is why the Roman Catholic Church is not yet part of the ecumenical movement despite increased cooperation and frequent ecumenical rhetoric. Instead, the Roman Catholic Church uses ecumenical forums to witness to its own version of truth and to call others back to the "only true mother church." Ecumenicity moved into interfaith dialogue only when attempts at missionary conversion failed and survival demanded that people live together in mutual respect. Then the question of religious prejudice was asked. Can Christians really define Judaism adequately? Can Christians define Islam, Buddhism, Hinduism, or any other faith system save our own?

Will dialogue ever be real and honest so long as evangelism as an attempt to convert is not surrendered? Is prejudice less prejudicial when it is religious prejudice? Without quite recognizing what it was doing, Lambeth, frequently over the protests of the conservatives, moved the Anglican Communion a step or two away from evangelism based upon our arrogance and a step or two closer to dialogue based upon our humility. Even in this ecumenical and interfaith arena, prejudice, understood as one power group defining another powerless group in terms of its own agenda, was countered.

Women alone will finally define women. Racial groups alone will finally define themselves. Homosexual persons alone will define homosexuality. Each religious group and faith tradition will ultimately be the arbiter of its own faith story and self-definition. That is what Lambeth began to assert behind the rhetoric of its seventy plus resolutions. That is a powerful message to permeate a lengthy agenda because it finally rests on the deepest of all biblical truths. It assumes that God has created all people in God's own image, that God has redeemed all people in the love of Jesus Christ, and that God has called all people to the fullness of life in the Holy Spirit. That, I believe, is the heart of the Gospel which was heard on four unique fronts at the Lambeth Conference of 1988.

– 23 –

Lambeth 1998: Christianity Caught in a Time Warp

September 1998

> "As you know it is my desire that there should be no attempt at the Conference to force the assembled bishops to vote in such a way that we are polarized."

That is a quotation from the archbishop of Canterbury in a personal letter to me dated May 7, 1998. Perhaps George Carey forgot he wrote it. Perhaps he changed his mind. Perhaps he intended to be deliberately misleading. Perhaps, when he saw the weight of conservative and evangelical support, he decided he no longer had to pretend to be a diplomat. Perhaps he judged defeating the "liberals and revisionists" as more important than keeping the Anglican Communion open to new possibilities, broad in its view of Christianity and constantly engaging the vibrant, emerging world. In any event he threw his weight verbally and visually behind resolutions that have in fact left this church polarized. Once more in the name of the God of love the church has managed to insult gay and lesbian people and to suggest to women everywhere that they are still a "problem" in the body of Christ.

For many Christians the 1998 Lambeth Conference of Anglican bishops was a tense, difficult, and negative experience. It proved to be an arena in which conflict was inescapable. We listened to calls to respect the cultures of emerging nations, but no attempt was ever made to respect the culture of the West. No one seemed to recognize that the church in the West has engaged our modern world with its challenging scientific and secular insights far more significantly than has any other part of the communion.

We lived at Lambeth with perceptions of reality so vastly different that the same words simply did not mean the same thing. We became aware that difficult local circumstances so deeply colored one's frame of reference that those outside those circumstances could never understand the words that were being spoken. So we dealt with charges and countercharges, with various attempts to claim in debate the high moral ground of identifying local operative truths with God's unchanging Truth. We dealt with Christians who had escaped genocide and with Christians who had participated in it.

We even endured the lecture of an official representative from the Vatican, Cardinal Edward Cassidy, who warned the Anglican Communion about how dangerous it would be to ecumenical relations with the Roman Catholic Church if we moved to consider issues on which the mind of that church was quite closed. We have heard similar themes at previous Lambeth Conferences from our Roman Catholic friends. The cardinal and those he represents seem not to realize that Rome's attitude toward women and homosexual people present barriers that make ecumenical union on our part both undesirable and impossible.

There were also moments of wonder and joy. There were new friends to be made like Dr. Stephen Laird and Dr. Stephen Shakespeare, young English scholars who offer hope to a coming generation. There were old acquaintances to be renewed — many of whom we had met on previous travels around this communion. There were thrilling stories of heroic Christian activity to be heard. Some parts of this communion live under extreme circumstances: the life and death struggle with Islam in some parts of the world; famine and sickness in others. In South Africa the whole society has moved through a kind of inner purging that accompanied the death of apartheid and the activities of their Truth and Reconciliation Commission bringing them to a remarkably new place in their history. Their bishops revealed a compassion and openness that heralds a new camaraderie in that nation's racial diversity. Archbishop Njongonkulu Ndungane, who has replaced the unforgettable Desmond Tutu in the primate's chair of that province, gives every evidence that he is a worthy successor. Younger bishops behind him, both black and white, are ready to step up when the next generation assumes the mantle of leadership.

Memories of past Lambeth gatherings seemed so poignant in retrospect. I thought about the bishop of London, now retired and no longer an Anglican, who stated in 1978 that there would "never be women priests in the Church of England." "Never" turned out to be a rather finite period of time as England now has thousands of priests who are women, and Lambeth 1998 welcomed eleven Anglican bishops who are female. I recalled a speech made by a Ugandan bishop in 1988 in which he stated that "AIDS is a white man's disease. It does not exist in Africa." But in 1998 the Lambeth Conference heard of whole African villages so ravaged by AIDS that its only citizens are children and some very old people, and of one African nation where 35 percent of its adult population is now HIV positive.

Homosexuality, barely mentioned in 1988, ten years later was destined to take the emotional main seat. We had to unload the stated misperception that it was the United States and Canada which were forcing this debate on the agenda. The fact is that it was the homophobic fears of the Third World seeking to condemn the very mention of homosexuality that made this topic the major item. Even American conservatives could not tolerate certain Third World statements made on this subject. A group of African bishops voted to expel from the communion, for example, any bishop who had signed the Koinonia Statement, a statement I drafted in 1994 affirming the place of openly homosexual people in the life of the church, now signed by more than eighty American bishops. Other Ugandan bishops likened homosexuality to wife beating, pedophilia, and bestiality. African bishops joined evangelicals from England, Australia, Canada, and New Zealand as well as American conservatives to pronounce homosexuality a sin for which repentance was required and without repentance they promised eternal punishment to anyone who was homosexual.

Buttressing every debate on every issue was an appeal to "Holy Scripture." Yet it was clear that those who employed this phrase meant something quite different from what most of us would mean. Many appeared to be oblivious to the last 150 years of biblical scholarship that has shaped Western Christianity. They still appeal to a literalized reading of this ancient biblical text to solve in a definitive way contemporary, complex moral issues. There seemed to be no acknowledgment of the fact that this attitude toward the Bible has been employed to condemn Galileo, Darwin, and Freud. Time has demonstrated in each case that this view of the Bible did not prevail. The Bible has also been used to justify slavery, segregation, and apartheid. Once again history's judgment has been that the Bible was wrong. This sacred book has been used to oppress women, to reject left-handed people, to bless the church's refusal to bury a victim of suicide, and to oppose birth control. Both church and society have moved so far away from these antiquated ideas that Christians are today embarrassed to recall this history. At this Lambeth Conference, however, the Bible was being used in a similar manner to uphold negativity and violence against gay and lesbian people. A literalized Bible with claims of inerrancy for its words has historically been a source of death far more often than it has been a source of life. Yet this kind of fundamentalism was clearly once again alive and well in this communion, making it all but impossible to build in our time a modern and relevant Christianity.

This conference caused me to feel that I was living in a time warp. The archbishop of Canterbury gave a talk on his vision for the church of the future. It revealed, rather, how far in the past his own life was rooted. I suspect that to the leaders of some of the undeveloped nations his words sounded visionary, but to me they were at least thirty years out of date. He and I simply do not live in the same world.

The most regrettable characteristic observed at this gathering of church leaders was the lack of honesty in communication. Making points rather than seeking truth seemed to be the agenda of far too many. Christians, no more and I gather no less than anyone else, will attack the character of their opponents rather than stating the way they differ from their opponents' ideas. It would be difficult to apply to what I saw at the Lambeth Conference the biblical standard that Christians "will be known by their love." I saw rather pettiness, dishonesty, spinelessness, spin doctoring, and absolute distortions of truth as the behavior of those who claimed to be disciples of Jesus. Those who called themselves evangelical journalists were the worst offenders.

The leadership qualities of our primates left much to be desired. The effective leaders were clearly the representatives of the evangelical wing of the church. Western leadership was disorganized, inept, incapable of working strategically, and without a common purpose. Their overt refusal to draft a minority statement when it was clear that their point of view had no chance of prevailing and in fact was almost certainly going to be overwhelmed meant that liberal bishops were reduced to making individual responses when the various hostile resolutions were passed. These individual statements lacked both power and persuasiveness and did not provide an effective place behind which opponents of the majority point of view could rally.

In those majority resolutions homosexuality was condemned as "nonscriptural," the cause of women priests and bishops was set back by a vote to be "fair to traditionalists," and evangelical fundamentalism was empowered time after time. In many forums we heard the church in our nation and America itself insulted as decadent, demonic, and no longer Christian.

I need to say that if this expression of evangelical Christianity is to define the Anglican Communion of the future, I do not want to be part of it. I regard this expression of the religious right as an irrational, hysterical stage in the death throes of Christianity. If we cannot reassert the Anglican genius that reason must be an equal factor with scripture and tradition in shaping the Christian message in every generation, then Christianity as we know it is doomed. The Lambeth Conference convinced me completely that my call for a new reformation in the church is right on target, and it showed me exactly why it is that Christianity must change or die.

– 24 –

Feeding the Flock Down Under

December 1991

Australia and New Zealand are literally thousands of miles away. They are, however, English-speaking nations where the Anglican Communion is deeply rooted. For that reason HarperCollins decided to introduce my recent books into the South Pacific. For three weeks of our vacation this past summer, Chris and I journeyed down under to fulfill a media speaking tour organized by my publisher. It was an expansive, deep-learning new experience.

In the twenty-one days available to us, I made ninety-four public appearances — fifty-nine in Australia and thirty-five in New Zealand. These included newspaper and magazine interviews, television and radio programs, and public lectures. We touched every major city in Australia except Perth and Adelaide, and every city in New Zealand. Privately I talked with bishops, clergy, and media people about the place and present health of Christianity in both countries, and I created dialogue and debate that, judging from my mail, is still vigorous in both countries.

Australia has a painful, shadowy history revolving around the original convict settlers and the European treatment of the aboriginal population. Today, however, it is a vast, modern, and beautiful country of some seventeen million citizens, organized around the two major cities of Sydney and Melbourne. The relationship between the institutional church and the secular society in this country is strange and complex.

I found in this nation a tremendous hunger for meaning, transcendence, and God. I also found in Australia a Christian church so conservative that, save for isolated instances, it was no longer in any significant dialogue with its world. The three major Christian groups in this country are Anglicans, Roman Catholics, and the Uniting Church — a merger of the major mainline Protestant traditions. The liveliest of the three appeared to be the Uniting Church. The closest to death was the Anglican Church. No church, however, seemed to speak with vibrancy.

The Anglican Church of Australia is dominated by the Archdiocese of Sydney, its largest and richest province. The roots of this diocese go back to the Anglican Protestants of Northern Ireland, who lived on their hatred of the Irish Roman Catholics. The most virulent aspects of that ancient conflict were simply transferred through migration to Sydney. In an attempt to preserve these ancient anti-Catholic prejudices, this part of our communion has become ultraconservative in a Protestant fundamentalist tradition.

The Archdiocese of Sydney has, therefore, not been a participant in the great debates on the role of women, liturgical reform, or human sexuality that have been engaged worldwide by our church. It is a rather narrowly defined diocese that insists that its clergy go only to its own diocesan seminary, which, of course, undergirds and supports its monochromatic viewpoint and which revealingly will not hire for their faculty those who are not its own graduates. Efforts at both mind control and political control are employed very successfully in Sydney. No one who isn't on the list proposed by the ruling clique is ever elected to anything at meetings of the synod. Old Harry Byrd never ran his Virginia fiefdom that effectively.

More than this, in the Australian General Synod, a 75 percent majority vote is required to pass legislation outright. If a resolution achieves only a two-thirds majority, it must then be submitted to all the dioceses. To become law, the resolution must then pass two-thirds of the diocesan synods and in each case by a two-thirds majority. So complicated and cumbersome is this process that most people do not have the energy to see a change process through to a successful conclusion. This means that a small minority can effectively thwart the democratic decision-making processes of the Australian church for an interminable number of years. The Archdiocese of Sydney has done just that for the whole Anglican Church of Australia.

The Archdiocese of Sydney also employs the threat of economic blackmail over the whole church when Sydney's views are not respected. The monetary threat has a paralyzing effect. The inability to bring change through the normal democratic processes means that many have given up on the church. This is especially true among the thinking members of Australian society. They hunger for God, for a sense of ultimate value, and for some place where life's deepest questions can be engaged — values functions that are normally found in church. When these things are not or cannot be found in church, a church alumni association comes into being. In a unique way this group, disillusioned and turned off by the church, became my primary audience. I seemed to speak not through the church, but over the heads of the church to the people of Australia.

HarperCollins successfully got my story and the story of my books to the media even before my arrival. *Newsweek* of Australia and New Zealand had done a major feature a week before I arrived. The magazine section of the major Melbourne Sunday paper had asked me to write an article for them for publication on the Sunday before I left the United States. Some two years ago I had done ten radio talk show programs via telephone from Newark with stations in every major Australian city. These were resurrected and rerun in anticipation of my arrival. There was an obvious eagerness in the media to give my ideas and my visit full play. Once there, this eagerness snowballed.

I had not been in my hotel for two hours when the first interview with Australia's only national newspaper took place. The interview began on a rather hostile note as the reporter probed for the obvious demonic nature Sydney church leaders had informed him that I possessed. But before an hour had passed he was listening, questioning, and even laughing. His photographer must have shot one hundred pictures while the interview proceeded. The next day a very positive story dominated page 3 of *The Australian*. After that, radio, television, magazines, and every other newspaper wanted to feature the one they portrayed as "America's unusual and controversial bishop."

I did a guest spot on a morning television show opposite the "Jerry Falwell" of Australia. I was interviewed by Ray Martin, Australia's best-known television personality, in a program format that was a combination of the *Today Show* and Phil Donahue. I was guest on the Australian version of *Meet the Press*. I filled one hour of radio time being interviewed by Terry Lane, Australia's most respected national host, and two hours of a national call-in show on Sunday night hosted by John Cleary, Australia's best-known religious broadcaster. This latter program was first set for thirty minutes, but was expanded to two hours because of public interest. Tapes of both the Terry Lane show and the John Cleary show were offered for sale by the radio stations and did, I am told, a record-breaking business.

This response in turn fed attendances at the public lectures that had been scheduled — two in Sydney, three in Melbourne, one in

Canberra, and one in Brisbane. The attendance ranged from 350 to 700 people and in every case surpassed by almost double the expectations of the sponsors. That was, in itself, exciting and fulfilling, but the most significant thing to me was not the number but the makeup of the crowds. By and large they were people who said they had not been inside a church in years. They were the alienated, the disenfranchised, the church dropouts.

Of course the conservative religious voices took notice — in both positive and negative ways. The archbishop of Brisbane was encouraged to think that five hundred people would come to his cathedral for a 1:30 p.m. lecture on a Wednesday afternoon, and so he began to question his priorities that were aimed primarily at keeping the faithful undisturbed. But the Diocese of Sydney priest who writes a once-a-week column for *The Australian* devoted his column for two straight weeks to a rebuttal of my thought in typical religious hyperbole, suggesting that I no longer believed in God and was a wolf in sheep's clothing. Significantly, at no point in either column did he deal with any issue I raised. When one cannot deal with the message, the time-honored method is to attack the messenger.

Since returning home I have received copies of various fundamentalist religious newspapers that clearly have been called into the fray because the media attention given to me was so extensive that they could not ignore the challenge. The result is that the Bible is being discussed in secular circles in Australia. When the Bible is seriously debated in public it has a chance at last to be heard, to be taken seriously, and to escape the literalistic imprisonment into which the church so often has trapped it.

Lest I paint too bleak a picture, be assured that there is a creative and alive remnant in the Australian church. There was a courageous priest in the Diocese of Sydney who hosted my first lecture, making thereby a statement of opposition to the mentality of his diocese. There was a priest in Melbourne who was as gifted as any ordained person I have ever met. He was open and alive, like a renaissance man who ached at the insensitivity of his religious tradition. There was a bishop in Canberra whose conscience drives him to contemplate an act of canonical disobedience that he talks about publicly. There was also an archdeacon of Canberra whose mind embraces the whole theological landscape. Finally, there were the women — one priest, many deacons, and even more among the laity, who struggle to live with integrity while their very being is discussed, patronized, and insulted by the church they love.

To these minority people I trust that I gave hope, the vision of a wider context of the Gospel, and the sense of history that is clearly on their side. It is deeply satisfying to think that in some small way I have touched these nerves and filled this vacuum on a continent halfway around the world and in another hemisphere. It is also affirming to know that at this moment some part of the world's population is, because of my visit, looking anew at the Bible, a book that has sustained and revolutionized the church for two thousand years. That same book, I am happy to assert, continues to feed my life daily with its Gospel of love and hope.

– 25 –

Face-Off in Vancouver

September 1993

The cathedral's doors were scheduled to open at 7:00 p.m. By 6:15 the line of people waiting to get in stretched over four blocks in downtown Vancouver. By 7:15 fifteen hundred people were seated in the cathedral as well as in the large room in the undercroft that was equipped with closed circuit television. Hundreds more were turned away. It was a Wednesday night in July of 1993. The attraction was a debate on Christian sexual ethics.

Neither debater was Canadian. From across the Atlantic came the best-known international voice of the evangelical wing of the Church of England, the tall, slender, gracious Reverend Dr. John Stott. This Anglican priest was for years the rector of All Saints' Church, Langham Place, in London, across the street from the BBC in Broadcasting House. The author of over thirty books, John Stott's name is a household word in conservative evangelical circles the world over. He was in Vancouver as a guest lecturer at Regent College, an evangelical lay training center of the University of British Columbia.

From the United States came the Anglican bishop of Newark, New Jersey, introduced as one who is also widely known throughout the communion, an author and a spokesperson for the liberal or progressive wing of the church. Bishop Spong was in Canada as a member of the faculty of the Vancouver School of Theology, also of the University of British Columbia.

This debate had caught the attention of the media who used the ice hockey phrase "face-off" to advertise the event. The people organizing the event played to that image. The debate was filmed for Canadian cable television. To heighten the drama, Dr. Stott and I were brought together in the dean's study for a televised flip-of-a-coin to determine the order of presentation. Dr. Stott called "heads." Heads it was; and he chose to speak first.

The format called for each speaker to present his point of view in a twenty-five minute address, followed by a five-minute response from the other speaker. Questions were then collected from the audience, and a committee decided which questions would be posed to each speaker in order to give balance to the evening. Dr. Stott and I concluded the evening with five-minute summations. Since Dr. Stott spoke first, I was given the position of speaking last. It was a warm evening, and the heat of the television lights added to the intensity of the occasion.

Dr. Stott's opening statement gave both autobiographical details and self-deprecating rhetoric about the English, including reference to the play entitled, *No Sex Please, We're British*. Then, with great integrity, he outlined his point of view. A text from Genesis referred to by Jesus, which states "a man shall leave his mother and father and cleave to his wife," was crucial to Dr. Stott's argument. This text ruled out all patterns of life except faithful, monogamous, heterosexual marriage, he asserted. He spoke of a personal responsibility not to compromise eternal biblical standards in order to conform to every new age. It was a well-delivered speech and a clear articulation of the classical position of the conservative evangelical point of view.

When I rose to speak I wanted to establish two things. First, I stated that I take the Bible seriously but do not apply its literal words to today's complex issues. Secondly, I stated that traditional biblical moral standards reflect the worldview and level of knowledge available to people living thousands of years ago and cannot be applied simplistically to our contemporary world. I reminded the audience of the role played in the perpetuation of slavery, apartheid, and segregation by Bible-quoting Christians. Slavery existed in the Christian nations of the West until the nineteenth century. Slavery's stepchildren, apartheid and segregation, continue, albeit in a weakened condition, in identifiably Christian nations to this day.

The Bible has been quoted throughout the twentieth century to keep women in subservient positions. Women could not own property in many nations of the Christian West until the nineteenth century. They did not vote in the United States until 1922. University education of women is a twentieth-century phenomenon. The professions have been quite slow in opening to women, with the priesthood of the church being one of the last bastions of male domination. We are still treated to the spectacle of watching a major Christian church in the world not only prohibit female ordination but daring to sit in all-male celibate councils and pronounce in the name of a male deity on the morality of what a woman does with her own body in the areas of birth control and abortion.

I reminded Dr. Stott that long after the writing of the text in Genesis that was so important to him, the Bible portrayed God as approving polygamy. Long after Jesus quoted that text in Genesis, women in marriage were still regarded as nonequal and as the property of their husbands. Real monogamy can be entered only where real equality has been achieved, and that is just now dawning in our generation.

I also questioned whether biblical authors, writing between 1000 B.C.E. and 135 C.E., were competent either to understand or to pronounce judgment on homosexuality. Those same writers assumed that epilepsy was caused by demon possession. I raised the possibility that the church needs to hold out to its gay and lesbian sons and daughters a model of faithful monogamous partnerships that both church and society would honor and bless.

Dr. Stott responded by reminding us that slavery had been opposed and eventually overthrown by Christians. The oppression of women was also opposed and is being overthrown by Christians. He would not, however, go on to admit that the persecution of gay and lesbian people is now being opposed and overcome by Christians. Indeed, he saw nothing but sin or sickness in homosexuality. There is only one moral alternative for homosexual persons, he argued, and that is to discipline their evil urges and control their lives rigorously by responsible celibacy. A faithful, monogamous, heterosexual, lifetime union was, for him, the only possible Christian ideal.

In my rebuttal time I wondered why it took these Christians nineteen centuries to conclude that slavery was evil, and twenty centuries to begin to discover the equality of women, unless slavery and second-class status for women both served the well-being of the white males who ruled the world without challenge for nineteen centuries and who made their actions seem moral by quoting from a Bible that reflected a patriarchal mentality. I referred to gay and lesbian couples I have known whose lives reflect a beauty that is coveted in many heterosexual marriages. I pledged myself to protect the integrity of gay and lesbian clergy and to encourage the recognition of life-giving partnerships for all God's children when they are faithful, monogamous, and holy.

The questions came next. Biblical literalists expressed fear that the Word of God was being undermined. A divorced woman asked Dr. Stott if there was no place in his value system for a divorced Christian. Homosexual persons asked how they could feel the welcome of Christ in a church that taught that they were sick or evil.

In his final summary, Dr. Stott began to suggest that I was not a Christian, that I did not believe in the Lordship of Christ or in the resurrection of Jesus. When I challenged him, he responded that I did not believe in the physical, bodily view of the resurrection. I suggested that belief in either the resurrection of Jesus or in the Lordship of Christ was not limited to Dr. Stott's particular views of those two truths.

In my summary I pointed to the changes that have come in our time. In the Middle Ages puberty and marriage were separated by one to two years at the most. In our day that gap is ten to fifteen years. The equality of sexes expressed in the equality of education and opportunity means that women are no longer forced to stay in abusive or unfulfilling marriages simply for economic security, so the rise in the divorce rate is inevitable, sometimes for very good and even moral reasons. I suggested that modern science was clearly coming down on the side of those who affirm that homosexuality is a normal but minority aspect on the scale of human sexuality, that it is a given not a chosen, and that the evil that homosexual persons have endured has resulted primarily from abuse heaped upon them by Bible-quoting moralistic representatives of Christianity. Even today the only groups who still think they can "cure" homosexual persons are conservative, right-wing, Christian groups. Their claims are not subject to verification by scientific standards, and many of them have been revealed as absolutely fraudulent.

A proper use of the Bible, I maintained, was not to quote its literal words but rather to look at its underlying principles, which then must be faithfully applied to life's changing circumstances. Those principles are that every human being is holy, created in God's image, every human being is loved and valued by God in Jesus Christ, and every human being is called into the fullness of life by God's Holy Spirit. When the church places its moral, ethical, and sexual decisions within this context, I concluded, every predatory relationship that violates the integrity of a powerless person will be seen as wrong, and every promiscuous relationship that treats a person as a thing will be seen as wrong. Christian morality will be determined by asking: Is this act holy, does it give life, is it true to who I am and to what I believe, and does it call another person involved in this act into life? To build a church where all are welcomed and where each person is helped to achieve this kind of holiness in every relationship is my goal as a bishop and a Christian.

The debate closed with an appreciative response from the packed assembly. Following a brief social gathering over wine and cheese, Dr. Stott and I shook hands and parted company. He was headed for Korea. I returned to the Vancouver School of Theology. Each of us remained eager to bear witness to our understanding of the church's mandate to proclaim the Gospel to the world. I suspect that the church has more integrity today because two of its servants who see Christianity quite differently dared to face these issues openly and publicly. In doing so we revealed that Anglican Christianity is not monolithic, that it is always in flux, and that this church will be a household of faith in which the real questions of life can be asked. It is a rare privilege in our day to be part of that kind of Christian community.

– 26 –

An English Reporter's Odyssey: Two Days in the Diocese of Newark

March 1994

The caller was Andrew Brown, religious editor for *The Independent,* which arguably is England's best daily newspaper, its circulation having now exceeded *The Times.* In the stereotypical manner of the English, he announced that his newspaper would like to send him to the United States to write a weekend magazine section feature on the bishop of Newark that would accompany the British launch of my newest book, *Resurrection: Myth or Reality?* His editors wanted him to help his English readers understand that peculiar part of the Anglican Communion called the Diocese of Newark. He wondered if he could spend the weekend with me, go everywhere that I was scheduled to go, and discuss issues with a variety of people. I was pleased and flattered to have this means of having the story of this diocese told in an influential way to the mother church of the Anglican Communion. At 7:15 p.m. on Friday, February 25, I met the flight from London and took my guest home for dinner and the beginning of the weekend odyssey.

On Saturday morning I organized the day so that we could view the work of the Diocese of Newark. Our first stop was at Christ Hospital, Jersey City, whose board I chair. Next we called at Grace Van Vorst, where the priest, Scott Kallstrom, and his wife, Bayla, introduced our guest to urban ministry. Andrew Brown saw flexible worship space, the way in which this church has attracted the artistic community, the children's programs that are housed in the gymnasium, and the support this church has given to entrepreneurial cottage industries begun in Jersey City. No member of today's Church of England ever confronted such a vision of what a church might do and be.

Next we drove to Trinity, Bayonne, where the rector, Gerard Pisani, and his partner, Dwight Tintle, have established a variety of outreach ministries: the "Windmill Alliance" for adult handicapped people; "Highways," a ministry to the poor which is supported by two thrift shops; and the "Umbrella Project" for unwed mothers and battered women. The corporation which this church has formed has just been granted the franchise for "Dunkin' Donuts," which it will develop as a new way of creating jobs and skill training for both the handicapped and the poor.

As we entered the parish house of this church, we discovered that we had interrupted a meeting of Narcotics Anonymous. It was almost more than this English reporter could take in. When Gerard Pisani described his future plans, the dazed look on Andrew's face grew more profound.

We moved on to Newark, making stops at the cathedral, Cathedral House, the House of Prayer, Apostles' House, St. James' Square, and St. Barnabas' Church. Here Andrew Brown was able to see the impact of our church on our city in terms of family shelters and family rehabilitation, low-cost housing initiatives on the site of the former St. James' Church, and the Resource Center that ministers to women and children with AIDS.

Driving through the Oranges we paused at the three "cathedral-like" structures — Christ Church, Church of the Epiphany, and St. Mark's — that anchor the main street running from East Orange to West Orange. As we drove I described the ministry in places we did not see, such as St. Paul's, Paterson, Hillsdale House, Rutherford

House, and Resurrection House. We ended our tour at St. Peter's, Morristown, one of our strongest and wealthiest congregations, where an ecumenical program to feed the hungry involves over one hundred volunteers and some five hundred homeless people as guests six days a week, supplemented on Sundays by the Church of the Redeemer in Morristown. Exhausted, and feeling the stress of jet lag, our guest crashed for a late afternoon nap.

For two hours before dinner Andrew interviewed me on my new book and my entire writing career. Were my theological concerns disturbing the church? Who constituted my audience? How do the people of the diocese respond to the theological controversies regularly generated by my writings? Could I really continue as a Christian if I regard the narratives of the empty tomb and the appearance stories of the risen Christ in the Gospels as legends? What is midrash and why does that concept illumine the Gospels in a brand new way? It has taken me a lifetime of study to reach the conclusions about which I write and the convictions that undergird my activity. In two hours I had to make one who had not read my sources understand my conclusions. It was a fascinating time.

That evening my wife and I tried to assemble a dinner party that would introduce our guest to a composite of our diocesan life, not an easy task when besides the host and hostess and our guest of honor we could only include five additional persons. But we worked it out. A leading suburban lay woman who has been deeply involved in many parts of the life of this diocese, together with her husband who has been senior warden and chair of the search committee in their parish, came to represent the main line constituency of this great diocese. A woman priest whose church is packed every Sunday and who twice has been a serious contender in another diocese for the office of bishop came to represent our support of women in every phase of the church's life. Finally we invited a gay couple. These two people are active at one of the Anglo-Catholic churches as well as in The Oasis (the ministry of the Diocese of Newark to lesbian and gay persons and their friends), and they have provided for the whole church a vision of inclusivity. The fact that this couple is also interracial added still another dimension of the quality of the portrait I sought to paint of our diocesan life.

The conversation before, during, and after dinner was rich and far-roaming. Time and again I wondered how this data was being processed inside the very English mind of our reporter.

On Sunday morning we rose early. This would be Andrew

Brown's chance to experience a day in the life of a bishop. The confirmation schedule made up a year ago placed me on this day in two churches of the Western Convocation: Christ Church, Budd Lake, in the morning and St. Peter's, Mount Arlington, in the late afternoon. Both are on the evangelical side of the church's life. Several people in Budd Lake had brought Bibles to church to follow the sermon and "to check on that bishop." I had anticipated that and had prepared a sermon on the symbol of three days from the Easter narrative. I had sixteen texts from the four Gospels marked to show how the symbol three days had grown and shifted from "after three days" to "on the third day." This analysis, I believe, lends weight to my conclusion that the three-day time span in which the Easter story is told is borrowed from Jewish mythology and was never intended to be a measure of chronological time. It is rather a theological affirmation that the Kingdom of God which was to descend from heaven at dawn three days after the end of the world has, in fact, come in the resurrected life of Jesus of Nazareth. The reporter interviewed a couple of worshipers after the service. "Did you understand what he was saying? Did it upset you or frighten you?" "It made me think" was the benign comment of one whose standard red-lettered international text of the Bible was prominently displayed under her arm.

Between the two services we drove Andrew Brown to the Delaware Water Gap and to the home of the two non-church-going friends who have helped found "Christianity for the Third Millennium," a project designed to reach people like themselves. This conversation focused on the issue of how the spiritual hunger so obvious in these latter years of the twentieth century can be met outside the present structures of the church since it is clear that it is not going to be met inside those ecclesiastical structures without a major new reformation.

Following the second service, my wife drove our guest to the airport while I remained for the parish dinner. They had an hour together in the car for conversation. Both are English and both understand something of the way the English reading public would receive this story. I would have loved the opportunity to eavesdrop on that conversation.

In a whirlwind period of forty-eight hours it had been my task to interpret to a jet-lagged English reporter the scope and meaning of that community of faith known as the Diocese of Newark and my particular vocation within it, which has now reached far beyond its borders. It framed for a moment in clear relief what it is that we are about in this diocese, and it helped me to understand anew the dimensions of my ministry as a bishop in the church of God. In my last convention address I sought to outline the scope of this ministry as it has evolved, to interpret for this diocesan family the demands on my life and time that this ministry now requires. The members of the convention heard that and responded by resolving that the ministry of this bishop beyond the boundaries of this diocese is part of the ministry of this diocese. It was deeply affirming, for I cannot step out of the role into which my episcopal career has carried me. The national and international demands of this career will probably not decrease. I would not care to engage these demands except as the active diocesan bishop of Newark. This frantically busy visit from a London religious reporter made that very clear to me, but it also made me know how very proud I was to show off this diocese and its enormously rich ministry.

– 27 –

Visionless in the Name of Unity

June 1994

Before this summer is complete, the Seventy-First Triennial Convention of the Episcopal Church in the United States will have convened, conducted its business, and adjourned. In some ways it is like a family reunion where friends meet to catch up with one another. In others it is a political gathering where issues are debated, votes taken, and elections held. It is also a worship-filled gathering where the pageantry of our ecclesiastical heritage is on display. As our church prepares to gather this year, an atmosphere of dis-ease that permeates to the core of all organized religion is very much present. Religious voices are increasingly angry. Denunciations are rampant. Blame is cast around freely.

In mainline churches financial resources are in short supply and vital statistics are declining. Every special interest group interprets these signs to its own advantage. But behind the explanations there is a stark picture of a church that no longer knows how to be itself. It is a church in retreat, a church in disarray; some would even say a church that is dying. When I look nationally for some understanding of this contemporary malaise, I find a yawning emptiness. Our church like most others would rather attack the symptoms and place Band-Aids on the cancer than to address the central reality. I see no truth at the heart of this church for which it is willing to die. Rather, I hear threats that if such and such occurs, this group or that group will leave the church, as if the future of the church can be secured only by chopping off those elements that they perceive to be creating the distress that they feel.

Church unity seems to have been enshrined as the highest value of church life, and in the service of that value debate is stifled and issues are suppressed. Those lives which have been called to stretch beyond their heretofore comforting and defining prejudices are no longer challenged to grow. At the same time those who are demanding a place at God's table are told to wait a bit longer until the levels of prejudice have been lowered and the church's recognition of them as people created in God's image will not disturb the church's cherished unity. Dioceses are cutting their commitments to the budget of the national church, developing various plans for local giving. They seem to think that a church that dies nationally today will survive locally tomorrow. History demonstrates that such has never been the case.

Our national leaders, rather than calling people to engage this critical moment, have decided to address this crisis by walking down a familiar pathway of abdication. They would send representatives to the "grass roots," to every diocese in the land to discover the needs, wishes, and desires of our people.

When I first heard of this plan, I could not believe it. It was, as Yogi Berra once observed, "déjà vu all over again." Does no one remember history? In 1970 there was a similar sense of pain that gripped this church of ours. John Elbridge Hines, in my opinion the greatest church leader in this century, had confronted the issues present in our national life. He had placed this church of ours at the side of the poor, the dispossessed, and the alienated of our society. He had developed in 1967, in the wake of America's urban riots, an initiative called the General Convention Special Program. It was a program of enormous risk, designed to empower the heretofore powerless black minority. In 1969 he had allowed the South Bend Special Convention to be interrupted by a group of black church people who demanded that the church stop doing business as usual and address the racism that continued to reign supreme in the body of Christ just beyond the church's empty rhetoric.

The reaction to these prophetic acts of leadership was predictable.

Conservative regions of this country from Virginia, where I lived at the time, to Florida and Texas began the task of punishing economically the leadership of the church by withholding their pledges. Of course, no one wanted to admit to being racist, so racism was clothed in the respectability of anti-communism. The communists, wherever they were, were considered a legitimate object of hatred and made the racist behavior seem righteous.

By 1970 the reaction had become so strong that the convention elected to the Executive Council a conservative anti-Hines slate led by the bishop of Mississippi, the Right Reverend John Maury Allin, and they began the task of removing the pain from the pews of the establishment. "Safeguards" were put into the General Convention Special Program to allow local vetoes of grants. There would be no more empowering of the powerless, for now the powerful could stop the programs, and stop them they did.

What tactic was used to achieve this surrender of authentic visionary leadership? It was a clever one. Conservative elements of the church convinced the leadership of the church that they must go to the grassroots and listen to the people! So out across the nation the members of the Executive Council trooped. When the survey was completed, a massive document, *What We Learned from What You Said,* was published. Not surprisingly, it called for the blessing of the status quo and for the gutting of all social action initiatives, except the safe ones like contributing to black colleges.

With the money that would be saved from these suspended controversial grants, a new investment in traditional-sounding and nondisturbing programs of Christian education and evangelism would be made. Even in these areas, the national church was to be only a responder, never an initiator. Bishop Allin rode this tide of reaction to his own election as presiding bishop three years later and for the twelve years of his term presided over the withdrawal of the church from the world. The only progress made during those years was on initiatives begun earlier that had such momentum that the forces of reaction could not stop them. I refer to the votes to ordain women in 1976 and to revise the Prayer Book in 1979. Both votes were achieved over Bishop Allin's active opposition, and far more of the church's energy was exerted to ease the pain of the losers than to celebrate the inclusion of the winners.

By and large, the church limited its vision to platitudinous rhetoric on safe subjects like Christian education and evangelism. With the election of a new presiding bishop in 1984, one would have thought that the church nationally was finally ready to engage its world again. The new presiding bishop was a man of a big heart and a voting record of unqualified support for the inclusion of minorities and for the ordained ministry of women. He was also one of only twenty-one bishops who had signed the minority statement in favor of full inclusion of homosexual persons into the life of the church in 1979. He began his primacy by stating that there would be no outcasts in this church. It was a hopeful beginning. But when the rhetoric was translated into action, the leadership of the church waffled.

When homosexual persons began to be welcomed into the life of the church on equal terms with heterosexual persons, once again the leadership blanched. Issues of conscience now suddenly seemed less important than issues of unity. Of course we found ways to legitimatize our prejudice. Homosexual persons replaced communists as the bearers of what many believed was a legitimate religious, righteous hostility. Strangely enough, monies began to be withheld once more in the same conservative parts of this church, like Virginia, Florida, and Texas. New calls for local options in giving were heard. "Restructure the presiding bishop's office so that it is pastoral [read powerless] and vest authority locally" became the new version of the old, old themes.

In 1993, to my absolute amazement, the leadership of our national church decided once again that they would go to the "grass roots" and listen to our people so that the programs of our church could be restructured in accordance with local need. I could not believe that we had not learned twenty-three years ago that walking down this road is to surrender any semblance of vision or leadership. It is an abdication to fear. So I refused to participate in this process. When the results were received, they surprised no one. For the second time in a quarter of a century, this church has laid out another visionless platform on which another future presiding bishop will be elected to unify the church in its irrelevance.

Why do we not recognize that an irrelevant church will die of boredom long before a controversial church will die from defections? Why do we not understand that a racist church, a chauvinistic church, a homophobic church, is not worthy of life? Why do we not see that this refusal of the body of Christ to confront issues, to stand for an unpopular truth, at the risk of alienating a segment of its prejudiced population is not a church that inspires anyone?

So here we are in the same rut we were in in 1970 and giving in to the same forces of reaction that led us into retreat twenty-three years ago. In the General Convention in Indianapolis, we will face these issues. With this method of preparation, however, we will almost inevitably choose the easy and painless path subverting truth to the call for unity! Despite noble rhetoric to the contrary that will seek to make virtue out of vice, we will gut the prophetic initiatives. We will refuse to name the pain in our society or to touch that pain or to enter that pain in order to bring healing. We will prefer to pretend that by ignoring the pain in society, we can enable the pain in our church to disappear. It will not. And in time we will discover that a church that stands for nothing save its internal health and unity is not a church that we respect, and its descent into death will be hastened.

From the cross of Calvary, I suspect that our Lord, who chose death over compromise, weeps for this church. In Austin, Texas, the last great leader of this part of the church, a man named John Hines, will, I suspect, also shed a tear. For unless these issues are addressed in this convention, we are inevitably laying the groundwork to choose again a presiding bishop who will be dedicated to easing the church's pain rather than the world's pain. Once again, we will miss the opportunity to choose a leader who will call this church into greatness and make room at God's table for all of God's children.

I wish I saw another possibility on the horizon. Regrettably, I do not.

– 28 –

Heresy! This Church Is on Trial!

December 1995

Heresy! This fascinating word is tinged with high levels of emotion. It harks back to a time in human history when conformity to certain beliefs was required and a willingness to participate in a debate that would challenge the authority of the church was not allowed. The word "heresy" brings to mind the trial of Galileo, the flames of the Inquisition, and the Tennessee conviction of John T. Scopes. Yet strange and anachronistic as it seems, this word is today being used in Episcopal circles by the right-wing members of our church.

What does heresy mean? It means that there is disagreement in the church over a major issue, and one side now wants the debate to cease so that they can force their convictions on everyone. It also means that there is enormous fear among religious people that the Christian faith to which they cling appears to be changing or even breaking apart. It is a sign that institutional religion is dying, and in its death throes; it is becoming self-destructive.

The issue, they say, is homosexuality. But that is more the symptom than the issue. Surely no one doubts that the church has had homosexual priests serving it since the birth of Christianity. That fact has been fully documented historically. There is no office in the Christian church from the pope to the archbishop of Canterbury to cardinals, bishops, priests, and deacons that has not been filled at one time or another by a homosexual person.

So when we press that issue, it fades into the issue of honesty, which has been sacrificed on the altar of institutional success. The church knows that homosexual persons have always served among its ordained clergy, but it does not want the world to know it. The church's ability to command respect, to manipulate life, to keep its coffers full would be threatened by such an admission, so dishonesty has been chosen instead. The policy of the ecclesiastical world on sexuality has always been a version of "don't ask, don't tell." If a homosexual person lives in secrecy and is never caught, then the service of that person to the church is both celebrated and honored. But if the person is revealed or caught, then removal, usually public removal, is quick and certain. This became so obvious when I heard a southern bishop say recently, "If one of my priests came out of the closet, he would be removed at once." However that same bishop hastened to add, "but I do not intend to start a witch hunt!" So survival in the priesthood has been accomplished over the centuries by encouraging clandestine, sneaky, dishonest, and dehumanizing behavior. It has demanded the sacrifice of truth. It has installed lying as a virtue. That is hardly the stuff of integrity.

But in this conflict there is something even deeper going on, for heresy also means false teaching. But how does one determine that a teaching is false? That requires the arrogant assumption that the ultimate truth of God from which heresy deviates is both known and possessed. To possess ultimate truth is to allow for no possibility of change and therefore it can allow no challenge and no growth. That is why conservative religious traditions have always asserted that "the faith" was not the product of human inquiry. It was rather revealed by God in some dramatic and complete way and has been understood and transmitted infallibly by the leaders of the church since its reception. There can be no such thing as heresy without this definition being operative. That is why the charge itself is so absurd and the people who hurl this charge are so naive and pitiful.

To anyone who has but the slightest knowledge of the intellectual revolution of the past five hundred to six hundred years such a claim reveals both ignorance and idolatry. Even the debate on issues of human sexuality today results from vastly new insights into gender identification, brain development, and the relationship of the Y chromosome and the male hormone testosterone to human development. If a willingness to engage this new data and to begin to act on the basis of a different and more enlightened understanding is to be condemned as heresy, then the church is publicly announcing that its mind is no longer able to entertain truth.

But issues around changing understandings of sexuality are not the only items in the expanding universe of knowledge that today challenges what the church once called "the Truth of God."

Even the Vatican has now declared that Galileo was correct and the church was wrong in that seventeenth-century dispute. But if Galileo was correct, then the whole worldview of the Bible is wrong! Recall that upon pain of his life Galileo was forced to recant his stated convictions that the earth was not the center of the universe and the sun did not revolve around the earth. The passage of scripture used to condemn Galileo was the story of Joshua, who stopped the sun on its journey through the sky to allow more daylight in which the victorious Jews could continue the slaughter of their enemies. Aside from the questionable morality of such a divine action, the Bible also assumed that God would and could manipulate the natural order to favor the chosen people.

Isaac Newton built on Galileo's insights and placed the final nails into the coffin of the view of reality espoused by the Bible. If the inability to believe in this premodern world of miracle and magic constitutes heresy, then everyone who has completed a fourth grade science textbook is either guilty or in denial. But that is not the only place where the implications of the Bible have been successfully challenged.

The biblical view of sickness as punishment for sin or as a sign of God's retribution has also died with the discovery of microscopes, germs, viruses, tumors, sterilization, and surgery.

The biblical view of the virgin birth died with the discovery of the egg cell in the eighteenth century. At that moment was born the recognition that every female, including Mary, is an equal partner with the male in providing the genetic content necessary for the formation of a new life. The virgin birth was based upon the ancient theory that all the woman did was to incubate and nurture the man's seed to maturity. If you wanted to talk of Jesus' divine origin in the first century, you only needed to remove the male from the birth process and to substitute the Holy Spirit for him. The virgin mother could remain, for she contributed nothing to the new life save the nurturing power of her maternal womb. So anyone who still asserts the literal biological nature of Jesus' virgin birth stands in violation of all we know about genetics. Thus, the perpetuation of this ignorance becomes the prerequisite for avoiding heresy, unless of course one hides once again in dishonesty.

The biblical view of human beings as fallen creatures, driven from their state of perfection by something called original sin, has also died, the victim of the work of Charles Darwin. One cannot fall from perfection if there is no finished creation. Darwin asserted that the created world is still expanding and human life is still evolving. If that is so, as the world of science today universally asserts, then neither the world nor any human life ever possessed a perfection from which we have fallen. This would mean that the assumption behind the traditional understanding of Jesus as God's divine rescuer becomes suddenly inoperative. So also does the sacrificial theology that the first Jewish Christians linked to Jesus of Nazareth in the primitive attempt to understand him as the paschal lamb or as the lamb of the Day of Atonement. Is it heresy for members of the church to face that bit of our intellectual revolution?

These and many other insights of an expanding knowledge have rendered great portions of the traditional literalized Christian understanding of the past to be nonsensical. A literal creed, an inerrant Bible, and an infallible pope are today inconceivably naive religious ideas. If facing these realities is the definition of heresy, then it is easy to understand why thinking people have abandoned the church in droves, leaving it to the emotional cripples, the fearful and dependent who scream heresy whenever their security systems are threatened. This is also why certain religious leaders like to control the flow of information to their people. They do not want the natives to get restless. They do not want people to raise questions they cannot answer. The more conservative a religious system is, the more its leaders will try to "protect the faithful" from challenging and threatening ideas, or challenging and threatening people. It is ultimately a hopeless and a losing task.

A Christianity that cannot engage the knowledge of the world in which it lives, that shouts its creedal affirmations defiantly as if they are self-evidently true, that believes the articulations of its faith convictions are unchanging and infallible, is a Christianity that will surely die. Yet that is the mentality that still uses the word "heresy" and that mentality today seeks to purge the church of those who are willing and able to grapple with the issues of the modern world. If this mentality is allowed to prevail, then there is no future for the Christian religion.

The Anglican Communion of which the Episcopal Church is a part, came out of the authoritarian religious systems of the past and stated its dedication to "scripture, tradition, and reason" as the sources of its authority. Reason certainly implied an openness to new truth, new insight, and new learning. If this church now decides that the category of reason must be subverted to a view of the Bible that undergirds only yesterday's religious convictions or to ancient Christian traditions that exclude new understandings, then the grand experiment called Anglicanism will have come to an end.

I cannot worship God without my brain participating in that worship. I cannot say the creeds with my fingers crossed. I will not be part of a Christian community that demands conformity to unbelievable understandings of yesterday's world. Perhaps I will discover another group of Christians who have been able to evolve in such a way as to keep both their roots in their original revelation while not sacrificing their citizenship in this century. The ability to live inside that dynamic tension is what I once thought was the mark of the Episcopal Church. But that definition is exactly what is on trial today. If this trial reveals that this community of faith is no longer able to be this kind of church, then I shall no longer be willing to be an Anglican.

– 29 –

If I Have Seen the Future of the Church, I Do Not Like It

December 1997

If I have seen the future of the church, I do not like it!

There are people who think that Europe or North America are the most secular parts of the world. But I would submit that this "honor" is held by New Zealand and Australia, which are primarily European nations transplanted into the South Pacific. Recent polls in New Zealand, for example, indicate that 84 percent of the population of this nation claims no affiliation with any organized religious body. Specific estimates for Australia were not available, but educated guesses by competent observers suggest that the percentage of religiously affiliated people in Australia is not significantly different. So the reality is that a majority of the citizens of both of these nations has moved beyond the boundaries of the traditional religious frame of reference. They are citizens of what Harvey Cox once called "the secular city." That, however, is only half of the problem. The other half becomes obvious when one analyzes the makeup of that decreasing minority who still do claim religious attachment. They are overwhelmingly of the evangelical, fundamentalist Protestant, or the conservative Roman Catholic tradition. They are basically ghettoized religious enclaves out of touch with the world in which they live.

These religious bodies still utter claims about how evangelical and conservative Catholic churches are growing while maintaining an arrogant, naive ignorance as to what is really happening in the broader religious picture. Almost inevitably these religious groups are fighting passionate rearguard actions over causes that have been overwhelmingly settled in the secular world. For example, they still expend primary energy debating the lack of fitness among women to serve in ordained capacities. They seek to demonstrate, in opposition to everything we now know in the scientific world, that one's sexual orientation is a chosen and not a given way of life. They appear to be dedicated to a simplistic view of Holy Scripture that assumes a literalness about biblical texts that has been abandoned by the academic world of scholarship for almost a century. In order to justify this mentality, they demonstrate a radical anti-intellectualism, which is marked by a defensiveness that frequently manifests itself in religious anger. They display an overt paranoia about the causes of their increasing irrelevance. They appear to believe that there is some organized conspiracy that is dedicated to their destruction. They imagine these enemies to be enormously powerful, and they refer to them with capital letters, as "The Militant Feminists," "The Gay Lobby," or "The Secular Humanists." They see themselves as a beleaguered minority battling for the truth of God, which they have confused with their distorted version of truth. They have become unpleasant, unattractive, and unappealing to the vast majority of their fellow citizens. From such a faith community modern men and women have fled in droves.

As I lectured across both of these countries while on my recent sabbatical study leave, I found an enormous spiritual hunger in the general population, but simultaneously a rising unwillingness to seek to satisfy that hunger in what have become the religious bodies of those nations. Time after time I spoke to standing-room-only crowds in places as diverse as Hobart, Darwin, Brisbane, Toowoomba, and Melbourne in Australia, and Auckland, Wellington, Christchurch, Napier, and Palmerston North in New Zealand. People came in those places to hear someone talk about God and Christ from a postmodern perspective. They came in order to raise the very questions they had not been able to raise in their churches before they left them. When they had tried to do so, before giving up on the religious enterprise altogether, they had received only the response of a threatened authority system that could not listen. They heard the clichés of antiquity that tried to settle all questions and disputes with the claim, "but the Bible says . . . " or "but the church teaches. . . . "

Representatives of this declining organized religious presence in both Australia and New Zealand certainly took notice of the response that I was receiving. They did not, however, act as if they recognized that we were engaged in the same enterprise. Instead, they saw me as one more enemy that they must discredit if their fragile hold on truth was to be maintained, and so they behaved in ways that could only be described as rude and offensive.

At a public lecture held in Wellington's Victoria University, hecklers in the audience interrupted prior to the question period with hostile barbs. My attempt to show how the story of the cross was constructed by the Gospel writers out of the primary Jewish sources found in Isaiah 53 and Psalm 22 got characterized as "Are you saying that the Gospel writers were liars?" In Hawks Bay I attempted to explain how the interpretation of the Christ experience grew from the writings of Paul (48–62 C.E.) through the elaborate theological explanations found in the writings of the Fourth Gospel (95–100 C.E.). Paul was content to exclaim simply that "God was in Christ reconciling," while the Fourth Gospel found it necessary to explain how it happened that this Christ was the preexistent word, or logos, of God, which had been incarnate in the person of Jesus of Nazareth. I was interrupted while speaking by hecklers suggesting that I might be the Antichrist.

In the heart of downtown Wellington on four successive Tuesdays at 12:10 p.m. I delivered a series of addresses known as the Lloyd G. Geering Lectureship. The audience at these lectures grew from 425 people on the first Tuesday to 550 people on the final Tuesday, necessitating a warning from the fire marshall that this building could not safely accommodate more than 450 people. So a new auditorium was opened and a public address system installed to handle the overflow. At the first of these addresses a small group of evangelicals frantically tried to corner a few of the listeners after the lecture was concluded to explain just why it was that I was wrong and thus not to be believed. At the third of these lectures evangelicals who were relegated to the room where a speaker system had been installed because of the overflow talked back loudly to the speaker system until the wrath of those who had come to listen silenced them. Walking out of that room at the end of the lecture, one of them passed an usher holding an alms basin. To the glee of his evangelical supporters, he proceeded to slap that basin so hard the usher dropped it, scattering coins and bills all over the floor. On the last Tuesday of this lectureship, when, to their dismay, the crowd was the largest in the history of that event, evangelicals prepared a sixteen-page handout, which they dutifully distributed to those attending as they departed. This handout was entitled, "Why Spong Is Wrong!" In it they attempted to defend a mindless biblical fundamentalism. I was enormously flattered by this attention, which certainly indicated that my message was being received.

This lectureship so engaged the Wellington public that the lead editorial in the *Wellington Evening Post* during my time there suggested that churches had been derelict in their duties by not bringing this knowledge about the Bible, which is readily available in the academy, to the attention of the people in the pews. This editorial further suggested in a rather overt way that religious people seemed to be engaged in a conspiracy of silence designed to keep their power intact. It was a terribly perceptive piece of secular journalism. When the lectureship was completed, two major stories were published on successive days in *The Dominion*, Wellington's (and probably New Zealand's) leading morning paper, seeking to interpret the meaning of the phenomenon of the crowds that had attended this public lectureship as an expression of a spiritual hunger no longer being satisfied by organized religious bodies. I doubt if the evangelical Protestants and conservative Roman Catholics were pleased.

In other places across the United States and Canada I have seen manifestations of this closed-minded, threatened, and uninformed religious mentality. It was apparent in the attempts that were made to "doctor" the content of a religious debate conducted in Vancouver when that debate was later published in an evangelical magazine to make the evangelical position look better than it did during the debate. It was apparent when an evangelical bishop actually changed a tape recording of a debate on homosexuality, conducted at the Virginia Theological Seminary, to cover his inept and ill-informed performance. It was obvious in an English evangelical newspaper just prior to our General Convention in July which ran a blatant and totally distorted attack on me for "closing urban churches" with their chief illustration being derived from the fire more than a decade ago that destroyed a congregation in Jersey City that had been dying for twenty years.

The reality is, however, that in the United States, Canada, and England this mentality does not exhaust the meaning of religion. There is still room in the Christian churches of these lands for differing points of view to find expression. These Western nations still have competent spokespersons for a Christianity that is engaging the issues of this modern world. Christianity has not yet become totally identified with an evangelical fundamentalist or conservative Catholic point of view. But the danger that we might be moving in that direction is present. It has already occurred in parts of Australia, especially in Sydney, and in most of New Zealand. If my experience in these two nations is accurate, a Christianity identified with right-wing fundamentalism will result in a massive exodus of thinking people from the churches of those lands. They will be turned off by a mentality they could never embrace. When the only voice of Christ that can be heard in the land is the voice of a strident anti-intellectual fundamentalism or semi-fundamentalism, thinking people depart from the church. That is a future scenario that I intend to resist with all of the power of my being.

So I return to my office as bishop of Newark planning to be very public in proclaiming a Christ who is engaging the issues of the real world in which I live. I will challenge openly the ignorance that is so rampant in our society in regard to biblical studies. I will stand against the stereotypical prejudices still present in Christian churches in regard to the full humanity of women and their competence to serve in any role the church possesses, including the papal office, and in regard to the full inclusion of gay and lesbian people in the total life of the church. Furthermore, to the degree that I am able, I will seek to get the theological debate of our generation into the public arena so that this secular society will know that the voice of Christ is broad, deep, competent, and not limited to the shrill sounds of those who think religion is a place where one can find security and, therefore, avoid the tensions of the modern world.

I call upon the churches of this diocese to join in this endeavor by adding to your regular worship life, if you do not already have it, an adult educational opportunity, and I ask our clergy to be willing to dedicate their primary energy to this function. Christian education for adults is not to be confused with teaching religious propaganda designed to shore up the religious answers of antiquity as if they are still relevant for our day. Christian education is rather an activity in which truth may be pursued come whence it may, cost what it will. It is an endeavor in which the spiritual realities of human life may be honestly explored.

If we do not do this in a competent and intentional way and do it immediately, then we run the risk that what I saw of Christianity in parts of Australia and in New Zealand is indeed what the church of the future will be like. Such a church will not be one in which Christianity, as I now know it, will ever be able to live. The need is urgent. The time is short. The issues are clear. Only your response remains to be determined.

– 30 –

A Wee Insight from a Bonnie Land

February 1998

The Episcopal Church of Scotland is unique in the Anglican Communion. The established church of Scotland is not the Anglican, but the Presbyterian. Elizabeth II is an Anglican and the head of the Church of England when she is in England. But when she is in Scotland, she is a Presbyterian and the head of the Church of Scotland. So the Episcopal Church is the name of the Anglican nonestablished presence in Scotland.

Most people are not aware that the Episcopal Church in the United States took its name from the Scottish Episcopal Church. Our ancestors in faith were not eager to be identified with things English following the war fought for American independence. Most of the Anglican clergy in the colonies had been Tories in that war. They were missionaries assigned to the new world for a term of duty, but their loyalties were significantly rooted in their homeland. So these Anglican clergy greeted the victory by the patriots with despair and returned to England in great numbers. That identification of England with our church did not make our church very popular in the fiercely independent new nation. The Anglican mission to the new world had been under the jurisdiction of the bishop of London. But he now withdrew all of his previous support by recalling those missionary priests under his authority and cutting off all financial sources. If Anglican worship was to continue in the new United States, it would have to find a way to consecrate its own bishops, to become indigenous in this new world, and to become fully independent of England. It was a critical moment in the history of our faith community.

The patriots who wanted to continue Anglican worship in their newly independent country finally got themselves together and chose a man named Samuel Seabury to be the first American Anglican bishop. The only problem was that Anglican tradition required that person to be consecrated by a minimum of three duly authorized Anglican bishops. There were no other bishops in America, so Dr. Seabury went to England to seek Episcopal ordination from the Church of England. He was not well received in the motherland. The English were still smarting from the war and the loss of their colonies. Their feelings were raw, and they were not eager to assist the upstart Americans in any way. So the bishop of London declined to provide ordination for Bishop-elect Seabury. Other English bishops followed London's lead.

Undeterred by this rejection Bishop-elect Seabury journeyed to Scotland and laid his case before the small disestablished Episcopal Church of Scotland. He received a warm reception. The Scots also had no great love of England and relished this opportunity to irritate their English tormentors. It is, to this day, a favorite indoor Scottish pastime. They also found much in common with this new American Anglican Church. It too would not be established. It too would be a small part of the pluralistic religious world of its nation, and it would have to make its way without State support. A genuine affinity began to develop between the two churches. So it was that from the Scottish Episcopal Church the first American Episcopal bishop was given his apostolic ordination. In a sign of both gratitude and growing identity the Anglican Church in America adopted the name of the Scottish Episcopal Church as its own name. That is why in this country we are the Episcopal Church rather than the Anglican Church. The Episcopal Church in the United

States also modeled its first Prayer Book quite deliberately after the Prayer Book of the Scottish Episcopal Church. The two have tended to walk in tandem from that day to this. History turns on such small episodes.

I go into this history because, while on my sabbatical study leave, I spent some time writing and doing research at the University of Edinburgh. When the primus of the Scottish Episcopal Church, the Right Reverend Richard Holloway, learned of my presence, he invited me to attend and to address the General Synod of his church, meeting in Oban very near Iona. I thus had the opportunity to attend and participate in my second General Convention of the summer, something I could not believe I was doing. Yet I found the experience fascinating. In my address I brought the greetings of the American Episcopal Church and the Diocese of Newark to my Scottish hosts. I rehearsed our common bonds in history and once again thanked them for their eighteenth-century hospitality to Bishop Seabury. I touched on the themes that consume our energy as a church in the United States, and then I watched the Scottish Church do its work. It was enlightening to see another national church deal with the same issues that our church has debated for most of the recent decades. They were talking about the full inclusion of women and homosexual people in the church's life. They were struggling with how to get out from under the pressures of institutional maintenance so that they could engage the world in significant mission. They were engaged with proposals to revise their present Prayer Book and with ways to reconstitute the episcopacy to make it more effective in the postmodern world. The primus has already proposed that Anglican bishops come to the Lambeth Conference in the summer of 1998 to hurl their miters into the Thames River as a sign of their willingness to rethink the role of the bishop as a sign of a servant ministry rather than as a crowned "prince of the church." It is a theme with which I deeply resonate.

The Episcopal Church of Scotland seeks to bear its witness amid tensions between its urban areas and its rural areas. It has deep divisions between its conservative members and its liberal members. It boasts a primus who is probably the best known and most controversial clergyperson in Scotland. He is the author of a number of books that are both provocative and challenging. He is about two years away from his retirement. It was quite instructive for me to observe these dynamics as they affected the debate of the Scottish Synod. It caused me to think deeply about my life and the life of the church itself.

The church is a strange institution. It inspires and it depresses. It is an intensely human institution, but it points to an intensely real realm which is transcendent and holy. It states its ideals powerfully, but it exhibits a curious and constantly disappointing pettiness. It was born in a dazzling revolutionary new spiritual awakening, but it spends most of its life resisting those who see God differently or who offer new models of thought for a new age. It proclaims that God so loved the world, which presumably includes all people, but it expends its energy trying to limit the church's exposure to those who appear to be different in culture, values, and way of life. It claims to serve the Prince of Peace, but its passions have fueled the cruelest wars and the most violent inquisitions in Western history.

In the service of the church's version of truth Christian leaders throughout history have been known to lie, cheat, twist truth, blackmail, murder, and steal. The assassination of the character of a religious opponent is almost standard operating procedure. One can become religiously disillusioned quickly if one's gaze never rises above the institutional expressions of Christianity. When one judges a faith community by attending the meeting of its national decision-making body, one is tempted to move in exactly that direction.

But this past summer as a member first of our General Convention and second as a guest of the General Synod of the Episcopal Church of Scotland, that was not my primary experience. I rather saw people in both settings torn between their security-producing ways of the past and a dawning new insight that could not be denied. I saw people recognizing that the definition of God by which they lived was no longer adequate and slowly but surely opening themselves to new possibilities. I saw people willing to set aside their prejudices against women and homosexual people as they embraced new data that rendered their prejudices no longer operative. I saw people living in this world, but in touch with the world to which all life seems ultimately to point. I saw the church at work — warts, blemishes, and all, but moving, ever moving to a new place where it has never lived before. Both the synod and the General Convention renewed my desire to be part of this institution, to be rooted in its past, as well as being compelled by its future.

While the Scottish Church met in Oban to deliberate, one of the issues that lay just beneath the surface was that there was no bishop in the Diocese of Brechin. Two election conventions had failed to elect any one of the nominees put forward. They were concerned about this. The divisions in the Diocese of Brechin between those compelled by the future and those rooted in the past had kept anyone from achieving a majority. However, a week later a successful election was held. The newly chosen bishop was a very attractive, outspoken liberal, dedicated to the church's involvement with the affairs of the world. The liberals clearly won, you say. Well, not quite. The new bishop has a name that roots him in the past. Perhaps that was what gave the conservatives solace. If you are ever in the Diocese of Brechin in Scotland, your bishop will be the Right Reverend Neville Chamberlain.

PART FOUR

Conversations with Other Faiths

– 31 –

A Hindu-Christian Dialogue

May 1984

When I was a child, the folk wisdom in my section of the country divided the world into three neat religious traditions: Christians, Jews, and pagans. The division within Christianity between Catholics and Protestants was related to with both humor and prejudice. The Jews were regarded as legitimate recipients of a thinly veiled anti-Semitism. References in the Bible that portrayed "the Jews" in the most negative way were never questioned.

The category "pagan" reflected the greatest ignorance and received the deepest scorn. Pagans were both those people in this country who had no religious affiliation and those throughout the rest of the world who were non-Christian. These distant people were those to whom romantic missionaries were sent for the purpose of conversion to our enlightened point of view. Their religious beliefs were caricatured as superstitious, magical, and inane. We had no sense of the beauty and vitality of Buddhism, Hinduism, Islam, Taoism, or of the teachings of Confucius. This provincial attitude prevailed before the advent of air travel, television, and instant communication. The world was vast, and the ignorance of local folk wisdom was not likely to be challenged by facts.

Today, only a half century later, contact and interaction with distant peoples have become commonplace. The airports in Bangkok, Dubai, Nairobi, Port-au-Prince, and Quito, for example, receive commercial, military, and holiday passengers every day of the year. In the process the world has become increasingly aware of the power and beauty of religious systems beyond our own. It is simply no longer appropriate for Christians of the West to ignore or to remain ignorant of the great religious traditions of the world. The era of arrogant Christian triumphalism is over.

When I traveled to India in February, one of my ambitions was to engage in dialogue with some Hindu scholars. I wanted to explore in an atmosphere of mutual respect the power, the beauty, and the depth of that religious system, which is at least a thousand years older than our Judeo-Christian faith story. That opportunity came to me in the town of Kottayam in an event sponsored by the Mar Thoma Seminary of that city. Three Hindu scholars were invited to meet with me in what I thought would be a private discussion, but what in fact turned out to be a very public event. A Christian bishop wanting to learn about Hinduism from Hindus appeared to be rare enough to capture the public imagination. So the conversation was attended by the seminary faculty, the seminary students, and the press. Despite that surprising context, those two hours were among the memorable moments of my life; and I developed such rapport with one of the Hebrew scholars, Dr. O. M. Matthew, professor of political science at Basileus College, that we met for private conversations on three other occasions and remain in active correspondence.

What I learned about Hinduism enhanced my appreciation for this ancient religious tradition. I saw a beauty in it that was enviable, and I found many points where Christians and Hindus are seeking to deal with the same human needs in remarkably similar ways.

Hinduism has no creeds or doctrines, and hence no spirit of missionary imperialism. It is more a way of life. It grows, changes, and assimilates when it meets new ideas. It does not resist, attack, or convert. Buddhism hardly exists in India today, because its essence has been absorbed by Hinduism. In a world of rapid and radical change, one wonders if any religious system that does not absorb and grow can hope to survive, or if our Christian claims to possess infallibility or ultimate truth are not signs of a brittle pettiness that cannot endure.

Hinduism comprises a wide variety of religious beliefs and practices. These are not judged as right or wrong, but as the manifestations of various levels of consciousness. To encourage a growth in consciousness is to encourage a change in the perception and content of religious beliefs. The differences that exist between the Hinduism of the simple Indian peasant and the Hinduism of the sophisticated Indian scholar are almost infinite. Yet internal Hindu religious arguments are almost nonexistent. Some Hindus literally worship sacred stones. Others are committed to local, almost household deities which have personalities and characteristics that are quite distinct. Beyond these regional deities are the great Gods of the Hindu system: Shiva, Shakti, Krishna, and Vishnu. Beyond these stands Brahma, whom some people attempt to describe. This is called Brahma with attributes. Beyond these descriptions, however, lies the one true God, Brahma without attributes. Pure spirit, indescribable, holy, mysterious, the ultimate One. No matter where a person is on the Hindu belief scale, all Hindus are regarded as embracing as much reality as they are able. No one is right or wrong; each is simply on a different level of consciousness.

Christianity is not dissimilar, though we seldom think of it this way. Many simple Christians embrace a religious system that is as superstitious and manipulative as the Hinduism of the simple Indian people. The next level of Christian consciousness manifests itself as biblical fundamentalism or ritualistic literalism. Denominational loyalty in the West can be likened to allegiance to regional deities in Hinduism. The coalescing of Christians into great families of faith would correspond to the major gods of the Hindu tradition. The abstract theological concepts of the philosophers, theologians, and ecumenical bodies move us close to the Hindu concept of Brahma with attributes. Finally, Christian mysticism and Paul Tillich's concept of the God beyond the gods of religious systems is analogous to the Hindu idea of Brahma without attributes — the holy God, one, mysterious, indescribably other. Perhaps the differences among Christians are not so much matters of doctrine or belief as they are differences in human consciousness and in our ability to think abstractly. Perhaps our task is not to be right or to prove others wrong, but to help one another to deepen our ability to embrace, on whatever level we are able, the wonder and mystery we call God.

Other points of similarity were noted in our dialogue. The Hindu concept of transmigration of souls or reincarnation and the Christian concepts of heaven and hell are both attempts to justify the unfairness of life that all people experience. The Hindu declaration, "you are Brahma," is not far removed from the Christian idea that every life is created "in the image of God." The Hindu path of righteousness called "yoga" is not far removed from the disciplines of the Christian life that we call "the way of the cross." Both religious systems address universal human questions: the traumas of existence, the loneliness experienced by self-conscious lives in a vast universe, the reality of death, the illusion of individualism. Hinduism sees a unity between the physical and nonphysical worlds, between the human and the animal, between the human and the divine. Such unities are also being explored in modern physics and psychology as well as by Christian mystics and twentieth-century theologians such as Teilhard de Chardin.

Christianity and Hinduism both seek from a sense of alienation to be at one with the universe. When we explore beneath the surface of religious language, we find a questing human spirit seeking the divine in the accents of the day and in the context of the religious system in which each of us lives. Beneath our religious diversity there is a remarkably similar humanity. I am convinced that a religious unity that we have not dared hope for might now be dawning. Perhaps in the next hundred years we will come to think of the religions of the world as being as similar to one another as we today think the denominations of Christianity to be. That would be a major breakthrough in consciousness. To me such is not only possible, it is highly desirable.

– 32 –

A Dialogue in a Buddhist Temple

January 1989

In the late fall of 1988, I worshiped God in a Buddhist temple. As the smell of incense filled the air, I knelt before three images of the Buddha, feeling that the smoke could carry my prayers heavenward. It was for me a holy moment for I was certain that I was kneeling on holy ground.

I am not a Buddhist, and do not expect to become one. I do not believe, however, that the God I worship has been captured solely in my words, my forms, or my concepts. Rather, these words, these forms, and these concepts have arisen out of the experience and history of my life. I walk in the tradition of the West. I find God present in the life of a first-century Jewish figure named Jesus of Nazareth. My understanding of that Jesus has been shaped by the life of the Christian church, but that church has been shaped by the cultural, political, and economic forces alive in two thousand years of Western history.

I do not know a universal Christ. I know a Western Christ and an American Christ. I know Christ who first challenged and, later, upheld the Roman Empire. I know a Christ who was translated into and helped to sustain a feudal system despite its division of human beings into lords and ladies on one side and serfs on the other. I know a Christ who kept civilization alive during the Dark Ages but at the price of forcing the world to obey the church. I know a Christ who was interpreted as the primary arbiter of good and evil, the judge who assigned the ultimate reward of heaven or hell.

This Christ became a major force in behavior control in the Western world and thus a source of the guilt that plays so large a part in the Western psyche. Guilt has produced such diverse things as good works, philanthropy, purgatory, confession, pilgrimages, and penance. An understanding of guilt constitutes the primary definition of human life against which the Christ story has been told at least since the days of Augustine of Hippo in the fifth century C.E. I know a Christ who has supported capitalism even while this Christ reached out to those who were ground into poverty by the capitalist system. When one steps outside the Western world that claims allegiance to the Christ, one begins to comprehend how that world has both shaped and distorted life for us all. A limited, not a universal definition of life available to us in the Western world has captured the Christ of the Gospels.

Surely the same process of acculturation has occurred in every great religious tradition. Obviously, the history and life experience of Jewish people has shaped and formed their understanding and practice of Judaism. The Jews created a religious cohesiveness that enabled their faith system to survive without a homeland from 70 C.E. to 1948 C.E. It is still today an identifying mark more powerful than citizenship. Russian Jews, American Jews, German Jews are still regarded by many as Jews first and Russians, Americans, or Germans second.

Islam has carried its prophet Muhammad through the particular history of the Middle Eastern nations. That history, without question, has shaped, formed, compromised, and distorted the meaning and power of Muhammad.

Hinduism and Buddhism, two traditions deeply related and yet quite distinct, have shaped the values, consciousness, and lives of millions of people of the East. These faith traditions have survived years of both political and religious imperialism. They have enabled peace and beauty to be established in many lives that endured crowded and difficult conditions in a less than perfect world.

My conviction is that the true God, the divine mystery, the essence of holiness, is within and beyond all of these ancient worship traditions. God is pointed to by all, captured by none. So, when I visit a Buddhist temple, it is not for me a pagan place, and its worship is not the worship of idols as I was taught in my early Christian upbringing. It is rather a holy place where human beings different from me have felt the presence of God. It is the point where for them the divine and the human have come together. I respect that holiness, and I want to step inside the lives of these brothers and sisters of the East to taste the culture, the meaning, and the understanding that they have found in their traditions. Only then can I feel and experience that which they feel and experience and perhaps ever so slightly begin to appreciate the worship that informs the values of their lives. So I worshiped in a Buddhist temple and prayed before a Buddhist shrine.

The monks were startled at my suggestion that they lead our Newark delegation in Buddhist worship. They declined, saying that Buddhist worship took much preparation and those of us who were not trained in breathing and in meditation would not understand. I nonetheless perceived that they were pleased that I had asked. It was then that I asked if I could pray at their shrine. They responded happily and gave way with enthusiasm. It was a moment I shall not soon forget. They seemed surprised that Christians would want to enter their understanding of holiness. Their previous experience of Christians had been quite different. By Christian missionaries they have been denigrated, made the targets for conversion, and generally told that they were inadequate, inferior, or evil.

When our tour was over the Venerable Kok Kwong, who is the chief monk of Hong Kong Buddhism, invited us to tea. At my request, he asked one of his monks, the Reverend Yuen Quing, to talk to our group about Buddhism. He did so in perfect English. He had been educated in the Anglican church schools of Hong Kong. But he contrasted constantly his understanding of Buddhism with what he said was Christianity. However, the Christianity that he described, and that he rejected, was a version of Christianity that I also reject.

It was a Christianity of an external God who manipulates life in answer to prayer and who reflects the value system of the oppressive West. When he finished his presentation, he asked me to respond. It was a rare, unexpected, and obviously not-planned-for opportunity. I had this chance to interpret Christ to Buddhists and to do so not in the traditional theological categories of the West, but as best I could within the values and thought forms of the East. I was glad that my life, at least to some degree, had prepared me for this moment. In 1984 I had engaged Hindus in dialogue in South India.

For thirty minutes, with each sentence being immediately translated into Chinese, I took their definition of the Buddha as the enlightened one, and tried to tell the Christ story in terms of their categories. If God is the source of life, as we Christians believe God is, then the fully alive Jesus reveals that God. So we Christians claim that God was in Christ not because of miraculous myths like virgin births and physical resuscitations, but because God is present in the life, in the love, and in the being of this Jesus. In him we see the God who could not be destroyed by death and who, both then and now, calls out of us the Easter faith. Go beneath the literal words we Christians use, I urged, words like "Jesus lives," or "death cannot contain him," or "we have seen the Lord." There you will discover a spirit of enlightenment not dissimilar from what Buddhists claim to see in their figure of Buddha.

I concluded by asking that Christians and Buddhists be true to what we each are, that we affirm our own unique values and explore with integrity our own faith systems. Perhaps we will discover, I suggested, that beyond the words and creeds that each of us uses, there is a divine power that unites us as holy people who worship a holy God according to two distinct holy traditions. I sat down to their applause.

To my surprise the Venerable Kok Kwong then rose to respond. I was told later that this was quite unusual for him. He thanked me and suggested that if Christians could accept what I had said, then Christians and Buddhists could walk side by side. In the continuing human struggle to break barriers, we have moved the small audience that gathered that November morning in a Buddhist temple in Lotus Valley in the New Territories of Hong Kong a step closer to the saving truth that we all seek.

We had also raised disturbing questions that Christians seem loath to raise, but questions that scream out for answers. Can we any longer claim a unique universal ultimacy for our Christ? Can we with integrity continue to support and engage in a missionary enterprise designed to convert? What is the meaning of that enterprise we call evangelism that seems to assume the narrow and traditional claims for Christianity that we have made through the ages? These are questions I have raised before. They are questions that continue to be traditionally answered in ways that I cannot accept. But the challenge before Christians today is to find new answers and more inclusive ways to respond to God's truth in our time. Faithfulness to Christ for me means saying no to the strictly defined alternatives of yesterday's religious enterprise, even while I seek to say yes to these truths into which I believe this century is calling all Christians.

Before any of my readers dismiss these startling possibilities, I suggest that they walk with an open mind into a Buddhist temple, kneel and pray before a Buddhist shrine, talk with a Buddhist monk, and sense holiness in the accents of an Eastern worldview. I did that, and when I did, my Christ grew in holiness and called me anew to my eternal journey into the fullness of God. I will not make any further attempts to convert the Buddhist, the Jew, the Hindu, or the Moslem. I am content to learn from them and to walk with them side by side toward the God who lives, I believe, beyond the images that bind and blind us all.

PART FIVE

Religion and Life

– 33 –

Does the Episcopal Church Welcome You?

October 1989

The catechism in the 1928 Prayer Book opened with the question of identity: "What is your name?" Then it moved to the issue of definition: "Who gave you this name?" The response proclaimed the church's teaching about our human life in Christ. "My sponsors gave me this name in baptism, wherein I was made a member of Christ, a child of God and an inheritor of the Kingdom of Heaven."

That was for many years the only catechism of the Episcopal Church. It was learned by and assumed to apply to all Episcopalians. No one ever suggested that there might be exceptions to this definition or that perhaps some people might have to be taught a different catechism. The church was proclaiming to all its people, black and white, male and female, lesbian, gay, and straight, what the church believes us all to be.

In the 1979 Prayer Book this inclusive quality was emphasized anew in the baptismal covenant where each candidate for baptism, confirmation, reception, or reaffirmation is expected to answer positively to this question: "Will you strive for justice and peace among all people and respect the dignity of every human being?" "All people" and "every human being" sound like inclusive words to me — words not intended to hide exceptions.

The Episcopal Church announces its presence in various locations across this nation with a readily recognized sign that bears the seal of our church and the familiar words, "The Episcopal Church Welcomes You." Presumably, the "you" means any person who reads the sign, for no list of exceptions is provided. That assumption was tested this past summer when clergy and lay people of the Diocese of Newark carried a banner in the New York City Gay Pride Parade proclaiming these words, "The Episcopal Church Welcomes You!" Those gay and lesbian Christians who have not been led by their experience to feel the church's particular welcome felt in that context the power of the Gospel that those words contain.

This church says it believes that in baptism all are made "members of Christ, children of God, and inheritors of the Kingdom of Heaven." We say we are called to respect the dignity of every human being. We publicly proclaim to the world that whoever you are, you are welcomed by this church. But somehow what the church says it believes and how the church acts are frequently not in touch with each other. Human prejudice seems to have the power to take stated ideals and to filter them into workable compromises where something less than our ideals becomes operative.

Prejudice is a powerful human emotion. It allows people to justify duplicitous and even evil behavior. Prejudice prevents us from seeing others as they really are. Prejudice requires that we view people within the stereotype that we have created for them. When prejudice dies we wonder how it was that we could have been so blind, so distorted. The ultimate power of prejudice is seen when it is allowed to shape our definitions of another person. How can we as a church reject anyone we have defined as a member of Christ, a child of God, or an inheritor of the Kingdom of Heaven? Yet, look at our history.

Western civilization, claiming to be overtly Christian, practiced slavery for almost nineteen hundred years after Christ. The Christian church shared in that sin shamelessly. When slavery died another evil, called segregation, took its place. The church also participated in apartheid. It still does. How could one who is a member of Christ, a child of God, an inheritor of the Kingdom of Heaven, be enslaved or segregated by Christians? It was allowed to happen because the operative definition of humanity in a slave-owning and bigoted society simply did not include the slaves. In this way, ideals were left intact and prejudice was left unchallenged.

The church has treated women in a similar fashion. Indeed, in many segments of the church today, we still do that. Women were marginalized by the church. We called the women of the church "the Auxiliary" until about twenty-five years ago, and we reserved for them only auxiliary and, therefore, powerless roles in the church. Women could not serve on vestries or be lay readers prior to World

War II. Women could not be deacons until 1970, priests until 1977, or bishops until 1989. Only men, said the church, were created in the image of God, so only men could represent God at the altar. When women are defined as less than human, ideals can be left intact and prejudice can be left unchallenged.

A similar fate has befallen the lesbian and gay male population. Unconsciously the corporate prejudice of both church and society has said that the homosexual population is not fully human, that the definitions of the catechism, the vows of the baptismal covenant, and the ideals of the Gospel do not apply to this minority. If gay and lesbian persons cannot be publicly ordained, if their holiest commitments cannot be blessed by the church, then the clear implication is that gay and lesbian people are not quite human, that they need to be changed or fixed and, if that is not possible, they need to be repressed and kept silent.

The power of one person to define another is an ultimate human power. It is so overwhelming that both definer and victim accept, at least for a time, the dehumanizing definition. In the one who has the power to define others this power creates a moral and psychic schizophrenia, for prejudice blinds the power people to the realization that what they have done is to define humanity in terms of themselves. Anyone who does not fit that definition can thus be categorized as subhuman. Such people are, therefore, exempted from the stated ideals of the defining majority with no qualms of conscience.

In Western civilization and in the official life of the church those who have possessed the power to define others have been by and large white, male, and heterosexual. Anyone who is not white, not male, and not heterosexual has had to live with an imposed pejorative definition. These power people have not been content simply to define human life. They have also defined the God in whose image they seem to believe only they themselves have been created. It is amazing how much that God of the Western world has seemed to be a white heterosexual male deity. It is no wonder that the houses of worship dedicated to such a God have discriminated against women, racial minorities, and homosexual persons.

Unconsciously, the assumption has been allowed to become operative that real humanity is only the humanity of the one who has the power to define. The result is that the church can talk about the goodness of creation, the universal love of Christ, the inclusiveness of the Holy Spirit, while at the same time participating in the enslavement and segregation of blacks, the oppression of women, and the inhumane treatment of homosexual persons. The primary purpose of prejudice is to create a stereotype and to impose a definition while keeping a clear conscience. To break the stereotype is to challenge the prejudice and, therefore, to trouble the conscience, which of course also means that the church is troubled and the nation is troubled.

Every successive wave of revolution in Western civilization has had its beginning in the refusal on the part of the oppressed group to accept any longer the imposed definition of the power majority. Revolution begins when oppressed people demand the power of self-definition. "I am not who you say I am. I am who I say I am." That is always the call to change and ultimately the call to revolution.

In the civil rights movement black Americans challenged the white imposed definition. We will not be "nonwhites," they shouted. We are black people. We will not be Erastus, Amos and Andy, Rochester, boy, Bojangles, or Uncle Tom. We are Africans — proud human beings. Black is beautiful. We will define ourselves, empower ourselves, organize ourselves. You will have to deal with us as we are, not as you think we are. We will be business and political leaders, social and athletic leaders. We will be managers and executives. We will be union members and leaders. We are and will be part of this nation and part of this church. We will even contend for the office of president of the United States, and presiding bishop of the Episcopal Church. You will have to deal with us. We will not go away. We will never again be excluded. The catechism applies to us. "We are members of Christ, children of God, and inheritors of the Kingdom of Heaven."

The feminist movement likewise began when women challenged the male-imposed definition of what it means to be a woman. No longer were women willing to be relegated to the biological functions of wife and mother. We will control our own bodies, women proclaimed. We will not be relegated to the world of schoolteachers, nurses, and secretaries. We will be bankers, lawyers, priests, and bishops. We will be scientists and senators. We will run for president and vice president. We will sit on the Supreme Court of the United States. Above all, women, not men, will henceforth define who a woman is. The catechism applies to us, women were saying. We are "members of Christ, children of God, and inheritors of the Kingdom of Heaven."

The rise within the Christian church of such organizations as Integrity and Dignity indicates that we are in the midst of yet another revolution. This revolution started the moment gay and lesbian people demanded the power to define themselves. The gay and lesbian members of our society have begun to throw off the shackles of the pejorative definition imposed on them by the power majority. "We are not who you say we are," the gay and lesbian population is saying. "We are who we say we are. We will not accept the stereotype you have imposed." Gay Pride is the emotional equivalent of Black Is Beautiful. Gay Pride stakes a claim for the power of self-definition. Lesbians and gay men are saying that the catechism applies to them also. We are "members of Christ, children of God, and inheritors of the Kingdom of Heaven."

Whenever the power of self-definition is claimed by an oppressed group, the power people have to adjust. When gay and lesbian persons insist on defining themselves, the straight world must begin to acknowledge its prejudice. That is happening today. Slowly but surely both church and society are learning to recognize that different is not evil — it is simply different. The dawning truth is that it is not abnormal to be gay, it is not deviant, it is not depraved, it is not sick. Homosexuality is a normal part of the rich variety of human life. Homosexuality has the same potential for health and wholeness as does heterosexuality. Homosexuality has been a part of human life since the dawn of humanity. Homosexuality is an aspect of nature found in almost every higher species of life. Far from being negative, it has greatly enriched the human enterprise. Homosexuality must break the stereotype in which it has been captured so that it can be acknowledged, accepted, celebrated, and appreciated.

All people take a step into wholeness when they can affirm and live out openly and honestly the deepest identities of their lives. We are called to demand of both church and society that the self each of us is be accorded justice, acceptance, affirmation, and protection.

So we call the whole church — bishops, priests, and laity — to the vocation of acting as the church says it believes. The time has come to remove the blinders of ecclesiastical prejudice and to affirm the basic dignity of every human being. The time has come to make real for all our people — white, black, Hispanic, male, female, gay, and straight — the imperatives of the Gospel. The time has come to assert the truth of the 1928 catechism: all of us are members of Christ, children of God, and inheritors of the Kingdom of Heaven.

The time has come to take seriously our own baptism vows to work for justice and peace among all people and to respect the dignity of every human being. The time has come to say to all those who have felt the sting of an oppressive prejudice, including the lesbian and gay male population, that the Episcopal Church does in fact welcome you. For, as the body of Christ, we will welcome all whom Christ would welcome, we will love all whom Christ does love, and we will serve all whom Christ would serve.

This church must listen to these demands and respond to these challenges, not because it is politically expedient or even politically wise. We must do it because the Gospel demands it. We must do it simply because it is right.

– 34 –

Christian Truth Requires Academic Freedom

December 1981

In periods of great upheaval and rapid historical change, religious institutions and movements seem to veer sharply to the right and to cover the radical uncertainty of the times with new religious claims of doctrinal certainty. The promise of a return to the security systems of yesterday is compelling, if misleading. In recent years we have watched the Missouri Synod Lutheran Church move into a tense, divisive fundamentalism. We have seen the rise of the Ayatollah Khomeini with his back-to-the-veil movement of Islamic fundamentalism that is also an undercurrent in Egypt and throughout the Middle East. We have witnessed the emergence of the religious political right of television-inspired Protestant fundamentalism in the United States.

In what appears to many of us to be one more manifestation of the same reality, we read the notice from the Vatican in September that the Roman Catholic seminaries of America would be investigated by a group of bishops for both operating efficiency and doctrinal orthodoxy. On the surface that may seem like a harmless housekeeping exercise, but when we look more deeply at the process, this ceases to be an adequate explanation. First, this is the only time the Vatican has asked the American bishops to conduct such an investigation. Secondly, this announcement has raised fear and anxiety among American Roman Catholic scholars, who clearly see in it a far more substantial threat. Many Roman Catholic seminary faculty members state quite openly that in their minds this investigation is one more hierarchical effort to intimidate the scholars, to discourage creative and free inquiry, and to compel adherence to a narrowly defined view of Christian orthodoxy.

My understanding of the role of a bishop requires me to defend the integrity of Christian scholarship so that the church might always be open to new insight and new truth. Without the impact on the life of the church of our own committed frontier-thinking scholars, this institution would quickly become stagnant and irrelevant, locked inside the formulas of antiquity. When ecclesiastical hierarchies become threatened by or frightened of their own scholars so that they seek to intimidate or silence them, then the church is in a very dangerous moment of life.

Roman Catholic bishops are quite properly sensitive to the authority under which they live. It is considered inappropriate for them to criticize publicly their superiors, so the prophetic voice or the minority voice of the Roman bishops seldom is heard in the public arena. To my knowledge, no American Roman Catholic bishop has risen to oppose this threat to scholarship and academic freedom now emerging from the Vatican. Similarly, none rose last year to defend Hans Küng.

My priestly and theological life has been greatly enriched by Roman Catholic thinkers who have been willing to open new doors of truth to me and to explore new terrains of faith with me. Had these thinkers been forced to live under the threat of censure by doctrinal purists, their creativity would have been muted and the spiritual growth of many of us would have been curtailed. Thus I feel compelled as a Catholic bishop of the Anglican Communion who stands outside the authority system of the papacy to speak out in defense of Roman Catholic scholarship and to warn the Vatican leadership of the shortsightedness and harm that seems inevitable if they persist in this thinly veiled attack on academic freedom and open scholarly inquiry into Christian truth.

In 1980 the removal by the Vatican of Hans Küng's official recognition as a Roman Catholic theologian signaled the dawn of a new attitude of theological narrowness in Rome. If the Vatican could censure and remove this world famous, articulate Roman Catholic thinker, then surely the lesser known figures are also vulnerable to the hierarchy's expectations. When this action is viewed along with the Vatican's harassment of the Dutch theologian Edward Schillebeeckx, the orders given to the Jesuits to curb their creative endeavors, and the attempt by the papal delegate to remove from Roman Catholic publications certain critical columnists, the pattern becomes quite clear. This September announcement of seminary investigation is one more step in the same direction. Almost every creative Roman Catholic thinker has at some point in his or her career felt the wrath and threat of the hierarchy. From Thomas Aquinas to Teilhard de Chardin to David Tracy, the suspicious ecclesiastical power structure has sought to guard itself from any theological questioning. Tragically that process has succeeded only in diluting the influence of the Roman Catholic Church in all areas. Our world today will not long take seriously the pronouncements on any subject of a church that demands narrow, doctrinal conformity from its most creative thinkers and at the same time debates such issues as whether the excommunication of Galileo ought to be lifted or whether the sale of indulgences ought to be continued. We need the powerful witness of the great Roman Catholic Church in our world today. That witness is diminished if the Roman Catholic Church is held in intellectual disrepute in scholarly circles, which will be the inevitable result of a continuation of this trend of activity.

On the ecumenical level this attitude also has serious ramifications. If, as these actions suggest, there is only one narrowly defined version of Christian truth so that diversity and scholarly inquiry cannot take place freely inside the Roman Catholic Church itself, then surely the Roman Catholic commitment to the ecumenical movement is compromised. The ecumenical movement assumes mutual respect for more than one approach to truth. If that is not acknowledged with honesty, then real theological dialogue becomes impossible, and all ecumenical conversations are really aimed only at conversion. Nothing will kill the ecumenical movement more quickly, yet the actions emanating from the Vatican are pointing in this direction.

I greet these recent developments with sadness and hope my brothers and sisters in the Roman Catholic Church will not long walk down the path to intellectual stagnation and ecumenical mistrust. I gladly step forward to raise my voice in defense of the great scholarly tradition that must always be a part of the proclamation of the Gospel among all Christians. I urge the Roman Catholic bishops of America to raise their voices of protest inside their own channels of communication before creativity and the free inquiry essential to the apologetic task of the Christian church in our day is stifled and the honest, public dialogue of the ecumenical movement is ended.

– 35 –

Apartheid: There Is Still a Slim Chance

September 1985

Inch by inch and day by day the tragedy of an irrational bloodbath comes closer in South Africa. There is a fatalistic and predestined air about it. Similar disasters have happened before in human history, and yet no one seems to have learned the lessons that would prevent grim repetition. South Africa seems caught in the grip of an irrevocable power that has assigned certain roles to be acted out without improvisation to the bitter end. South Africa's president, P. W. Botha, appears to believe the myth of his own propaganda—that the unrest among the blacks is caused by communist agitation and therefore must be responded to by a show of force. He tightens the screws in the name of security. Martial law is declared. Human rights are suspended. Even funeral processions are banned. Funerals, he naively argues, have become political events, as if any activity surrounding a death in the midst of a budding revolution can be anything other than a political event.

In the ranks of the black South Africans it is a difficult and cruel time of self-purging. Among oppressed people there are always those who survive or who think they can keep the peace by serving their oppressors. Many South African blacks, by motives both innocent and calculated, are guilty of collaboration with the enemy. They have been employed as police and as minor government functionaries. Their duties have not always served the best interests of their own people, but these roles were understood and tolerated when there was no hope.

Those survival strategies, however, are condemned today. This is the moment of revolution, and those who collaborate with the enemy become the enemy — perhaps worse than the enemy. The pent-up rage of the oppressed people turns with murderous frenzy upon those they now target as traitors. Sometimes mob execution is captured on live television. It is a chilling and riveting scene. The suspect is taken, his or her clothes are ripped off, gasoline is poured on, and a torch is lit — all in living color. The government uses these atrocities to justify an even harder line. Military force is necessary to curb such violence, they insist, blindly oblivious to the fact that the real violence is an inhumane, cruel apartheid, imposed with an iron hand by whites upon blacks.

The government announces that they will negotiate with no black leader who urges civil disobedience, or condones violence, or seeks to overthrow the law and order that crushes the blacks. That stance successfully rules out negotiating with anyone. The only blacks who fit the government's criteria have no black following and represent no black constituency. How does one negotiate with a person who represents no one? Is the government intransigent, blind, evil, or just stupid, one wonders.

Even the Reagan administration, certainly not identified around the world as a liberal government, officially announces that apartheid, and not the reaction to apartheid, is the real issue that needs to be faced and removed. But once that proper diagnosis is articulated, our leaders retreat to the failed policy of "constructive engagement," where, joined by the Thatcher government of England, they walk the sidelines of this moment of history as if there is a hiding place of inaction for any who hold the responsibility of power. The United States and Great Britain together are quite capable of exerting the political, economic, and moral pressure necessary to dismantle apartheid peacefully. They are not yet willing to do so. The only alternative left to the victim of this system is to smash apartheid violently. It is incomprehensible that even heads of state, outstanding successful politicians, do not understand the elementary lessons of political oppression. The tribe of white South Africans is afraid. Well they might be. Human oppression inevitably reaps its own whirlwind. The whites fear that if political power flows back to the blacks, revenge for the violence whites have meted out to blacks will be the payment required of them. That fear becomes a more certain prospect with each passing day. The whites are also victims of apartheid, for oppression not only cauterizes the spirit of the oppressed people, it also kills the very humanity of the oppressors.

Yet there remains a tiny ray of hope. In times of revolution there is a grace period — a fleeting moment when change can still be accomplished with goodwill. Perhaps it's not too late for this possibility even though most observers believe the clock on South Africa stands at one minute before midnight. Moderate voices still seem to be hanging on to shreds of credibility among the masses of increasingly angry black people. It will not last. Everyone knows that. Yet, unable to embrace the urgency of the moment, no one acts on it.

Who are the South African black leaders? Who can speak for the black people? When I visited South Africa in 1976, the universally acknowledged leader of the black people was Nelson Mandela, a man who has now been in prison for twenty years. My contacts today confirm that he continues to be the one recognized as the black chief of state in absentia. Imagine the political power one must have to maintain the political leadership of a people when he has had no direct contact with those people for twenty years! It is reminiscent of the power of the Ayatollah Khomeini, exiled by the shah of Iran to Paris, but never exiled from the hearts of his followers. Mr. Mandela speaks to his people through his wife, who lives under a ban, through his children, and through his friend Bishop Desmond Tutu. But it is he who speaks. Unless he is executed or is debilitated through torture or injury, Nelson Mandela will, in all probability, be the first head of the black South African government, and Desmond Tutu will be its spiritual leader. But this can happen only if change comes quickly.

How does one convince a government that the only way to save its life is to give it away? That action, so much at the heart of the message of our Gospel, is in fact the only way to avoid the tragedy that is imminent in South Africa. Sometimes the Gospel is good politics.

The lessons of history are so very clear. No people will remain powerless forever. Power is either shared or it is taken away. Oppression always breeds revolution against and hatred for the oppressors. Revolutions once begun have a life of their own, which cannot be contained. Why is it that these oft-repeated, almost obvious dictums of history are not recognized, or heeded, or used to transform this tragedy and to offer a peaceful hope for the future of that troubled land?

The present South African government is doomed. It will surely fall. The only real question is when, not if. Perhaps a more urgent question is how. Will it be a voluntary stepping down, a gracious giving away of oppressive power? Or will it be a violent overthrow with power being seized by the oppressed masses? Will it be a direct confrontation or will it come through the expensive process of sabotage and guerilla warfare, that will bleed the nation dry, leaving it spent and in despair? If Desmond Tutu and Nelson Mandela retain the power of their leadership, there is yet a slim chance for peaceful transition. But, peaceful or not, there must be and there will be a transition. No one should misunderstand that.

Bishop Tutu is one of those wonderfully shameless Christians who seems capable of living out the Gospel's mandate to love one's enemies in either victory or defeat. But if he is judged by his constituency to be politically impotent or incapable of bringing about peacefully the necessary change, his people will quickly relegate him to the ash heap of history as a modern-day Uncle Tom. Then the mantle of leadership will pass to another generation and another style, in which any attempt to mediate the injustices of that system and to bind white and black together will be replaced by an absolute passion to destroy not just the system but those who have devised it. It will be a fight to the finish. The result is predictable. There will be first a white government of increased oppression, then a black government of victorious vengeance. That is the inescapable scenario of revolution. It has been played out in the United States, in Russia, in Cuba, in Kenya, in Zimbabwe, in Iran, and in many other places. As the folk song says: "When will they ever learn? When will they ever learn?"

– 36 –

Racism Reborn

March 1987

"Go home, niggers!" The words have a strange and jarring sound. They are painfully anachronistic; they belong to another era, another world. Yet, we have heard them in 1986 and 1987 in the United States of America in such diverse places as urban New York City and rural Georgia. The voices that shouted these words bear witness to a tragedy and provide our corporate life with trauma and embarrassment. The New York shooters were at first white teenagers, though later their seniors took up the cry. These teenagers left a party in Howard Beach and came upon three young black males whose car had broken down in the neighborhood. The whites attacked and beat the blacks, causing the death of one of the victims, who ran into the path of an automobile in an attempt to escape this abuse. The perpetrators of this crime then returned to their party to brag about their victory. The cheers disappeared only when they were arrested and charged with murder.

The citizens of Georgia who shouted, "Go home, niggers," were dressed in the clown suits of the Ku Klux Klan. They carried the stars and bars of a dim and distant past. Their contorted faces and their clenched fists revealed anger and rage. These people were citizens of Forsythe County, located just north of Atlanta. They had been raised in an environment that purposefully kept alive the race hatred of the past. In 1912, in Cummings, Georgia, a village of two thousand people in Forsythe County, a white woman was beaten and raped.

Before she died she named three black men as her attackers. One of these men was captured and lynched; the other two were tried by a kangaroo court and hanged before a cheering mob. The remaining black people in that county faced such overt hostility that they all moved out. No black has lived in Forsythe County since. But the story of that 1912 episode has been told over and over as the years rolled by, finding in each generation a receptive audience. So hatred festered and racism lurked barely beneath the surface, waiting for an episode that would trigger an explosion. This nightmare of a newly alive racism reveals once again that there is something sick, distorted, even evil, in the human psyche on which an ever present prejudice feeds. These recent events make us aware that only a thin layer of civilization covers the primitive and irrational fear that we harbor against those who seem different, those who threaten the identity of our tribal security system. We had hoped that the dark shadows of our racist past had been uprooted, but now we are not so sure. There are those who suggest that these episodes constitute only a momentary eruption, that they are surely isolated vignettes. They see them as the expression of an intransigence that demands a final fling before it retreats into the archives of our dismal past. Racism, they assert, is in the last stage of rigor mortis. There are others, however, who believe that these events are nothing less than a new demonstration of racism's enduring potency, a new reminder to civilized people that the ancient cesspools of intolerance are always capable of breaking out to pollute our lives anew. I am convinced that the latter is the more viable truth. The back of racism has, in my opinion, not yet been broken. It has been engaged, some of its excesses curbed, and some of its potency dissipated. But it has not yet been destroyed.

Whenever a series of circumstances act to invite racism back into the public, it is quite capable of producing a new manifestation of virulence. If this conclusion is accurate, then it behooves us to look at our corporate life for clues to understand how we, consciously or unconsciously, have encouraged this latent racism to find new incarnations in the late 1980s.

Peeling back the layers of racism, we can identify at least three sources that feed these impulses. First, there is the negative layer of fear. In the dominant white society, black has almost always been a synonym for evil. The blackness of night was a terrifying experience to our ancient forbears who found themselves victims of nocturnal predators until they learned to brighten the night and to sleep protected by the glow of fire. In our folklore sinister characters, witches, and satanic figures all are dressed in black, while heroes and angels wear white. Darkness is used to set the stage for horror shows. The black sheep of the family, the black cat of superstition are other examples of the way the fears of antiquity feed the latent racism in the deep recesses of our psyches. Making conscious what is unconscious is one step toward exorcizing this demon. Redefining black as something quite beautiful is still another.

The second layer of racism is found in the economic realm. Prejudice assigns its victims the menial positions in the economic system. In the biblical tradition, the aliens in the population were forced to be the "hewers of wood and the drawers of water." To create a perpetual servant class is a goal designed to serve the needs and comfort of the dominant group. So prejudice always has economic consequences. When that economic pattern is broken, dislocation and threat inevitably occur. When blacks compete with whites equally for a finite number of jobs, the primitive feelings in the heretofore dominant but now threatened group are exacerbated. This threat is less apparent when the economy is expanding and more apparent when the economy is stagnant or contracting. In recent years America's economy has been kind to those at its top and center of the ladder, but it has been cruel to those who struggle to gather the crumbs that fall from the table of the economic machine.

It is at the lower end of the economy that the confrontation normally occurs between those seeking to break out of the prejudiced patterns of the past and those who stand to be replaced when the victims of yesterday arise. So, in periods of economic duress, the fears of those who might be replaced are clothed with the jargon and feelings of racism. The ones who are perceived to have created the economic insecurity become the unwitting victims of an irrational anger. That, too, is an element that allows latent racism to make a public return.

There is a third level to racism, however, that may be the most provocative reason that these strange echoes of the past have returned to haunt us in 1987. It is found in the role of leadership and in the willingness of those who set the standards of propriety for the entire body politic. When the former secretary of agriculture, Earl Butz, was reported to have told a joke that was blatantly racist, he was removed from his position. The leaders of the nation were in that action proclaiming that racism was unacceptable and those infected with it might well be warned to hide it deeply in their own personal closets. But if the leaders and value setters for this nation begin to waffle on this crucial issue or to send out signals that are interpreted to be racist, the effect is predictable. Such a stance proclaims that racism, especially well-perfumed racism, has become acceptable and may therefore be expressed in public. In subtle ways, those in power are perceived to be pronouncing absolution over attitudes that without that absolution would remain unacceptable and would therefore be tucked away in hidden places. When Dwight Eisenhower refused to give his verbal support to the Supreme Court decision outlawing segregation, he guaranteed the confrontation in Little Rock, Arkansas. People take their cues from leaders — and leaders set the tone for the whole society.

Why has racism become acceptable enough in the late 1980s that people are emboldened to shout, "Go home, niggers," in public and even before cameras that will carry their revealing words around the world? Is the present eruption of racism just an accident for which blame is inappropriate? Or is it a direct response to policies that have in effect suggested that racism is to be tolerated or even blessed in this nation?

What signal goes out to a nation when the Reagan administration seeks to give tax-exempt status to segregated schools? What message is received when this administration tries to put an end to the Voting Rights Law, or when it is publicly critical of affirmative action programs? What is heard when the administration guts the Civil Rights Commission, stacks the courts with hard-line right wingers, and appoints a chief justice who has both a record of intimidating minority voters and a racially exclusive clause in his home ownership contract? What perception enters the field of human behavior when our president continues to support a nation committed to a race-hating apartheid even over the opposition of his own party in Congress? If vigilance is required to keep the baser instincts of human life restrained, then it is certain that the relaxation of that vigilance or even the perceived acquiescence to these base emotions will loosen the chains and allow the beast of racism to roam the nation's streets once more. When Howard Beach, Forsythe County, and other more isolated episodes erupt at the same time, we must look to see who gave our people permission to let racism find public expression once again. It is not a comfortable vision.

There is a deep psychic base to racism. There is an economic component. There is a public perception of what is allowable. These three have coalesced in recent days. Our task must be to cage the beast of racism once more, to understand anew the reasons for racism, and to address the causes of racism with effective power.

For those of us who are Christians this is a matter of doing nothing less than keeping our sacred vows. For racism violates the promise we make in the baptismal covenant: "Will you strive for justice and peace among all people, and respect the dignity of every human being?" To this we respond, "I will, with God's help." And so we will and so we must, for Christ's sake.

– 37 –

Banning Abortion

January 1981

Speaking at the conclusion of the recent gathering of the American College of Roman Catholic Bishops, Archbishop John Quinn of California, the outgoing president, in the name of his church called on President-elect Reagan to move quickly to implement his campaign platform pledge to seek a constitutional amendment to ban abortion. At a public rally earlier this month in Trenton, New Jersey, the Reverend Jerry Falwell, who has emerged as a leading spokesman for fundamentalist Protestantism, reasserted his frequently voiced support for a constitutional amendment to ban abortion.

As the Episcopal bishop of Newark, I would like to state that I will do all in my power to resist and oppose any attempt to pass a constitutional amendment to ban abortion. Furthermore, I want the public to know that the leadership of the Christian church is not united in support of such an amendment. Spokespersons for religious groups frequently seek to create the impression that their position is the Christian position or the moral position and therefore anyone holding an opposite opinion must be either non-Christian or immoral. For those people I lift now another voice and another perspective on this complex moral issue.

Let me first assert that my opposition to a constitutional amendment to ban abortion should not be misinterpreted to mean that I embrace the position popularly called "freedom of choice" as the only other alternative. Abortion is a reality that cannot be treated lightly or disposed of quickly. A simplistic, cavalier treatment from either of the presently drawn sides would be inadequate.

To all people who hold life to be holy the question of the legality and morality of abortion causes great anxiety. We must recognize first that the act of aborting a fetus is ipso facto destructive. Those couples yearning to conceive a child and yet unable to do so tend to see abortion by those who can conceive as incomprehensible. Any parent who has lost a child finds it extremely difficult to imagine that anyone would deliberately choose abortion. Many examples could be cited of decisions to abort that have become the source of a lifetime of regret.

Increasingly permissive attitudes about abortion reflect this society's diminished appreciation for the holiness of all life. Abortion intrudes into the mysterious, frightening, and still not scientifically answered debate over the moment that life begins. People who are willing to terminate life or quasi-life simply because it is bothersome or burdensome will soon be part of a society that will find it easier and easier to develop reasons that will justify the taking of other lives for similar reasons at the other end of life's spectrum. When life itself ceases to be viewed as holy, all lives are endangered.

I would resist those who say that the only legitimate basis for a decision to abort is the mother's wish and right to control her own body. It is a rare pregnancy in which the vital interests of the mother alone are at stake. The unborn child, the father, the web of relationships in which every person lives, and even the state as the guarantor of life are undeniable parties to the decision. The inescapable seriousness of the act of abortion with its emotional, physical, and mental impact on people must never be lost.

Yet despite the seriousness of the subject, I am convinced that the answer cannot lie with those who would make abortion illegal in every instance. Such a solution must be opposed, and I will do so in the public arena as a Christian and as a bishop. To me there are clearly situations in which the maintenance of the life of the fetus is more destructive to the people involved and to society at large than its destruction. Victims of rape and incest should not be denied the choice and the right to have an abortion. Cases in which it is medically proven that the fetus is irrevocably deformed, damaged, or retarded must have the choice and the right to abortion. There is throughout this country and throughout the world widespread ignorance about birth control. We will face active opposition to birth control on religious grounds by the same groups that oppose all abortion. These two realities greatly complicate the lives of the poor. Poverty, large families, and still another pregnancy may well create emotional harm among the poor that few of the middle class can imagine. To claim that every child conceived has the right to be born but to live in a country and a world that allows poverty and starvation to continue unabated is a double-mindedness that cries out for judgment.

There are other complicating issues in the arena of public morality. Those who respond to a woman who conceives a child out of wedlock with scorn, condemnation, and moral indignation have, I believe, no right to deny her a legal escape from the public ridicule they create. What kind of vindictive spirit is it that wants to punish the unwed mother and distort her life forever under the humanitarian guise that carries the slogan "the right to life"?

From whence does the naivete come that assumes that making abortion illegal will end abortion? Clearly that will not be so. What will happen is that illegal abortions will be performed in shadowy places under less than clinical conditions and in many cases by unscrupulous practitioners. The lives of many women will thus be placed in jeopardy. They too have a right to life. This country tried once before to impose a moral norm on the people of this land. It was called Prohibition. It did not work. Surely the lesson from history is clear.

In the gray area between simplistic absolutes, the following things are clear to me:

1. Abortion is a grave act that touches the essence of life's sacredness and intrudes on what many regard as the prerogatives of God and should be undertaken only for serious cause. The lives of everyone involved must be considered in the decision.

2. Birth control is a legitimate and moral alternative in an overpopulated world facing limitations on food and a decline in the quality of life. And it is time the Christian church said so. Any legislation which would limit abortion that is not accompanied by legislation to disseminate widely information on birth control and its use in responsible family planning in this nation and throughout the world would be counterproductive and would border on being immoral.

3. Making abortion illegal would create enormous harm and cost in the lives of many women. It would also, I believe, prove to be as degenerative to the essential holiness of life as the right to life people now claim for the practice of abortion.

I call upon our political leaders to move with wisdom in the area of protecting the holiness of all life. A constitutional amendment to ban abortion would not serve that purpose.

– 38 –

In Defense of Assisted Suicide

January 1996

What gives life its value? What gives life its meaning? If value and meaning are removed from life before life ceases to exist, is it then still life? Do potential value and potential meaning attach themselves to fetal life that is so embryonic as to be only potential, not actual? Who has the right to make decisions about life that is only potential? Is it the society? Is it the affected individuals or the bearer of that life? Does the sacredness ascribed by the religious systems through the ages to human life reside in our biological processes? Is biological life itself sacred whether it be human or otherwise?

It is around these questions that debates swirl in this century on such ethical issues as euthanasia, assisted suicide, birth control, abortion, animal rights, the use of animal organs and parts in human attempts to combat diseases, vegetarianism, and many environmental concerns. In most of these debates the emotional content is high. The person operates on the basis of an unstated but assumed answer to these questions that is passionately held. Frequently that answer is so deeply related to the core of the person's being that it allows no opposition. So the result is argument, not dialogue, and heat, not light. One of these issues is today coming before the society with increasing rapidity, and it requires of the Christian church a response. Is active, as well as passive, euthanasia an acceptable practice within the ethics of Christian people? To state it more boldly, is assisted suicide an ethical option for Christians and, if so, under what circumstances? At our Diocesan Convention these issues will be a major focus of debate.

The first thing that must be noted is that these issues are peculiarly modern ones. A century ago and, in most cases, even fifty years ago, these issues would hardly ever have arisen. Throughout Western history, society in general, and the medical profession in particular, has been passionately dedicated to the preservation of life. The assumption commonly held was that life was sacred, that it bore the image of God, and that its limits had been set by God. Because of this deep sense of the sacredness of life, even suicide was rare in this religious tradition,

So deep was this conviction in the Judeo-Christian world that murder was not only prohibited among members of the same tribe, but it was also surrounded by powerful disincentives. In the biblical code, when murder occurred, blood retribution was the legal right and moral duty of the victim's nearest of kin. To escape immediate vengeance and to determine whether or not extenuating circumstances existed, cities of refuge were set up for those who accidentally killed a fellow Jew. In these centers, the killer could find temporary sanctuary until the case could be decided and the verdict rendered by society. If the murder was in fact accidental, then innocence and freedom were established. But if not, then guilt and the delivery of the killer to the family of the victim could be pronounced.

Of course the killing of an enemy was not covered by this prohibition. Thus the Hebrew scriptures had no conflict in proclaiming that the same God who said, "You shall not kill" as part of the Ten Commandments could also order Saul to slay every "man, woman, infant and suckling," among the Amalekites (1 Sam. 15:3).

But in that world surgery was limited to the sawing off of a limb. Antibiotics were unknown. Blood transfusions could not be given. Organ transplants were inconceivable. Intravenous feeding was unheard of. Finally, machines or medicines that could stimulate the heart and lungs could not be imagined. The time of death did seem to be in the hands of God. Human skill could do little to prolong it. So the idea grew and became deeply rooted in the psyche of the whole society that the sole task of medical science was to prolong life. That was a noble value, then and it remains so today.

The realities of our world, however, have changed dramatically. That which was inconceivable, unimaginable, and unheard of is now a part of our contemporary experience. We have extended the boundaries of life to where the values and definitions of yesterday collide with the technology and skill of today. That is why the debate on assisted suicide now looms before us, and that is why this generation must question the conclusions of the past.

Let me pose the complexities of this issue by asking a series of questions. In what does the sanctity of life reside? Is life sacred when pain is intense and incurable? Is it a value to drug a patient into insensibility for pain while continuing to keep him or her alive biologically? At what point does the quality of life outweigh the value found in the quantity of life? Is life's meaning found in the physical activities of the body or in the relationships of the person whose physical body is alive? If those relationships can no longer exist, should the body be allowed to continue functioning? Who should make the life and death decisions in this world? Should that power be given to doctors? But doctors today are less and less involved with patients as medicine becomes more and more impersonal and complex. Since doctors still profit from hospital visits to their patients, we must recognize that there is a financial incentive to doctors to keep lingering patients alive. Should this decision be left to the family members? But there are cases in which family members have profited from the death of a relative. Family members have been known to kill a parent or a spouse when they had a vested interest in that person's demise. Should that decision then be left to chaplains, rabbis, pastors, or priests? But the religious institutions today are too weak to carry such a responsibility, since perhaps half of the population of our nation is today not related to any religious institution. It might also need to be said that even members of this professional group of "God bearers" have not always been strangers to self-serving corruption. Can the decision be left to the individual involved? Certainly that person needs to be involved in that decision if at all possible, but can it be solely the decision of one person? Should extraordinary care for terminally ill persons be allowed to bankrupt families? Where is the point where such care becomes destructive to the economic well-being of the remaining family members? Because this generation is now capable of certain procedures, is there some moral necessity to use those procedures? Given the interdependence today of the health of the whole society through insurance rates, Medicare, and Medicaid, extraordinary measures to prolong life universally applied would bankrupt the whole nation. Already this nation spends more than eighty cents of every health care dollar in the last year of a person's life. Should such life supports then be available only to those who can afford them? Would we then be equating the sacredness of life and the values that grow out of that concept with wealth? If health care has to be rationed, as it increasingly is in the managed care contracts, on what basis are extraordinary procedures to he withheld?

The values of yesterday are colliding with the technological and medical expertise of today, rendering the conclusions of the past inoperative for the future. That is why questions abound and debate rages around the issues of life and death at both ends of life's spectrum. Even the word "murder" is being redefined in this debate. Is a doctor who performs an abortion a murderer? Is Dr. Jack Kevorkian a murderer? Should he be prosecuted for assisting people into death when hope for those persons has expired? Is it murder for a father, who can no longer bear to see his child in intense pain or lingering malaise, to take matters into his own hands when all conscious function has been lost? Is it murder for a wife of long years to order no further food to be given to her dying husband in order to speed his death? Would it be different if she placed a plastic bag over his head? Would one be more moral than the other? The lines are so vague, the decisions so awesome, the fear so great, the values of the past so compromised by the technology of today, that by not facing these issues consciously, the society will drift into decisions by default, and a new uncritical consensus will become normative. The debate must be engaged and Christians must be part of it.

I, for one, am no longer willing to be silent on this issue. I, as a Christian, want to state publicly my present conclusions. After much internal wrestling, I can now say with conviction that I favor both active and passive euthanasia, and I also believe that assisted suicide should be legalized, but only under circumstances that would effectively preclude both self-interest and malevolence.

Perhaps a place to start would be to require by law that living wills be mandatory for all people. A second step might be to require every hospital and every community to have a bioethics committee made up of the most respected leadership people available to which a patient, family members, doctors, or clergy persons could appeal for objective help in making these rending decisions. My conclusions are based on the conviction that the sacredness of my life is not ultimately found in my biological extension. It is found rather in the touch, the smile, and the love of those to whom I can knowingly respond. When that ability to respond disappears permanently, so, I believe, does the meaning and the value of my biological life. Even my hope of life beyond biological death is vested in a living relationship with the God who, my faith tradition teaches me, calls me by name. I believe that the image of God is formed in me by my ability to respond to that calling Deity. If that is so, then the image of God has moved beyond my mortal body when my ability to respond consciously to that divine presence disappears. So nothing sacred is compromised by assisting my death in those circumstances.

So into these issues Christian people must venture. It is a terrain fraught with fear and subject to demagoguery by the frightened religious right. That is why the mainline churches must consider these issues in the public arena where faith, knowledge, learning, and tradition can blend to produce understanding. This diocese will begin this process at our convention.

– 39 –

The Environment Begs the Question: Servant to Humankind?

June 1991

In the Adam and Eve myth in the book of Genesis, God spoke to the first human beings, exhorting them "to fill the earth and to subdue it." In time these words were incorporated into the sacred text of the Jewish people. Still later this sacred text came to be thought of as the literal words of God, and all of its attitudes were invested with the authority of this God. That, in turn, has led to some dire consequences.

Our faith ancestors lived with realities quite different from our own. "Give us this day our daily bread" was a prayer of actual need in a world without supermarkets, refrigeration, or transportation systems that could bring fruits and vegetables from around the world in all seasons. For those folk the sustenance of existence had to be wrested from a hostile environment.

Our forebears viewed the environment, under a variety of guises, as the enemy. Some said the material substance itself was evil. Others said this world "has fallen into sin." Still others suggested that the physical world was the realm of Satan. But whatever the theological content, the underlying thought was that human survival, even at meager levels, was dependent on the human ability to subdue the world. So very real was that need that hostile aggressive words, aimed at the environment and reflecting that struggle, found their way into the worship life of the Hebrew people.

One wishes that our ancestors in faith might have produced something different from this war-like environmental mentality. Even a pluralism of differing attitudes that could have vied with one another for supremacy as the circumstances of life in this world changed would have been helpful. Other attitudes did emerge in different parts of the world. Anthropologists suggest that the earliest of the religious traditions of human beings viewed the earth and nature not as an enemy to be subdued but as a nurturing mother to be embraced. The vestigial remains of this conviction lie in the fact that human languages the world over call the earth and nature both by the title "mother."

Native American folklore, for example, contains stories of a people who apologized to and gave thanks for a tree before it was felled to provide fuel for the winter. Totem pole legends expressed the interconnectedness of human life and animal life. The slaying of the buffalo was a liturgical and ritualistic act to remind the Native American of the interdependence of all life. So deep was their sense of being related to the rest of nature that the decimation of the forest or the extinction of the herd was beyond their imagination. This tradition believed that trees, rivers, mountains, animals, birds, fish, and even the rocks were meant to live as one single, multifaceted organism with the Great Spirit filling everything with holiness.

The Western world, however, following the direction of the Bible, has reflected that tradition that viewed nature as an enemy to be conquered. A line was drawn in Western thought between human life and all other life. In time this line produced an overvaluing of human life and an undervaluing of all else. This peculiar Western megalomania asserted that human beings were not only superior to nature but they were somehow not even part of nature. In the grip of this belief system Western men and women have acted historically in such a way as to create our present environmental crisis.

Since our religious system produced this attitude, is it not reasonable now to ask that same religious system to provide us with the means to counter, correct, and redeem that which it created? Such a process might begin by our searching anew among the artifacts of our religious heritage to discover if that call to fill the earth and to subdue it might have had a biblical context different from the one we have always assumed. In this manner perhaps a new entry point can be achieved.

The goodness of creation is the background to the biblical command to subdue. The biblical sense that God's spirit had been poured out on all flesh, not just human flesh, is also part of our story. The destructive aspects embodied in the command to subdue the earth did not succeed in eliminating this sense of the goodness of all the created order. Today, however, only the form of the Judeo-Christian tradition continues, while the religious content of our age has become an overwhelming secularism. The good life — the highest goal of the secular faith — is the driving force that removed the goodness of all that God had made from the desire to subjugate the earth.

The secular world has achieved this subjugation through advanced technology. Coal has been pulled out of the hills, oil pumped out from the ground, and fossil fuels used extravagantly, raising, thereby, the standard of living for those who owned or shared in the means of production. The industrial age was ushered in with the creation of a mobile society built on convenience. This process developed wealth which, when it spread, created the middle class — a specifically Western institution with which most of us identify ourselves. In the relishing of relative affluence that seemed to know no bounds, secular people began to assume that because all was well with them then all must be well with the world.

But suddenly a snake appeared in this garden of Eden. Its form was that of chemical wastes that seemed impossible to destroy, garbage that threatened to choke our lives, air that was no longer healthy, water that was no longer pure, and a shrinking ozone layer that hinted of Armageddon in a brand new form. The reality of these destructive, life-threatening forces now bombards our consciousness daily.

In the grip of our appetite for consuming, this century has won humankind's battle. The environment has been made our servant. We have obeyed the command of the holy God and subdued the earth. Now, however, we are being forced to recognize that this victory is also killing our life. In this emerging catastrophe there is revealed yet again one more reason why our Bible, our Christian holy book, must be rescued from the clutches of fundamentalism.

To counter this destructive behavior the other parts of our Judeo-Christian tradition must be rediscovered. The scriptures not only teach us that this world is God's world and that it is good, but also that this goodness lies in the delicate balance of mineral, plant, animal, and human life in the totality of the environment. That is the theological reality that needs to inform life now and to feed the decisions this generation will be called upon to make.

Dr. James Hansen, head of NASA's environmental concerns, has suggested that recovering nature's balance and interdependence will not be easy because it forces people to submerge self-interest in the name of corporate interest. It requires a radical shift in human values that most people today are simply not willing to make because the cost is too high. The price paid for such a shift will be the loss of individual convenience. It will necessitate a maturing human interdependence which will make our nationalistic sword-waving look like kindergarten brawling. It will require the removal of the self from the central position of every person's private universe.

There is no political consensus today to support such a change in the operative values of human life. This generation is much more like the biblical character of Esau who was willing to sell his future birth right to satisfy his immediate hunger. Desire now was for Esau more important than life later. So it also appears to be for twentieth-century Western men and women.

History shows us that profound shifts in behavior never occur voluntarily. It takes an overwhelming disaster to make change acceptable. Only in tragedy is a new consensus born and a new set of values created. My fear is that this is exactly what lies before us ecologically. I am not alone in this fear. Some people in the scientific community believe that we may have already moved so far down the path of environmental destruction that the impending disaster itself will not come soon enough to bring the changes that could save our world. These scientists believe that this disaster will simply announce that time has already run out and that no remedial action we might take would be effective. For them, the sentence of doom has already been pronounced and humanity lives awaiting the day of execution.

But there are others who do not believe that we have passed the point of no return. For them, and I count myself among them perhaps more in hope than in knowledge, some response is needed now. To preserve our sanity and to feed our prayer that it is not too late we must act today as if our actions can and will make a difference. We must continue to act until events proclaim that time has run out on the human enterprise. Therefore, I propose three actions by which the Christian church can address these issues effectively.

First, the church needs to confess publicly that it has been guilty of giving divine approval to the exploitation of our universe. The church and its Bible have historically participated in the problem that today confronts us as an environmental crisis. So the institutional church must face the world with the humility that asks forgiveness and places honesty at the top of its public agenda.

Secondly, a major factor in the destruction of our environment is overpopulation. Major portions of the Christian church have viewed any form of birth control other than abstinence as sinful. This attitude grew out of a time when disease and disaster regularly decimated human life and thereby controlled the population growth. The continuous advances in the development and production of drugs and technology have removed these plagues of humanity. Without a balancing change in the human reproduction habits, overpopulation will first destroy national boundaries and political stability and then it will exhaust fuel and food. That in turn will destroy the ecological balance and the quality of life for all people. Overpopulation will then exhaust the oceans, the forests, and the ozone layer. Finally it will destroy the world.

For these reasons the Christian church in all of its expressions must immediately rethink past practices and change old patterns. Responsible family planning is a requirement of our mutual survival. The failure by any Christian body to endorse birth control methods must be viewed today as an act of immorality. That stance is no longer even a morally neutral position. There can be no compromise on this issue. This is not Catholic bashing, as some ecclesiastical figures will surely claim. It is simply the realization that no antiquated religious system can be allowed to compromise the human struggle to survive.

Thirdly, the time has come for the church to articulate a new socially responsible value system for our world. We cannot live with an ethical base that does not reflect the changing world. It is no longer moral to say that if one can afford it, it must be okay. The cost to the future of conveniences today must be a factor in our decision-making. The gap between the rich and the poor within and among nations must be narrowed. Present imbalances carry with them the seeds of our mutual destruction. The church must address these issues and offer an ethical system that engages these realities.

That is the minimum platform that I believe the Christian church must adopt to have the credibility and integrity that will justify its continued right to speak to this world. I appeal to the clergy and laity of this diocese to address immediately these concerns.

– 40 –

Homosexuality

November 1985

"Mom and Dad, I must make you aware of a part of my life that you may not understand. I am gay." "Bishop, there is something that you need to know about me since I am a priest in your diocese. I am a homosexual person."

With these words in many different settings in recent years, men and women have identified publicly and owned personally their sexual orientation. It has happened so frequently that we have developed a widely understood code phrase for such disclosures. We call it "coming out of the closet."

Homosexuality is a minority position on the spectrum of human sexuality, but it is a significant minority. The best estimate by sociologists and psychologists is that a constant 10 percent of the population is gay. Recent biological studies indicate that a corresponding percentage prevails even among the higher mammals. Most people do not translate that data emotionally. They are not able to admit to themselves that in every group of ten people the statistical probability is that one person will be homosexual. This means that most families have at least one gay member in either the immediate or extended constellation. Gay people are all around us. They are our physicians, our business associates, our clergy, our sisters, our brothers, our children, our friends, sometimes, tragically, even our wives and husbands. For the most part they choose to remain invisible, yet they are present. In silence they bear our slurs, our definitions, our derogatory jokes, while trying to smile and keep their emotional equilibrium. It has not been easy for them. It never is easy to be different, to be misunderstood, to be feared.

The English historian A. L. Rouse states in his book on homosexuals in history and literature that such well-known figures as Erasmus, Dostoyevski, Tchaikovsky, W. H. Auden, Richard the Lionhearted, Lord Byron, Herman Melville, and many others, were, in fact, gay people. John Boswell, a social historian at Yale University, has chronicled in scholarly detail the history of homosexual persons in the life of the church. His list includes popes, archbishops, bishops, abbots, priests, and deacons. Anselm and Lanfranc, two well-known archbishops of Canterbury, and Aelred, recently added to our church's calendar, as indicated by a reading of their diaries and correspondence, were clearly homosexuals. Anthropological evidence has been cited to demonstrate that holy men, shamans, medicine men, and other similar persons in ancient tribal life were, in large measure, homosexually oriented people. They were accepted as a kind of third sex, encouraged to wear distinctive cross-sexual clothes (like vestments), and given permission to behave in a different manner. The priestly status among our prehistoric forbears seems to have been frequently achieved at the price of living out a neutral or reversed sexual role. The shaman or medicine man was thus considered "safe" to leave with the women of the tribe while the men went away on the hunt.

There is certainly ample evidence to demonstrate that homosexuality is not a new or modern phenomenon. It has been part of the human experience from the beginning of recorded history and has clearly been a factor in shaping the life of the church. Indeed, one could argue that the emphasis on celibacy in the Christian priesthood, particularly in the Western church, has made that vocation very appealing to those who were homosexually oriented. The leadership of the Christian church throughout history has included substantial numbers of ordained homosexual persons.

There have been times and places in which these facts have been accepted in a rather commonplace fashion, without either passion or fear, as very ordinary human realities. "Platonic love," now a description of a nonpassionate male/female relationship, was, in fact, originally a rather benign description of a homosexual relationship. Most of the early Roman emperors were known to be either homosexual or bisexual. In his book, *The History of the Decline and Fall of the Roman Empire,* Edward Gibbon suggested that of the first fifteen Roman emperors only Claudius was entirely heterosexual. There have also been times and places in which homosexual persons have been treated with such unaccepting hostility that the homosexual minority was forced to live in secret and in constant dread that if they were exposed they would be persecuted and even put to death. The demeaning word "faggot," which literally means a small stick used for fuel, comes from the era when gay people were burned at the stake.

Most of the emotional negativity toward gay people rises from two primary sources. The first is the anxiety that one's own sexual identity is not secure. The second stems from the debilitating worry that some homosexual person will lead our children into the homosexual lifestyle. Neither anxiety is based on rational data.

The medical world has recently removed homosexuality from the list of mental diseases. Most experts in this field lean heavily toward a genetic explanation of homosexuality's origin. If that is so, the gay person has no more control over his or her sexual orientation than others have over being left-handed or red-headed. If environmental influences could be permanently dismissed as causes of homosexuality, much of the irrational fear would disappear and the ability to accept persons who elicit that fear in us would begin to grow. Contemporary biological, psychological, and medical opinion increasingly affirms this position. At the very least we can say that homosexuality appears to be a regular part of the human sexual reality, normal in the sense that its presence is the norm of the human experience, abnormal only in the sense that it is not the norm for the majority.

There is no doubt, however, that the manner in which the heterosexual majority relates to the homosexual minority creates other powerful forces which do, in fact, twist and warp human beings. The majority viewpoint still implies that homosexuality is a disease, a perversion, or a sin. We heap judgment and vilification upon those whom we presume to have willfully chosen this "distorted" style of life. We organize our society and social mores according to this unfounded prejudice. We refuse to undergird and support responsible decisions made by gay people to bring both love and stability to their lives. We do not accept homosexual couples into our lives openly. We do not see in such relationships commitment, trust, love, beauty, and the desire to grow together—the very qualities that bring about wholeness in all human beings. Our society offers little sustenance or encouragement to the gay couple as they seek to create a mutually supportive union. The result is that permanent relationships are difficult to establish among gay people. The alternative is short-term relationships, the destabilizing world of gay bars, sexual promiscuity, and shallow lives. It would not be different among heterosexual people if we lived in a society that did not bless and encourage faithful monogamous marriages. Most therapists and physicians do not believe that homosexual persons are capable of changing their sexual orientation. What can be changed and what must be changed is the way in which the straight world relates to the gay world. That change is long overdue.

Into this welter of confused emotions and prejudiced fear has now been injected the disease known as acquired immune deficiency syndrome, or AIDS. This disease, which breaks down the body's immune system, is afflicting the gay population in this country in a concentrated manner. At this moment there is no known cure. The final result seems to be a painful and inevitable death. A growing hysteria has invaded the public consciousness, greatly increasing the latent phobia in the population against homosexual people. Children who have contracted AIDS at birth through an infected mother or through a blood transfusion are not welcomed in public schools. Funeral homes have been known to refuse to prepare AIDS victims for burial. Medical people have been known to refuse to treat AIDS patients. Establishments that cater to the gay population have been harassed by police and closed by court order. Insurance companies are canceling medical insurance on suspected AIDS sufferers.

My sisters and brothers, this church of ours must be open to the whole human family. Gay people must hear through the words and deeds of the church that they too are children of God. All of us together must work to develop a means within our society to enable all people, heterosexual and homosexual, to live normal loving lives within the boundaries of their sexual orientations and to place the fears and hysteria that surround AIDS into a context of fact and reality. AIDS may turn out to be a momentary passing epidemic. It also may be a new bubonic plague. At this moment, no one knows the final outcome. It must not, however, become an excuse to unleash another wave of irrational hostility on the gay population of our world.

– 41 –

Debating Sexual Issues

December 1986

At the fall meeting of the House of Bishops a resolution was introduced asking the bishops to issue a clear, unequivocal statement upholding the traditional biblical standard of sexual morality for the members of our church This standard was defined by the framers of that resolution as celibacy outside of marriage and faithful monogamy inside marriage. A caveat was attached, explicitly forbidding homosexual unions on any basis. The resolution failed for two reasons. First, a similar resolution, passed in 1979, is still the operative position of this church. Secondly, a major study in human sexuality is underway in our church and is scheduled to come before the General Convention in 1988.

Since the official prevailing view of the church on questions of human sexuality is unchanged, why, one must wonder, would the bishops be asked to reaffirm it? The answer to that question lies, in all probability, in the observed fact that this sexual standard of the church is not upheld in either society at large or within the church. Many people, including devoted laity, priests, and bishops, find it difficult to support that standard. The church is also discovering today that the field of human sexuality is not a simple uncomplicated arena where moral precepts are easy to formulate or follow. This is not because the leaders of the church have lost their moral courage but because the issues have become increasingly complex. Indeed, both life-science scholars and biblical theologians find it difficult either to identify or to support something that might be called the biblical norm on sexual matters. There is no doubt that the Ten Commandments state clearly and succinctly, "You shall not commit adultery."

Those people unfamiliar with biblical scholarship believe that this simple proclamation should be quite sufficient. Or is it? The society of Israel that received and upheld that law was significantly different from our society in four unique ways.

First, polygamy, not monogamy, was the accepted norm for the marriage patterns of that day. Solomon, who had one thousand wives, could and did uphold the injunction against adultery. Secondly, women were considered mere chattel or property, and were bound by the commandment against adultery in a way that men were not. A man committed adultery in Israel only if he violated another man's marriage. A woman committed adultery if she violated her own marriage with anyone else. Thirdly, the life expectancy of that day was relatively brief by our standards. To reach forty years of age was a remarkable feat. There were almost no postmenopausal years. Few couples lived long enough to experience the empty nest syndrome. Fourthly, puberty occurred much later than it does in our time, and marriage occurred much earlier. With an anticipation of death in one's thirties, for example, it would not be sensible to wait until age twenty-five to get married. One tended to enter marriage shortly after puberty. Those generations of people would never have understood our long culturally imposed separation between puberty and marriage that now stretches from ten to fifteen years. They would also have regarded any attempt to encourage virginity for that long a period after puberty to be both nonsensical and unnatural. Can we then take this ancient injunction from its very different context and apply it in the complexities of our world? It is at least an interesting question.

If it is the mind of the church to define acceptable sexual practices as abstinence outside of marriage and a faithful monogamous relationship inside marriage, then Christians must come to terms with the inconsistencies between practice and precept, and recognize that the standard we proclaim is violated with increasing and substantial frequency. How shall that data be interpreted? If the church by official proclamation expects brides and grooms to come to the altar as virgins, what does it mean when the vast majority of our couples who come to be married are not living in accordance with that position? Has the world become so corrupt, so decadent, that debauchery has become the norm? If that is a proper conclusion, then the church should speak a mighty word of condemnation to this generation. A reaffirmation of the traditional stance that few are observing hardly seems mighty enough. An alternative might be to admit that our standards reflect an inadequate response to the complexities of human sexuality and changing cultural values. If this alternative is worthy, then we must engage seriously the difficult task of determining contemporary values to which we can be committed in the midst of the gray morass of uncertainty, relativity, and situationalism.

It is impossible to believe that this generation will retreat from the emancipation of women and return to the oppressive stereotypes of the past. If virginity prior to marriage is to be the rule, then clearly it must be the rule for men and women alike. Even in the heyday of Puritan moralism, no such expectation of the males pertained. There will be no double standard in setting ethical norms in this generation. This society will also not stop using contraceptives. This means that the fear of pregnancy that served as a powerful deterrent no longer curtails sexual activity. Women have thus been freed from the anxiety of connecting sex with childbirth. That also is not likely to change.

Does this church as an institution want to say that the satisfaction of sexual desire is now a legitimate reason for marriage? Is celibacy a special calling to a tiny minority, or is it the expected lifestyle of those who find themselves divorced, widowed, or unmarried? Time after time pastors tell of counseling with people who decide to break the stated rules of the church. Should two widowed elderly people, living in a retirement home, be told to live in sexual abstinence because they discover that marriage will reduce their Social Security checks and that they cannot afford such a reduction? If they initiated a sexual relationship without benefit of wedlock, would that be condemned as immoral by the church? How does the church react if two responsible young adults decide to live together prior to marriage? Is there not a possibility that this decision reflects not an immoral attitude but a deep valuing of the marriage bond and a desire to test the relationship before making a permanent vow? If we were to entertain such new possibilities would life be enhanced, or would moral chaos he encouraged?

Is a young woman whose husband is paralyzed and rendered impotent by an automobile accident doomed to be sexually abstinent for the rest of her days? Is the only alternative to leave the marriage and seek another mate? Suppose she wants to stay in that marriage and discovers she can do so with sensitivity and caring, and without resentment for her husband, but only by having as a sometime companion and lover a widower twenty years her senior who has himself decided that the continuing grief he has for his deceased wife makes remarriage an inappropriate option for him? Is that immoral? If so, on what basis? Who is hurt by that behavior? Who is helped?

If we are able to determine once and for all that homosexuality is a normal minority position on the spectrum of human sexuality, then why cannot the heterosexual world accept committed homosexual relationships? Most of the evidence from the life sciences now indicates that no one causes another to be gay, nor does one actually choose a particular sexual orientation. We simply are what we are, and we awaken to it. Can we impose a standard of celibacy on people who are gay that we do not and cannot impose on those who are not?

In the midst of the changing patterns, what can we do to make commitment the basis of our ethics and then to define commitment so powerfully that the basic Christian affirmation of the holiness of life will be well served? Such a decision-making process might result in a position short of sustaining what traditionalists call the Christian standard, but would it not put us into dialogue with practices that our society by consensus now affirms in its corporate life? How can the church give support to married couples that would assist them in keeping their marriage vows? Can a sanctity be restored to marriage that will slow down or stop both divorce and marital infidelity? Can the church require faithfulness in the normal marriage without requiring virginity before marriage, or abstinence for those whose marriages have ended? Or is it all one package indivisible? Where should our primary energy be placed: on commitment or on the attempt to restore standards that society has abandoned?

Can these issues be raised by the church and debated with sensitivity rather than judgment? Can we find a way to preserve the values that lie behind the traditional standards if the standards themselves are modified by a changing world? Or is the only allowable task that of recalling our wayward society to an unchallenged stance of virginity before marriage, faithfulness in marriage, and celibacy whenever marriage ends?

I would like to invite the people of the Diocese of Newark into a significant dialogue on these issues. It is my hope and expectation that the corporate wisdom of Christian people in the Episcopal Church throughout this diocese will find a way to speak a word of meaning and hope to those who struggle to be faithful to God in the midst of life's ambiguities.

– 42 –

Women Priests: Rome to Canterbury – Extraordinary Letters

September 1986

An extraordinary and revealing exchange of correspondence between the pope and the archbishop of Canterbury was released to the public just this past summer. It shows that the debate within the Anglican Communion concerning the role and place of women in holy orders has now reached both the world stage and a central place on the agenda of ecumenical conversations.

John Paul II initiated this exchange in December of 1984 in a letter to Robert Runcie that was couched in all of the nuances and niceties of ecclesiastical diplomacy. His purpose, however, was quite clear. The pope wanted to make sure that the leadership of the Anglican Church was aware that the ordination of women to the priesthood and episcopacy would constitute a "threat" and "an element of grave difficulty" in the quest for Christian unity between our communions.

Two things were unusual about this papal intervention. First, the Roman Catholic Church, in the person of this pope, obviously cares about what happens in a non-Roman communion in a way that has not existed before. Secondly, this communication makes it obvious that the Roman church still reflects a triumphalism informed by the implicit claim of infallibility. The response of the Anglican Church to these two issues should be to receive the first with joy and to challenge the second with power.

It is a joy to welcome the caring of our sister communion even when that caring takes the form of entering and participating in the internal dialogue of the Anglican Church. In the name of ecumenical unity, Rome has now publicly placed its influence on the side of those members of our church who oppose the present Anglican drive toward sexual inclusiveness in the ordained ministry. In the process, Rome has established a fascinating precedent. The pope himself has suggested that the quest for ecumenical unity is of such value that it justifies the attempt by the partners in an ecumenical conversation to influence the internal wrestling and the decision-making process of the other. If that is to be the standard for the ecumenical dialogues of the future, then ecumenicity has achieved a dynamic new level of realism. Anglicans tend to think of the Roman Catholic Church as monolithic. That perception hides from Anglican eyes the pluralism that enables arguments to rage within the Roman church. Power ebbs and flows throughout history, and this has always been true inside the Catholic tradition. Today the hierarchy of the Roman Catholic Church is in the hands of its most conservative elements. From the pope and his appointed "guardian of the faith" Joseph Cardinal Ratzinger on down the line, the liberal position within that church is being muted by increasingly conservative attitudes and increasingly conservative appointments. The liberal spirit that marked the reign of John XXIII, however, is still present, silent and underground but nonetheless alive, and someday it will rise again. If Rome can enter the internal debate in the Anglican church on the conservative side, then surely Anglicans can enter the internal debate in the Roman Catholic Church on the liberal side. The winds of change and the forces of modernity will finally infiltrate even the most resistant structures. The present position of the Roman church on women and ordination will not be eternal. The degree of caring within the Roman church about the Anglican position on the ordination of women that is powerful enough to prompt the pope to write the archbishop of Canterbury opens the ecumenical dialogue in hopeful ways. That dialogue can now become serious, and at long last the real issues of our division can be engaged. Anglicans can only rejoice in that.

The second attitude revealed in this remarkable letter from John Paul to Robert Runcie is an implicit Catholic triumphalism that must be challenged. Rome does not set the sole agenda of the ecumenical movement. The pathway to Christian unity does not lie in Christianity's "errant children" returning to the one true universal mother church. There are issues between Roman Catholics and Anglicans that from the Anglican perspective can only be regarded as "threats" and "elements of grave difficulty" in our quest for unity. Among them would certainly be included: Rome's continued insistence on mandatory celibacy as well as its all male priesthood; Rome's opposition to birth control in a world beset by the problems of overpopulation; Rome's limit on intellectual freedom as witnessed by the hierarchy's repressive treatment of such leading Roman Catholic thinkers as Pierre Teilhard de Chardin, Hans Küng, Edward Schillebeeckx, Charles Curran, Leonardo Boff, and David Tracy, whose scholarly pursuits have led them to challenge Rome's narrow version of Christian truth; Rome's single-minded opposition to all abortion that takes public form when nuns are threatened with expulsion from their orders for signing an advertisement that called only for a public debate on the issue; and, finally, the doctrines and dogmas that Rome unilaterally has added to the Christian tradition: the immaculate conception, the bodily assumption of the Virgin Mary, and the infallibility of the papacy. If, in the name of the goal of Christian unity, Rome now feels free to participate in the Anglican dialogue on the ordination of women, then surely, in the name of the same goal of Christian unity, the Anglican perspective on these issues must be allowed to become part of the internal discussion that today marks the Roman tradition. Such an agenda would challenge powerfully the idea that infallible truth is the possession of any portion of God's church.

The relativity of truth is as established today in theological circles as it is in the world of physics. A study of the history of Christian thought reveals that Christian theology emerges out of debate and compromise within the church as Christian thinkers interact with their understanding of truth as well as with the culture and the times in which they live. Only later, long after the smoke of the battle has cleared, do these debates get codified into doctrines and dogmas that are called infallible. Then those who have no sense of history proclaim that they were received by revelation.

The ancient infallibility claims of the church, whether of papacy or scripture, are defended today by no one other than the spokesperson of the competing Christian institutions. No reputable scholar takes either claim seriously. Genuine dialogue assumes a pursuit of truth through joint discussions. It cannot occur if either party to the dialogue assumes that infallible truth is their solitary possession. Whenever that assumption has been present in the ecumenical movement, dialogue has been replaced by attempts at conversion. Such attempts are hardly worth the time and cost that the churches of Christendom give today to the ecumenical enterprise, nor will they ever produce any result other than high levels of frustration. This Rome-Canterbury correspondence enables Anglicans to face with clarity the real choices that are inherent in the ecumenical movement. Is the institutional unity of the Christian church a goal worth pursuing if the price of that unity is the continued sexist oppression of women? Will not the future reveal that sexism in the Christian church today is one more dark and embarrassing chapter to be placed beside anti-Semitism and the support of slavery that once enjoyed official ecclesiastical sanction? Our Roman Catholic brothers and sisters need to understand that the Anglican Communion will never return to an exclusive male priesthood. Women priests in the not-too-distant future will become bishops of this church. If these realities result in the ending of unity talks between Anglicans and Roman Catholics, then so be it. Ecumenical cooperation can continue in many areas even when the quest for ecumenical union has ceased. A church and a priesthood freed from the sexism of the past is, to me, a higher good than ecumenical unity. Someday that sexism will also be purged from the Roman Catholic and Orthodox parts of Christianity. Then the ecumenical conversation can be resumed with integrity. Time is certainly on our side.

I rejoice that I serve a church in an age where these issues are drawn with such candor and clarity. I shall seek sexual inclusiveness in every area of the church's life even if the cost of the inclusiveness is the sacrificing of the hope for Anglican-Roman unity for the time being. This church that I am privileged to serve and to represent will also, I am convinced, take such a stand.

PART SIX

God, Jesus, and Christianity

– 43 –

A Free Man

January 1979

Two thousand years ago the historic figure Jesus of Nazareth lived his life. It was a life of relatively short duration, only thirty-three years. At most only three of those years were devoted to a public career. Yet, that life was a source of wonder and power to those who knew him. Tales of miraculous cures surrounded him. Words of insight and wisdom flowed from his lips. Love and freedom were the qualities that marked his existence. Men and women who knew him were called into being by him. Those laden with guilt discovered, somehow, the joy of forgiveness in him. The alone, the insecure, the warped and twisted found him to be a source of peace. He possessed the courage to be what he was. He is described as the freest man that history has ever produced. Jesus seemed to have no internal needs that drove him to prove himself — no anxieties that centered his attention on himself. He rather had an uncanny capacity to give. He gave love, he gave selfhood, he gave freedom, and he gave them abundantly — wastefully, extravagantly.

Lives touched by his life were never the same. Somehow life's secret, its very purpose, seemed to be revealed in him. So empty was he of human need that when people looked at him they saw beyond him; they saw through him. They saw the source of all life, the source of all love, the hope of all fulfillment. Power such as this they had never known before. In many ways it was an eerie, unearthly power. Human life alone could not have produced it.

Finally the life of this free man was taken away from him. More accurately, so fulfilled was he that he laid his life down. He gave it away in love deliberately. He did so, loving those who took his life from him, revealing that his love could embrace all the hostilities of human life and still not cease loving. He did so to demonstrate that nothing we do and nothing we are can finally be unlovable or unforgivable. Even when we kill the giver of life and love we are still loved by him. Such a life could not help but transcend human limits. For this kind of love can never be overwhelmed by hatred; this life can never finally be destroyed by death. All of this was experienced in the historic person called Jesus of Nazareth.

Is it any wonder they broke the barriers of human concepts to understand him? They called him the Son of God; they said that God was in him reconciling the world unto himself. The world was never the same after this life had entered it. He split history in two. We date our civilization from that moment.

He gave love and forgiveness. He gave acceptance and courage. He gave life and he filled that life full. Only one in touch with the source of life and love could do these things. So people began to see that this Jesus revealed the source of all life and the source of all love to them. Even more they came to believe that he was the source of life and love itself. In Jesus God had been met living in human history.

Then they began to write about him. But when they did they confronted a problem. How could the human mind, the human vocabulary stretch far enough to embrace the truth of this life? How could mere words be big enough to tell of this godly meaning? So inevitably, as they wrote they lapsed into poetry and imagery to capture this truth. When this life entered human history they said even the heavens rejoiced. A star appeared in the sky. A heavenly host of angels sang hosanna. The Judean shepherds came to view him. Eastern Magi journeyed from the ends of the earth to worship him. Since he revealed the fullness God, God must have been his father in a unique way, for human life alone could not have produced this life. These were the birth traditions that the adult historic power of this man inspired.

Our modern nonbelieving world reads this story and, assuming a literalness of human language that the biblical writers never intended, say, "How ridiculous! How unbelievable! Things like that just do not happen. Stars don't suddenly appear in the night. Angels do not entertain hillside shepherds with songs. These things cannot be true."

"How right you are," we Christians must respond in honesty. On literal levels these things cannot happen nor do they happen, but to our doubtful, nonbelieving world might we Christians not suggest that they look at these traditions on another level from a different perspective — for lives that have been touched by his life, the ones who know the power of this Jesus? When we read these accounts we recognize the poetry, the imagery. We see here interpretive truth and we say how right! How profound! How natural! When life meets God and finds fulfillment one can see sights never before seen, one can know joy never before experienced, and one can expect the heavens to dance in celebration.

The story of Christmas as told by the biblical evangelists has a profundity beyond the rational. It portrays a truth beyond the scientific; it points to a reality that no life touched by this Jesus could ever deny. The beauty of our Christmas story is bigger than literalization could ever produce. For when this Lord is known by our lives, when love, acceptance, and forgiveness are experienced, when we are whole and free and affirmed people, truly the heavens do sing, "Glory to God in the Highest," and on earth there is "Peace and Good Will among Men." Hence, we Christians rejoice in the transcendent beauty and truth of this Christmas story. To our nonbelieving world we issue an invitation to come stand where we stand and look through our eyes at the babe of Bethlehem. And perhaps then they too will join all the faithful ones who come amid the imagery of our Christmas stories year after year for one purpose only: to worship the Lord of life who still sets us free, who still calls us into life and being. O come, we urge, come let us adore him.

– 44 –

Our World Is a Changing Kaleidoscope

November 1982

The urban Northeast, which embraces northern New Jersey, stands on the front lines of a rapidly inbreaking future. We are privileged to live in a cascading experience of vibrancy, contrasts, dynamism, hope, despair, diversity, dreams, and pain. Many of us feel buffeted by change, displaced and alienated from the fractured, security-giving traditions of the past, and uncomfortable and uncertain amid the still-emerging patterns of the future. All around us is a sea of revolutionary change in values, standards, and mores.

Our world seems to shrink in size daily as it becomes more and more radically interdependent. The traditional candle of faith appears to flicker dimly while we walk through a barren wilderness in search of meaning. Some of us relate to this world by pretending it is not different, others by actively denying the painful change process. Tragedy comes when we cannot embrace what is happening to us and therefore cannot live creatively in our present opportunity. This response is not infrequently the plight of the church, and it becomes obvious when the church speaks to our world out of assumptions that people no longer make or when the content of the message reveals a worldview that no longer exists.

To sharpen this issue, look at the assumptions and the worldview of the thirteenth century, the great age of faith that shaped so much of our Christian content, and compare that time with our own.

People in the thirteenth-century believed unquestioningly that this planet was the center of the entire universe. The earth was flat, but its distances seemed vast. Just above the earth was the dome formed by the sky beyond which everyone assumed the holy God dwelled. God was in God's heaven, exercising full control over all life. Prayer was an intimate exercise addressed to this close-residing deity. The unspoken assumption that fed the life of prayer was that God could and would intervene directly in our world in answer to those prayers to fix whatever was amiss, to save, to heal. When that divine intervention failed to save or heal, the people of that day were absolutely certain that the victims would enter the heavenly realm of eternal life, which all seemed so very near.

The thirteenth century was an emotionally closed, cozy, fixed world. The steeples of the Gothic churches seemed to reach into heaven itself. They made God's presence rich and sure. Through the priesthood and the sacraments, eternity and grace were thought to be captured and made readily available to the faithful. No one doubted this scheme, and the power of the church was enormous. Many people still yearn for or pretend that we live in that kind of world.

But, dear friends, such is a delusion. Today the human consciousness of every one of us has expanded a thousandfold. We are a post-atomic, post–space travel generation. This tiny planet is not perceived by anyone to be the center of the universe. The earth seems to us rather to be hung as an almost insignificant ornament in a vast infinity of space. Heaven does not feel close or real. God does not seem intimate. Life itself is threatened with extermination either by the atomic bomb or by environmental deterioration. Confidence in life after death is eroding. To be human today is to be radically insecure.

The church's power is questioned on every side. Attendance is declining, except in those churches who traffic in closed minds. Faith is a fading power. Promises of future glory fall on doubting ears and seem empty. Certainty is vanishing. Dynamic pluralism is a fact of our life. Diversity of beliefs, values, and standards abounds so that we are forced to wonder what is true or lasting or real.

In the inner city the hopelessness that grips the lives of men and women who no longer drug their pain with heavenly visions feeds a restless militancy. They have identified as their enemy the historic patterns that have produced poverty and oppression. They demand that these patterns be addressed now, and any institution that does not share the urgency of that cause is dismissed as part of the oppression. If Christianity wants to live in the inner city, it must speak and act now.

In the suburbs there seems to be a conscious need to hide from the pain of the city, to deny the injustice of our system, to pretend that change has not surrounded us. But such denial is itself denied by our behavior. Here, too, religious certainty has eroded. The songs the church sings no longer seem to communicate with the same power to suburban lives. The secular spirit has permeated our values.

The stability-giving institutions of yesterday such as marriage, schools, community, and patriotism are in full retreat. The roots which once related us to our past now seem so shallow. All of life appears transitory. The church, which years ago bound us to itself by providing us with a backdrop of unchanging truth against which we could live our lives from birth to death, now seems itself caught up in a maelstrom of transition. Insecurity abounds.

In our metropolitan area all of these forces are alive. Cultures are colliding; values are being debated; God is not assumed in our consciousness; the church's power is shrinking; life's very meaning is questioned. Our world is a kaleidoscope of changing symbols. It is here that we are called to work, to live, to witness. Here we must build churches that can embrace, baptize, and transform this world. Can you imagine a more challenging time to be alive or a more exciting place in which to live? I am convinced that our generation is the crucial pivotal generation in all of Christian history.

How pleasant it would be if only we could chant our liturgies and recite our creeds as if they still had a kind of magic power that would turn the tide. How peaceful it would be if we could pretend that we live in an age of faith. But that is not our choice, unless we prefer to be deluded.

In the life of this diocese, clergy and laity alike are embracing the whirlwind, walking into the storm, engaging our dynamic world in vigorous dialogue. Our task as a church is to equip the people of God to face the issues of our day effectively. We cannot hide from our opportunity. Our church must be willing to try new options and wild experiments. We are being asked in this new day to run the risk of failing with the new forms rather than to guarantee our failure by clinging to the old forms. We exist not for the people within the church but specifically to bear witness to those who are outside the church.

To the extent that our understanding of God continues to be based on the manipulative superstitions of the past, it will die and no ritual will save it. To the degree that the church continues to claim an infallibility, whether of inerrant scripture or of the papacy or of any sacred tradition, it will be defeated.

If we lived in the isolated and rural sections of the South and West, we might for another generation get away with playing yesterday's religious games. But this is the Diocese of Newark, the metropolitan New York area. We live on the frontier of change. What we need in this diocese is not escape but courage that is so strong that we will be empowered to engage the task at hand. We need a commitment that is so deep that we will never waver. We need a vision that is so broad and so open that we will never be able to cease walking forward.

I suspect it will never be comfortable or easy to be a Christian in the Diocese of Newark, but it will also never be dull or tedious. I invite you to share in this excitement by offering yourself, your leadership, your resources.

– 45 –

Challenger: Technology Fails Us; Does God?

March 1986

In 1969 when the first human being set foot on the moon, an elderly woman asked, somewhat incredulously, "Mr. Spong, do you really think that man was walking on the moon?" "Well, yes," I answered, "we've seen it on our television screens." "Well, I just don't believe it," she responded. "I don't believe God would let anybody get higher than God."

It was one of those indelible moments remembered because it poignantly captured something of the mystery and fear associated with space exploration. It is not easy to embrace a vision of the universe that leaps beyond the human capacity to imagine or the human ability to understand.

The vastness of space is an awesome concept for human beings, for the corollary of such vastness is the apparent insignificance of human life in the created order. So long as we believed that the earth was the center of the universe, we could also believe in the intimate protection of God. If God dwelt just beyond the sky then we could assume that we lived our lives under the constant surveillance of those graceful divine eyes. We were certain that God saw and recorded all that we did. From time to time this God would intrude into the affairs of this planet to heal, bless, punish, or judge. It was to this intervening and all-powerful God that the prayers of the believers through the ages were addressed. Apart from the concept of divine intervention much of the content of our prayers was meaningless.

Human beings tried to fit everything that happened to them into that theological framework of the intimate intervening God. It was our stated conviction that everything had a rational purpose, an understandable explanation, or was, at least, a mysterious reflection of the will of God. Though the sky seemed immense, it was nevertheless a comprehensible magnitude. What we now call meteors were named "falling stars" in that day, reflecting the belief that stars were heavenly lights, hung decoratively in the sky. Though far away, they were still close enough that occasionally one might drop to the earth and be recovered. This manageable world with its great God who lived just beyond the sky and who could be blessed, praised, and served forever, formed the context for human behavior until the late Middle Ages.

In the fifteenth century it began to dawn on the human consciousness that this was not so. This thought revolution began when Copernicus insisted that the sun, not the earth, was the center of the universe and that the earth actually revolved around the sun. Though this proved an inadequate description of the physical universe, it was a giant step toward the accepted modern worldview. As this truth gained credence the central significance of the earth was radically reduced. In response to this brilliant scientific conclusion the Christian church condemned Copernicus as a heretic. Despite that institutional rejection this idea was established. Galileo built on Copernicus's work, and the contemporary field of astronomy was born. As his reward, Galileo was excommunicated and forced to recant by an unrelenting church. History, however, remembers his name far more readily than the names of his misguided ecclesiastical authorities.

The march of science does not linger to allow small religious minds time to adjust, and slowly but surely the realization emerged that the planet Earth, home of the human consciousness, was in fact but a speck of dust in the created order. Space travel finally brought this idea into full human awareness. Today we know that there are, in our single galaxy, hundreds of billions of stars, most of them larger than our sun. Beyond that, there are billions and billions of galaxies in the universe. This planet Earth is tiny. Human life is fragile and often it feels very, very lonely. God does not seem quite so intimate, nor so powerful, nor so caring as once God did. Unable to tolerate a sense of powerlessness, we have shifted our confidence from the power of the divine God to the power of human technology. To technology we now look to find the courage to keep the dreadful angst, the debilitating sense of human insecurity in check.

And now technology has failed us. When the *Challenger* spacecraft exploded before the eyes of millions of watchers throughout the world, people responded with horror, fear, dread, anxiety, and endless interpretation. The graphic explosion was shown on television over and over again. The seven passengers were transformed into folk heroes after whom the moons on the planet Uranus might be named. The business of the nation was postponed, and people everywhere plunged into various expressions of grief. It was a telling response. Less than a month earlier a Boeing 727 had crashed, killing three hundred servicemen returning from a tour of occupation duty. In terms of loss of life this was a far greater tragedy, but it did not elicit the emotional response felt throughout the country when the *Challenger* exploded. The fact that this was a space flight was not itself sufficient to account for the reaction. Space probes have become so routine that the names of the astronauts are no longer household words as they were in the days of John Glenn and Neil Armstrong. Many people were only vaguely aware that another space flight was scheduled. Even President Reagan, when first informed of the explosion, inquired, "Is that the one the schoolteacher was on?" A tragedy in the space program alone is not sufficient to explain the response.

The trauma we felt as individuals and as a nation resides, I believe, in that sense of human dread that surrounds our knowledge of space. It rises from a recognition of the fragile vulnerability of human life—alone in the universe, unprotected by an all-good and all-powerful God. It is the despair that recognizes that human technology cannot be counted on to keep us safe, to keep life under control, and to keep anxiety in check. The destruction of the *Challenger* spacecraft brought each of us face to face with our own insecurity, with our mortality, with the impotence of our God concept, and with the impotence of our God substitute—technology. The only note of resurrection that was voiced throughout this tragedy was the constantly reiterated commitment that we would rise again with success on the next space venture. It was small comfort, but interestingly enough, it was the only comfort.

In our attempt to understand our corporate response the most important clue, I believe, is in the public outcry that focused on the children who had viewed the disaster. Because a civilian schoolteacher was aboard, the involvement of children had been particularly solicited. Two lessons from space had been scheduled to be transmitted to schoolchildren all over the world. Space travel was to be taken from the stars and placed in the classrooms. Now, instead of viewing our technological success, our children had been forced to see tragedy and failure. In an instant their eyes had beheld an unexpected, uncontrollable disaster which brought death. What would they think? How would they be affected? How would it be explained to them? Even President Reagan inserted in his address to the nation a paragraph directed to the children. "I know it is hard to understand that sometimes painful things like this happen," he said. "It is all part of the process of exploration and discovery. It is all part of taking a chance and expanding man's [sic] horizons." His words addressed a need that all adults seemed to feel.

Somehow we wanted to protect our children by patching up for them the illusion that life is rational, predictable, and that everything has purpose despite the fact that we adults abandoned that illusion long ago. Somehow we wanted to save our children from being contaminated by the adult sense of human loneliness in the vastness of space and of human impotence in the face of an incomprehensible universe. Somehow we wanted to protect them from coming to the same conclusions which now dominate our lives, to keep them from seeing what we see. In the explosion of *Challenger* some part of God died again — both the God who watches over, guards, and protects human life, and the God of human technology who binds the dreadful forces of the universe and makes them serve the rational purpose of human ends. Above all, we did not want our children to awaken to our levels of anxiety. We were sure our children could not handle that, for we are also sure that we are not handling it. The space tragedy destroyed our pretensions and removed our masks of certainty. The apocalyptic vision was terrifying, and the grief and depression were overwhelming.

In this moment of national tragedy it becomes starkly clear that a great theological crisis is abroad in our nation and in our world. The God most of us worship is revealed as too small to be God for this day. Some relate to this crisis by withdrawing from the world and clinging to the religious suppositions of previous generations, not recognizing that they have created for themselves a God who is an idol around whom must be built the myth of infallibility or that God cannot survive. Others relate to this crisis by withdrawing from any propositions about God and by becoming fatalistic citizens of the secular city. They are the shallow and cynical stoics who hope for lucky breaks in life so that they might achieve at least moderate happiness. Then there are those who can neither live with the old religious platitudes and the old God concepts, nor can they abandon that mysterious sense of the God who creates, enlivens, and gives meaning to the human enterprise. It is to this group that I believe our church must speak. How can we sing the Lord's song in this strange and complex world? Any organized religious structure or any single congregation that is not addressing these questions is simply not speaking to the major issues of our day. Any church that spends its energies answering questions no one is asking while ignoring this primary source of human anxiety will not long survive.

If we are to find a faith by which we can live today and a God in whom this generation can have confidence, then we must be willing to be led into the wilderness where our ideas about both God and life can be tested, refined, and remolded. That wilderness will be filled with change, risk, and uncertainty, but there is no alternative open to us except to enter it.

Ours is a dreadful, exciting, anxious, exhilarating time in which to be alive as Christians. I trust that those of us who constitute the church today will be both faithful and courageous in responding to the call that is ours simply because we are alive in this generation.

– 46 –

Embracing the Exile

December 1987

There are times when I feel as if I live in a period of exile. I look around for familiar landmarks from which to get my bearings, and there are none. I seek paths that might lead me to my destination, but the way forward is not clear. I turn to find ways by which I can retrace my steps to my known past only to discover that my footprints have been covered over and the way back has been obliterated. I am caught between that which is no more and that which is not yet. There is pain and anxiety in such a time, but also in these moments there is the opportunity for growth and hope. New occasions do teach new duties. I discover, to my delight, that I am not a solitary pilgrim in this wasteland of transition. "Exile" has become for me the most descriptive word by which to understand the present condition of Christian thinking as well as the contemporary experience of the Christian church.

Those verities by which Christians have traditionally defined life are today under siege. As theologian Paul Tillich once observed, the foundations of both our faith and our world are shaking. Confidence that human beings know who God is has eroded substantially in this century. The security that once came from the experience of prayer has largely departed the modern scene. The assumption that somehow the Bible provided us with certainty and answers has increasingly been abandoned. It is a scary, anxious time for believers.

These are not new realities but the intensity with which they are being felt in our generation is new. That intensity is manifested in a vigorous denial that fuels the anti-intellectualism of the new religious right in both its Protestant and Catholic forms. It is also manifested in the lethargic drift of people out of any commitment to the religious enterprise and into both a shallow secularism and an ethic of pleasure.

A primary reason for this drift is that the major religious assumptions are still cast in a premodern form that defies our postmodern credibility. The heart simply cannot be committed to what the mind rejects. The religious institutions appear in large measure to count on the demonstrated human need and desire to believe that is so deep in the psyche in order to continue to place adherents into the pews of our churches. We have failed to provide those who raise different or deeper questions either with a serious hearing or with new possibilities. Representatives of organized religion continue to quote ancient authorities far beyond the time of their believability. The church seems to depend on and even to encourage a continued ignorance. It is a rare educated individual who is moved by such antiquated religious claims as papal infallibility or biblical inerrancy. It is not encouraging to those who seek faith to observe that the church seems blissfully unaware of changes in the landscape of knowledge that are so vast that yesterday's creedal formulations or ethical prescriptions are simply irrelevant. Sanctifying our ignorance does not make it less ignorant.

This modern dilemma emerged in Western consciousness at least as early as the writings of Sir Isaac Newton in the seventeenth century. Newton discovered order in the universe that was so regular and so mathematical that all religious claims of divine intervention were called into question. This order appeared to be impersonal and oblivious to the human condition. Indeed, the belief in humanity as the "image of God" or even as the focus and purpose of God's creation, was called into question. Newton gave us a clockwork universe and reduced our concept of God to being the one who wound up the clock and hurled it into space, where it ran with the immaculate precision of its creator, but in a manner insensitive to individual human need. As this concept permeated the human consciousness, the power of prayer, based as it was on a pre-Newtonian mentality, was compromised.

The human creature whose mind could contemplate the universe and who could be self-conscious about his or her place in that universe was confronted with an existential loneliness and anxiety that had not been known since the dawn of civilization. Human beings were coming of age and discovering it to be a painful process. The childish myth that perceived God as a divine parent who would do for human beings what loving human parents would do for their children began to fade.

The impact of Charles Darwin pushed this process of secularization along dramatically. Darwin made us aware of our link with all forms of life as well as the vast expanse of time that has marked the life of this planet. The Christian understanding of life that began in the goodness of an instantaneous creation, was marked by a fall into sin, and finally required the rescue of a divine savior no longer fit an understanding that suggested that for 450 million years life had been evolving from lower to higher forms, from biological determinism to heightened self-consciousness.

Since World War II the exploration into space and the development of the field of astrophysics have further accelerated these anxieties. The vastness of time and the immensity of space both served to remove to even greater distances that cozy sense of a God who hovers over this tiny planet to protect it and those of us who live within it. Under the cumulative impact of modern science our thought of God became more and more impersonal, less and less satisfying emotionally.

When religious people turned to their sacred scriptures for consolation they found themselves instead filled with an even greater sense of the loss of God. That book, written between 940 B.C.E. and 150 C.E., presupposes a pre-Newtonian mind-set that no one today presupposes. The biblical God could talk with Adam, warn Noah of an impending flood, destroy Sodom and Gomorrah for their evil ways, bring upon Egypt supernatural plagues, part the waters of the Red Sea for the children of Israel, rain upon them manna from heaven, and help them conquer militarily the land of Canaan.

Even in the Christian part of that biblical story the narrative understands many experiences within the context of the magic and superstition of the ancient world. The New Testament tells us of a virgin birth, voices from heaven at baptism and transfiguration, the stilling of a storm, walking on the water, the curing of epilepsy and deaf muteness by casting out demons, the turning of water into wine, and the resuscitation to life of those who had died. It understands the Christ event in terms of an invasive God. Often the literal form of this narrative so offends our understanding of the way we experience life to be that we simply dismiss it as unreal. Even more often the church rehearses these narratives with no attempt to help us get beneath the words, as if to suggest that we must relate to them literally. Those who cannot do so walk away sadly and enter the faith crisis of modernity.

Complicating matters even further has been the reality that over the last two hundred years our society has grown past, and will no longer be bound by, the social attitudes found in the Bible. These attitudes reflected the corporate wisdom of an ancient world that was completely comfortable with the institution of slavery, the second-class dependent status of all women, and a blanket condemnation of whatever these ancient people did not understand. These attitudes have largely been abandoned by our world, but their presence in the pages of scripture that we have been taught to think of as the literal "word of God" makes us either defensive or disillusioned. We modern Christians find ourselves living in the strange world of a scientifically oriented secular society, and like the psalmist of old, we too wonder how or if we can "sing the Lord's song in a strange land." To work in this religious wasteland has been the vocation of my lifetime as a Christian. The books I have written, the articles I have had published, the study I have done have all been attempts to bridge the gap between the faith insights of the ages and the contemporary understanding of our world.

The first step for me has been to separate eternal truth from its literalistic bondage so that the insight to which the limiting words pointed could be examined from a new perspective. The second task required that I enter the knowledge explosion of our secular age as deeply as I could to embrace the questions and conclusions of modern biology, physics, and medicine so that dialogue might be engaged honestly and intelligently in the search for the truth. In this process the biblical image of exile has emerged for me with enormous power. I am not the first member of my religious tradition to know the chilling angst of exile. The Jewish people, my spiritual ancestors, were, like me, also removed from everything they had ever known, loved, or trusted. These Jewish men and women entered this same mood of radical insecurity. They lived in a world that admitted no certainty, offered no capacity to plan, and knew no semblance of power or potency for their values. The exile elicited from the Jews two primary responses. Some of them developed a religious hysteria that was marked by tenacious clinging to the rituals, routines, memories, and religious myths of the past when life was believed to have predictability. When they could not move beyond these symbols, death and the loss of meaning overwhelmed them. Others were forced into an incredible growth in their understanding of both God and life. Those in this latter category did not experience the death of God or even the loss of faith as their conservative critics expected. Rather, the exile enabled the God worshiped in Judah to be transformed from a tribal deity into a universal deity. It enabled the Jewish people to dream of a God beyond the limits of their provincial minds. This God would call them into a new vocation by which all the people of the earth might worship "in spirit and in truth." By enduring the exile, admitting the loss of certainty, allowing the death of their concept of God, there was a painful stretching transition into new truth that in time was recognized as saving truth.

The exile thus becomes for me a contemporary symbol of considerable power. The church in all of its manifestations is called today, I believe, to enter the exile, to abandon yesterday's security symbols, to embrace powerlessness, to seek truth in new forms, to meet a divine presence that can interpret our world as adequately as the now abandoned religious myths of a premodern world interpreted the world of yesterday. The call of the exile is to find God, to discover Christ, to engage prayer, to know life's fullness as intelligent men and women who accept the world as we know it to be. That is a challenging assignment. Perhaps only a saving remnant of the church can respond to this vocation, but someone or some group, no matter how small, must respond, for the future of Christianity quite clearly hangs upon their willingness to do so. The experience of exile calls those who find themselves pilgrims in this barren land, or refugees from a beleaguered church, to identify themselves, come together, and build a community that will learn how God can be worshiped while we journey to a place that as yet we are not able to see. Of course it is scary to face the fact that this is who we are and where we are, but it is also honest, and it does not participate in the popular religious delusion. For me it is the only option for faithfulness.

– 47 –

No Neat Answers

May 1989

It was a dark and somber Holy Week. Walking the way of the cross took on a realism that all of us seek to avoid. The first toll of the bell was sounded on Saturday morning before Palm Sunday, when at about 1:30 a.m. Kimberly Stanton Hegg, the daughter of David and Judy Hegg of St. Peter's Church, Morristown, was killed instantly in an automobile accident.

Kimberly was twenty-six years old and newly launched on a career with Mobil Chemical Corporation. She was bright, articulate, and vivacious — combining in proper proportions a sense of humor, a commitment to feminism, and the charming impertinence of youth. She was the oldest child and only daughter of the rectory family. This life, so exuberant and expansive, came to an abrupt halt as her car ran off the road and into a brick wall. The presumption is that she went to sleep at the wheel for but a moment. But in that moment the elements of fate and chance combined to send a searing pain into the lives of a mother, a father, two brothers, and countless numbers of friends. That moment also forced into the consciousness of many the eternal questions of meaning, purpose, and God.

Five days later Kirk David Casto, the twenty-nine-year-old son of David and Joyce Casto of St. James', Upper Montclair, died of leukemia. It had been for Kirk a long and painful battle with a dreaded disease. For some time his parents had watched his strength dissipate and his body waste away. Kirk had overcome many obstacles in his short life, but this one he could not overcome. His hopes, his expectations, his dreams for the future were destined to be aborted. He left a mother and a father grieving for their oldest son and two younger brothers newly aware of the shortness and uncertainty of human life.

Clergy families are certainly not immune from pain, death, or bereavement. Still it is an unusual set of circumstances that would decree that the firstborn child of two clergy families in a single diocese would depart this life within five days of each other and during that part of the church year when Christians contemplate the meaning of the passion and death of the one we call Lord. It had not occurred to me before this Holy Week that Jesus, called the firstborn of the Father, was at the time of his death according to the tradition just four years older than Kimberly Hegg and just one year older than Kirk Casto.

These two young lives were an inescapable presence for me during Holy Week. When I listened anew to the cry from the cross, "My God, my God why have you forsaken me?" I heard it inside the grief that the Hegg family and the Casto family must have felt. To have a loved one taken from you leaves inevitably a sense of profound emptiness, a feeling of having been abandoned. When I hear in the passion story the scornful cry of the crowd beneath the cross saying, "He saved others, himself he cannot save," I knew afresh something of the humanity of Jesus and simultaneously something of the impotence of God. It is the same impotence that parents feel when their child has gone beyond the parental power to protect. It is the same impotence that doctors feel when a patient's sickness is beyond their technical and scientific skill to save or even to relieve from pain. It is the same impotence that pastors feel when they are called upon to comfort those whose lives have been torn asunder by grief or when death seems so unfair and so uncaring.

That sense of impotence we deal with in many ways. Some of us quickly move on to other things that we can control, allowing the dark silence of loneliness to haunt us as little as possible. Some of us become calloused or hardened so that the next time we must deal with what we cannot change it will not hurt quite so badly. Some of us become very busy saying our prayers or chanting our liturgies so that we can pretend we are making a difference. Some of us grieve and sink into a depression that warps the rest of our days. Some of us seek the escape of alcohol, drugs, or hysterical religion—all of which serve to dull the pain but never to eliminate it. All of us wonder, reflect, wrestle, and contemplate whether or not life has meaning.

For Christians, and I suspect especially for clergy, the tragedy of premature death creates almost inevitably a crisis in faith, for it reveals that the answers we have been taught through the ages are simply not adequate. Is God unfair? If not, is God powerless to prevent this pain? Is life at the mercy of fate—cold, cruel, impersonal fate? Archibald MacLeish, in his play *J.B.*, put it this way: "If God is God he is not good. If God is good he is not God." What have we Christians to say to these things?

My first response is to dismiss the simplistic pious religious answers that seem to abound in such a tragic time. I am repelled by a God who is said to need the likes of Kimberly and Kirk in the nearer divine presence. So needy a God could not be God for me. In the early days of my ministry I watched a simple godly lady trying to comfort a sobbing nine-year-old boy whose father had just died. "Johnny," she said, "God wanted your Dad to be with him." Looking with tear-stained cheeks at this woman, Johnny replied, "Well, damn God!" I have never forgotten either the look on her face or the honesty of Johnny's reply. Any God who needed a little boy's father more than the little boy was a demonic force worthy not of worship but of the condemnation that Johnny pronounced. Out of the mouths of babes comes wisdom, I noted.

I am also not impressed by those who suppose that there is some larger unknown pattern into which tragic death fits with meaning. The God I worship is not weaving some gigantic tapestry that requires the dark shadows of human tragedy to bring out its brilliance. I do not expect to be enlightened someday by the realization that the deaths of Kimberly and Kirk had meaning and purpose that I do not now understand. I do not believe that death at age twenty-nine from leukemia or at age twenty-six in an automobile accident is an expression of God's will. Surely God desires life, health, and wholeness for those created in this God's image. The religious answers we have devised through the ages to defend God in the face of human tragedy seem to me to fail miserably.

Does this mean that God is not in control? Does it mean that there is no God? Is life itself but an accident of physical and chemical forces without ultimate meaning? Are we alone in the vast universe guided by a mindless fate? Is our only consolation the realization voiced by the cynic who says, "Those are the breaks"; "That's the way it is"; "Too bad, tough luck"? Is there no ultimate meaning or no guiding purpose? Many people in their innermost being believe this and live on the basis of this even if they cannot admit it to themselves. They are the ones who have felt existentially the vastness of space and the insignificance of life. They have comprehended the brutality and the accidental quality of an evolutionary process called the "survival of the fittest." Human beings have embraced the mathematical certainty of the laws of the universe that admit to no chance, manipulation, magic, or miracle. They understand the tricks a fragile psyche can play on the rational processes: imposing meaning where there is no meaning, inventing God where there is no God, discovering purpose where there is no purpose. Many people live in such a place. Some of them know it, admit it and state it clearly. A significant number know it but cannot admit it and spend much of their lives denying it or pretending that it is not so.

For me, honesty requires two things. First, I must reject those easy religious answers that have been offered in various forms through the ages. Secondly, I must live in the modern world accepting the knowledge that this world has thrust upon me and forcing any appeals to God that I might make through the crucible of this knowledge. I cannot pray as a pre-Newtonian person. I cannot think as a pre-Darwinian man. I cannot pretend that Freud never lived. I cannot close my eyes to the world of subatomic physics or astrophysics. If God is to be real for me, if divine purpose and transcendent meaning are to believed, then this God, this purpose, and this meaning must come to me in the contemporary world of my knowledge and experience. God cannot be mine at the price of tempering reality or hiding in some anti-intellectual retreat from modernity.

I suspect that the God who is God is beyond the human capacity even to imagine. I suspect that all we can know of God is but a fleeting glimpse, a momentary point of view. Throughout history the religious establishment has pretended that these glimpses and insights were revelations of the whole divine power. Armed with that illusion, we have executed as heretics those who disagreed with the majority insight. We have fought religious wars to establish our truth over a competing truth. We have claimed for our revelation an intimacy that surely no human truth can possess. When tragedy strikes in the form of premature death, it strips away the facade of these deceptive and false claims and forces us to admit how little we know, how uncertain we are. The authority of religion itself wavers.

The first step into comfort for bereavement, I believe, is to face this reality openly. The second step is to allow our grief to be real, to refuse easy answers and quick panaceas. The third step is to walk into the pain of life with a willingness to experience it fully until we learn from it something of who we are. Finally, for me, comfort and hope are born when I take into the moments of bereavement all that I know of God and allow faith and pain to confront each other. The power of life, the depth of love, the timelessness of meaning are all aspects of the divine. As a Christian, I see these qualities preeminently present in Jesus of Nazareth, who is for me the human face of God, fully alive, fully loving, fully being, and, therefore, revelatory of what transcendence is all about.

So when death overwhelms me, I dare to affirm life. When love is taken from me, I dare to affirm love. When my being is diminished by the loss of one who has enriched my life, I dare to have the courage to be all that I am. I recall that Jesus, the life through which I see God, was himself a victim of hostile forces who killed him at age thirty. I remember that he was not able to save himself and neither was the God he knew so intimately. I will walk with this God. I will shout in defiance when the meaninglessness of premature death embraces me. I will continue to love, even though the more I love the more I know I will be open to the pain of losing that love. I will dare to risk all in the gamble of living fully, because in the depths of living I find holiness to be present and God to be real.

I do not offer this as an answer. Ultimately, there are no neat answers to which we can cling. I offer it rather as a philosophy of life. It is the only way that I am able to be both a citizen of the twentieth century and one who, by the grace of God, believes himself called to be a Christian.

To this God of life I commit Kimberly and Kirk as well as the pain of grief, despair, and separation that engulfs those who loved these two young adults. There will be many who will find this stance ever so inadequate. At this moment in my life it is all I have to give. I can assure you only that for me the God with whom I live is real and the strength that comes from this God is sufficient. To journey through life with this God is the privilege of those who have learned to walk by faith.

– 48 –

Yes, Virginia, There Is a God!

December 1991

The jolly old elf named Santa Claus is ready to make his annual visitation. Young and old alike recognize his beard, red suit, paunch, and that endearing twinkle in the eye as he invades store windows, street corners, magazine and newspaper advertisements, and television.

Children literalize this seasonal symbol by writing Santa letters, sitting on his lap to recite a list of desires, and putting food by the hearth on the night before Christmas to feed him and the reindeer. Parents participate in this literalization by using the figure of Santa to control the behavior of their children for at least a month. Children are told that being good will bring rewards on Christmas Day and being naughty will bring deprivation or even punishment. Who wants coal in their stocking?

At some point in the early life of a child the literal fantasies that gather around Santa Claus explode. Perhaps a wiser, older brother or sister bursts the bubble; perhaps a parent makes a slip of the tongue; or perhaps the child's growing perception of the world can no longer be contained within the boundaries of this myth. Gradually, Santa's sleigh does not look big enough to carry toys to all the children in the local school, to say nothing of all the children in the world. A growing understanding of time forces the realization that to visit all the chimneys in one's block would complete the hours of the night before Christmas. The ability of Santa to read his mail, keep his lists, make his toys, pack his sleigh, and cover the world, even with the help of Mrs. Claus, the elves, and Rudolph, finally overwhelms credibility even in the life of a young child.

When that moment of truth dawns and the child dares to announce his or her new conclusion about Santa Claus, there is a sense of sadness in the household. Many parents mourn the loss of innocence and the end of fantasy while others seek to deny the child's new understanding and to call that child back into literal belief for at least one more Christmas season. Tragically, some parents announce to their children that without Santa Claus there can be no Christmas, thus blaming the loss of the magical holiday on the child. The best response uses this opportunity to help the child move beyond the literal mind-set into a deepening awareness of both symbol and myth. Many are familiar with a piece of our Christmas folklore written by Francis P. Church and run in the *New York Sun* in 1897. It begins, "Yes, Virginia, there is a Santa Claus and ten times ten thousand years from now he will continue to make glad the heart of childhood."

When I think about the role assigned to Santa Claus during the Christmas season, I am amazed by the similarities between the father figure of the North Pole and the holy God of heaven as this God is so frequently interpreted in the common mind. Many people envision God as one who is "making a list and checking it twice" looking for "who's naughty and who's nice." Many of the prayers addressed to God are similar in form and content to letters that children write to Santa Claus. These prayers tend to tell God what is wanted and to remind God of how good the petitioner has been so as to be deserving of the divine generosity. God is regularly portrayed, even by the church, as a year-round Santa who rewards good behavior and threatens to punish bad behavior. For many, the concept of heaven is a sophisticated version of the ultimate Christmas goody delivered to those whose lifetime behavior was deserving. Similarly, the concept of hell is a sophisticated version of switches and ashes for those whose lifetime behavior is worthy of ultimate punishment.

The analogy can be even more revealing. Compare a child's dismissal of the literalized myth of Santa Claus with the adult's dismissal of the literalized myths of his or her religious tradition. Both emerge from the rising consciousness forged by a growing knowledge and experience of the world that renders the previously believed content no longer credible. Furthermore, the literal view of Santa constitutes a detriment to maturity for the child just as a paternalistic, understanding God serves to keep adults in a status of pious infantilism. This simplistic approach feeds the craving for dependency and eschews the task of taking responsibility for one's own life, destiny, and well-being.

A child trying to imagine Santa's sleigh to be big enough to carry toys for the children of the world is not much different from an adult trying to imagine Noah's ark capable of housing two representatives of all of the world's animals. A child's small sense of the universe that envisions Santa covering the world in one night is not much different from the modern adult's small sense of the universe that depicts God living just above the sky watching over and protecting vulnerable human beings. It is surely no more incredulous today for a child to imagine Santa's reindeer streaking through the sky than it is for an adult to imagine a literal star that moved through the heavens to lead wise men to a spot in Bethlehem, or to believe that angels populated that same sky to sing (presumably in Hebrew) to a group of hillside shepherds.

This connection between what Santa Claus means to a child and what the traditional understanding of God means to an adult was driven home to me when a college student confessed to me that he lost his faith in Santa Claus at age six and his faith in God at age sixteen. He concluded, "I don't know which one I miss the most." God has been presented so often in the life of the church as a kind of heavenly Santa Claus that this sort of confusion is all but inevitable.

In the mainline Christian traditions in the twentieth century we are now experiencing radical social and cultural religious change. Some people speak of it as a paradigm shift; others as a coming of age in our understanding of God. Whatever we call it, it is an uncomfortable experience. Like the loss of Santa Claus to a child, the shattering of the traditional view of God heralds the loss of innocence and the end of fantasy to many an adult.

Because of the emotional similarity, the responses are often the same. Adults unable to accept or to deal with the vision of the shattered Santa Claus–God myth retreat into a hysterical fundamentalism. They offer to one another and to the world the illusionary comfort and assurance that the Santa Claus-God still lives, undisturbed by the march of science or the maturing of humanity. They condemn with vehemence the critics and the skeptics of their literalized symbols and proclaim that the old-time religion is still good enough for them. This approach is enormously appealing for a period of time for it holds out the promise that the innocence of childish belief systems can be sustained. Ultimately, however, it fails, for neither Santa Claus nor a Santa Claus–type God can live comfortably in a modern adult's consciousness. Fundamentalistic religion is reminiscent of those parents who try to preserve the Santa myth intact for their children for one more Christmas.

There are also those adults who say that if God, like Santa Claus, is not the divine presence as portrayed in generations past, then there is no God at all for them. They turn bitter and reject all things religious to take up full-time citizenship in the secular city. These dropouts are reminiscent of those parents who say if there is no Santa Claus, there can be no Christmas at all.

Finally, there are those who recognize that, like Santa Claus, everything we know about God has to be in part mythological. There is no human mind nor ecclesiastical tradition that can capture literally the awesome mystery of God's fullness. A god who could fit comfortably inside a limited human brain would not be a god big enough to be God for all time. In people's faith story God is always growing and expanding, and a myth that is ever developing is an essential part of believing. In every age it is the human destiny to walk by faith — not by complete, literal knowledge. We see God only through a glass darkly. The content we attribute to God is a frail human construct that points to a truth it cannot finally capture. When we literalize that construct we become more idolatrous, not more religious. But we cannot live without that construct for it is a symbol, a myth that drives us beyond the limits of words toward that presence to which our words can only point.

Santa Claus stands for the spirit of Christmas that finds its greatest pleasure in giving rather than receiving. It is a spirit that binds the human family together on at least that one day of the year, a spirit so powerful that even opposing armies in the field have been known to suspend hostilities on December 25. In like manner the word "God" stands for an ultimate truth that drives us beyond our symbols to the edges of our imagination. The word "God" stands for the power of love that lifts us out of our self-imposed prisons and shows us what human life can ultimately be. It points to the source of life that challenges us to walk beyond every human limitation into a reality deeper and richer than our literal minds can contemplate. The word "God" represents the ground of being seemingly present when each of us dares to be the all we were created to be. To glimpse this understanding of God is to move significantly beyond the religious symbols of the past that perceived God as protective parent figure in the sky. It is to force us to question the Santa Claus-God to whom we have so frequently offered prayers that sounded like "Dear Santa" letters.

When human life comes of age, the parent God is no more adequate than a literalized Santa Claus is to a maturing child. Hysterical fundamentalism will not revivify our childish images of the divine.

Abandoning Christianity because the literal myths of the past are no longer believable will not give us either life or maturity. A faith by which modern men and women can live today and tomorrow is born when we learn how to walk into the depths of our religious symbols and how to develop the ability to see spirit rather than letter. Only then are we emboldened to move beyond the binding rules and concepts that are limited by our understanding into the open-ended vastness of the God we seek.

Yes, Virginia, there is a God. But God is not the man upstairs who pulls strings, sends sickness, or rescues the good while punishing the evil. God is the symbol for our deepest human yearning. The Christian life is at one and the same time a journey into this God and a journey into the depths of our humanity.

Because our journey begins inside a Christian context, our guide for this journey is the one we call the Christ, in whose total humanity the divine and holy God was believed to be revealed. We are drawn to his awesome integrity, his total openness, and his radical freedom that enables him to give his life away. The God that this Christ offers is a God who calls us to endure life without flinching, to trust the source of life even while dying, and to live with courage inside the full dignity and integrity of our humanity. This God is no Santa Claus, for that symbol cannot embrace the cross where goodness is killed and experience the sense of abandonment that death always brings.

Each Christmas a new group of children move from fantasy to reality in their understanding of Santa Claus. In our century a whole generation of adults are moving from fantasy to reality in their understanding of God. Will the church be the community of faith that helps that transition to move from letter to spirit, from literal notions to transcendent truth? Or will part of us turn to fundamentalism in a vain attempt to keep yesterday's myths alive while the remainder of us, in bitter disillusionment, abandon the religious enterprise altogether? The future of Christianity depends upon our ability to walk through this crisis as old symbols die and new symbols emerge to take their place.

I will listen to the echoes of life until I can hear the angels sing; I will journey inwardly until I can discover Bethlehem, where Christ can be born in me; and finally, I will live my life in such a way as to be a light in the world's darkness that can lead twentieth-century wise men and women to know that Christ in whom God can still be met.

– 49 –

The Lord Is Risen...He Is Risen Indeed!

April 1992

"The Lord Is Risen...He Is Risen Indeed!" These words, lying at the heart of the Christian story, possess an authentic, original quality. They do not narrate; they only proclaim. They rise dramatically out of the ecstasy of that first experience of resurrection. They lay claim to a truth that has defied rationality and stretched credibility since the dawn of the Christian era. The twentieth century listens to these words with doubt, speculation, and even disbelief. I understand that, for there is much in our sacred story about which one must be skeptical. But as we approach the Easter season I want to assert that, as a citizen of this same twentieth century and as one who is not afraid to doubt, I believe that Jesus of Nazareth, the one who was crucified, the one who died and was buried, lives. God has raised him up.

I do not make this claim lightly, nor do I deny the questions that the expanding knowledge of the last two thousand years inevitably poses for the faith assertions of modern men and women. For example, I take seriously the pioneering work of Sir Isaac Newton in the seventeenth century, whose discoveries did much to remove from human consciousness the categories of magic and miracle. Before Newton, almost any phenomenon that lay beyond the scope of human understanding was attributed to supernatural forces operating inside human history. Much of the Bible was written from this supernatural understanding with stories of God intervening in history to send plagues on Egypt, to part the water of the Red Sea, to feed the multitudes in the wilderness, to heal the sick, to raise the dead, and to protect the church. I am post-Newtonian in my thinking; nonetheless I affirm that God raised Jesus from the dead.

I also take seriously the radical criticism of Christianity made by Sigmund Freud in the early years of this century. I recognize the anxiety that death creates in the hearts of self-conscious and self-transcending human beings. I know that wishing it is so is quite often the creator of an account that it is so. I am aware that much of the language in which the Christian story is framed reveals unconscious desires, oedipal conflicts, and superstitious assumptions. Yet it is as a post-Freudian person that I continue to assert that God raised Jesus from the dead.

I am a student and devotee of the historical-critical approach to

Holy Scripture, and as such I am deeply aware of conflict, contradiction, and exaggeration in the biblical narratives about the resurrection. More than once I have traced the developing tradition of Easter from Paul, who wrote from 49 to 62 C.E., to the fourth Gospel, which appears to have reached its final form about the year 96 C.E. That literary journey through the first century reveals both irreconcilable details and an expanding tradition in the biblical narrative itself as it seeks to describe the Easter events. The Gospels disagree on who went to the tomb at dawn on the first day of the week, on whether or not the women saw the risen Lord, on the number of angelic persons who delivered the Easter message, on whether it was in Galilee or Jerusalem where the disciples first met the risen Christ, and on whether that meeting took place on the third day or at some unspecified later time. The Gospels also disagree on the relationship between resurrection, ascension, and Pentecost, and on whether the body of the risen Christ was physical or nonphysical. All of these incompatibilities I have charted. I have also traced the presence of growing legends in the resurrection accounts. So it is as one who is aware of these textual anomalies that I assert my belief that God raised Jesus from the dead, that the Easter claim is true, and that life not death is our ultimate human destiny.

I am also a student of the Hebrew roots of my Christian faith. I know that when Easter dawned in the lives of the first disciples the language of their own faith tradition was the only language in which they could describe the event. So I am not surprised to find Jesus' death and resurrection interpreted in terms of the perfect sacrifice offered by Jewish people on the day of the atonement, or as the paschal lamb slain on the day of the Passover. I know that the Hebrew scriptures shaped the way Jesus came to be understood. The servant figure of Isaiah who bore the sins of the people, the son of man figure sketched by the prophet Daniel, and the psalms that described the enthronement of the king all became the images by which Jesus was interpreted.

I have also pressed the Gospel narratives deeply to discover in their stories of Jesus the echoes of the stories of Abraham, Moses, Hannah, Elijah, Elisha, Solomon, Judith, and many, many others. I have begun to see how sacred stories of the past were used to tell of sacred moments in the present. It is as one who takes seriously this process of subjective biblical interpretation that I continue to affirm that God raised Jesus from the dead.

My convictions about the truth of Easter arise from two things.

Out of the past comes a sense of the undeniable original power of the Easter experience that roots my faith in history. Out of the present comes my contemporary sense of the reality of transcendence that this postmodern world has only begun to explore. When these two realities are merged, I believe that a case for the resurrection can be made for our time.

First, we look at the past. No matter how one interprets the data of the first Easter, there is no question that it reflects enormous power. A man was executed. His followers were scattered in fear and despair. They either went into hiding or returned to their remote life as Galilean fishermen. They had no reason to believe that there was any future for the movement in which they once had shared. They had every reason to believe that their continued participation in this movement would be life-threatening. Yet some moment of incredible power occurred that reconstituted this apostolic band, called them out of their cowardice into courage, out of the safety of hiding into the danger of public proclamation. Something transformed this heretofore unimpressive band of people into a community of such self-confidence that whether they lived or died, whether they were tortured or imprisoned became quite secondary to their compelling need to tell others of the lordship of Jesus, whom they were convinced God had raised from the dead.

The disciples were all Jewish males who had been taught from their infant years that God only was holy. Yet, driven by the Easter experience, these Jewish disciples were forced to broaden radically their understanding of God until Jesus became for them a part of all that God means. These Jewish people who, upon pain of death, refused to bow their heads to any power less than God suddenly began to direct their prayers to Jesus. I watch in wonder as the day they came to associate with the resurrection challenged the Jewish Sabbath for supremacy as the new holy day in the unfolding drama of the Christian story.

Only enormous power could change both the beliefs and practices of Jewish people. This power was present in whatever occurred when Christianity was born. I acknowledge that power. I also recognize that the Easter experience lived in memory and by word of mouth for thirty-five to seventy years before it achieved written form. How inevitable it is that the details would vary widely and even that the various accounts would be exaggerated and contradictory. These accounts do, however, point to an experience that could not be doubted.

When I take this witness and turn to my own modern world, I am seeking a context, a vocabulary, and perhaps even the concepts that people of my generation might use to process the Easter experience. What words would we use today if Jesus' resurrection had occurred in twentieth-century Western life instead of in first-century Jewish life? In this question I recognize that there is nothing objective about either first-century Jewish words or twentieth-century Western words. What is objective is the experience behind the words, the reality that made the words necessary in the first place.

I suspect that if I stood in my generation before an empty tomb and entered into the meaning of Easter, and then had to narrate that experience to my friends, I would be equally lost for words. I would grasp, as first-century Jews did, at whatever way I understood transcendence. I might begin with the learnings of my life that suggest that once I escape the limits imposed on me by the culture, prejudices, and mind-set of modernity, I too can have visions. My world has taught me that when I risk, venture, and dare to walk beyond the definitions that have bound me, a new future beckons me. In that future, truths that once were hidden and realities that once were unseen emerge. New horizons appear and new visibility occurs. In this new place I listen as if for the first time to Jesus' words that some people have eyes to see but do not see.

I also know what it means to give my life away, to live for another. I know the vulnerability that love always creates. Love lowers our barriers and exposes our fragile security systems. Love opens us to move beyond ourselves into transcendence, timelessness, and eternity, which are just alternative ways of saying that this love moves us into God. Standing here I can listen anew to the words of the Epistle of John, which assert that God is love and that those who dwell in love dwell in God. Then I look anew at the Gospel portrait of Jesus as love incarnate and see things about him I had never seen before. I see love that is infinite and indestructible. I see Jesus living out this love as he embraces the lepers, Samaritans, women, gentiles, executioners, betrayers, and even those who forsook him and fled.

This love then emerges as the essence of his teachings. From him I learn that divine love is not fair. It can be as generous to those who worked but one hour as it is to those who have borne the burden and heat of the day. It embraces the prodigal son who wasted his father's substance in a life of debauchery as surely as it embraces the elder brother who always did his duty. It values the single lamb that strays from the flock as much as it values the ninety-nine sheep that stay securely inside their boundaries. When this picture of divine love is experienced and when it can be heard in his words and seen in his life, then I can understand why people claimed that when they met Jesus they met nothing less than the holy God.

In this context I see Easter as so much more than just a supernatural miracle. Easter has become the touch of a new reality that breaks into my consciousness. It is a reality centered in a living God defined as self-giving love. The life of Jesus becomes the revelation of the nature of this God as boundless love. Only then do I begin to understand that death cannot destroy Jesus because death cannot destroy the love of God. God raises Jesus into the very selfhood of God because that is who Jesus is. This is what our faith story asserts. Even more personally, the faith story holds out to me the promise that when I live inside the powerful love of God, death cannot destroy me either. As Paul asserts, the one who raised Jesus will also raise us into the divine presence and thus into the divine and eternal life.

This Easter claim then makes sense to me because it makes sense out of both Jesus' life and my life. Easter has thus become for me an invitation to stand before the crucified one where love is most deeply portrayed and then to enter the meaning of that love as its recipient. Only then does Easter become both a proclamation that Jesus lives and a faith assertion that God has raised him from the dead. Inside this truth I discover that even someone like me, prone to be a skeptic, living in the last decade of the twentieth century, cannot deny the power or the reality of Easter. So I assert that I believe in the resurrection of Jesus and I commit myself to live my life as one who can accept vulnerability and love wastefully, for in doing that I enter Easter and I become a resurrected person.

– 50 –

Propaganda or Education? A New Vocation for the Church

October 1995

The fall of the year is traditionally a time of intense institutional activity in the life of the church. Sunday school classes and the youth group are reorganized. The adult education program is advertised. The plans for the every-member canvas are announced. Social events are scheduled and attempts are made to invite the faithful into the various programs that are offered. These activities consume enormous energy on the part of both clergy and lay leaders, and each September there is great hope that this will be a successful church year.

However, if one charts the trends present in institutional religious life, it becomes apparent that those traditional activities have a declining appeal to the people they are designed to serve. Studies reveal that, before the program year is complete, the church leaders will once again be discouraged. If one looks at these activities over a longer perspective, it is clear that the decline is precipitous. It is a demoralizing time for leaders in institutional religion.

That discouragement becomes more ominous when one looks at recent opinion polls on American religious sentiments today. In this nation there appears to be a very high level of religious feeling, a yearning for God, for spiritual things, for meaning, and for a sense of transcendence. However, few people who express these desires believe that any institutional religious entity is the place where one can go to explore these dimensions of life. So we have a society in which the interest in things religious is growing while the interest in organized religion is declining. One wonders what this means, why it is so, and what the future holds for an institution like the church.

To begin to formulate an answer, we might examine, first, some of the presuppositions that still operate, perhaps not always consciously, in the structures of the church. One of those presuppositions is that the church has a duty and a responsibility to provide its people with a variety of religious answers. The assumption has been made that the leadership of the church was in possession of those answers, perhaps by divine revelation. But the world has evolved to a place where this assumption is no longer trusted, especially since this very claim of ecclesiastical authority has been used in the past to suppress the questions that religious people want to ask. Today's spiritually hungry world would like the freedom to probe new experiences, new understandings, and new realities. People yearn, not so much for answers in this generation, as to have their questions honored and explored. Perhaps my daughter was right when she informed me years ago, "Dad, the church keeps answering questions that I don't even ask anymore." So far removed from the real issues of life has the church grown that those who have abandoned its life now appear to regard the church as irrelevant, and those who have not left its sacred walls frequently regard the church as boring. The only exception to this rule appears to be in that right-wing of Christianity where a passionate hysteria is promoted to remove doubts and to create the momentary illusion of well-being in an otherwise frightened world. But when either this passion or those simple answers are challenged, this form of religion inevitably turns angry and vindictive and reveals an empty despair. One has only to listen to the fear-mongering of a Patrick Buchanan or the veiled threats delivered through the constant smiles of a Ralph Reed or a Pat Robertson to have this confirmed. These observations raise for me the dramatic question as to how the church in this moment of history can fulfill its vocation.

Christian leaders might begin to address these concerns by seeking the difference between what believers call Christian education and what religious critics call Christian propaganda. It is my conviction that these two have been so deeply confused over the centuries that in the minds of most people they are the same thing. Indeed, the more established the church has been in the power structures of the society, the more propaganda has masqueraded as education.

When the Western world conceived of itself as "Christendom," the dominant religious tradition was understood to speak with the literal voice of God. The leaders of this tradition identified their understanding of God with God and claimed for it an infallibility. Hierarchical pronouncements and institutional interpretations of what the church called "God's scriptures" were clothed with inerrancy. Church leaders from the papal office to the local priest presented themselves to the people as the source of answers. As such, they tolerated no questions that relativized the authority of their conclusions. The educational function of the church was actually propaganda designed to impart "the true faith," to explain the intricacies of doctrine, and to discern the correctness of scripture. The assumption was abroad that if one mastered these things one became a true believer. Vestiges of that mentality are still present in the life of the church today, and it is that mentality which contributes mightily to the church's growing irrelevance and to the decreasing appeal found in normative church activities. The people resent being propagandized. The church refuses to educate.

Christendom as an organizing principle of our society no longer exists, whether the institutional church recognizes that or not. Christendom has been replaced by the secular city. In that secular city the authority of the church is at best badly compromised and at worst nonexistent. The secular city came into being, at least in part, because the church, in the defense of the ultimate authority of Christendom, fought and lost battles against Copernicus, Galileo, and Darwin, just to name a few. The once unchallenged moral authority of the church has been devastated by its defenses of slavery, apartheid, and segregation, by its persecution of heretics, by its opposition to the emancipation of women, and by its hostility toward gay and lesbian people. For these reasons neither the intellectual nor the moral authority of the church is today intact, and efforts to relate to this present day out of the propagandizing authority of the past are pitifully inept. The church may well still make pronouncements, but the fact is that very few people are listening. That is one major reason why the programmatic activities of the church today are in trouble and have declining appeal. That is also why a whole new concept of how to be the church and how to engage the task of Christian education in our generation needs to be born. That might begin by drawing a clear distinction between propaganda and education.

The assumption of Christian propaganda is that the church possesses the "truth," so it is designed to give people the right answers. Christian education must be done in a secular society and be designed to help people ask the right questions.

Christian propaganda assumes that there is a fixed goal to which a person's life is properly destined. Christian education is open-ended and invites a person into a journey into the largely undefined mystery of God. Its destination is thus not clear. It offers no fixed guideposts and no detailed maps that we can follow along the way.

Christian propaganda calls its adherents to master the content of the Christian faith as if that content were self-evident and totally set. Christian education suggests that truth is always relative and that ultimate and unchanging truth is finally unknowable except "through a glass darkly." Thus it proclaims that the sources of the authority in the life of the church, such as the scriptures, the creeds, and that body of doctrines, do but point to God; they never capture God.

Christian propaganda invites one to be secure and seduces its recipients into the belief that the church can provide that security. Therefore, Christian propaganda aims to remove doubt and to claim certainty. Christian education, however, invites one to embrace insecurity as an essential mark of our growing humanity, to walk courageously into it, to celebrate doubt, and to recognize that certainty is nothing but the pious face of ecclesiastical idolatry. Christian propaganda invests the Bible with inerrancy. Christian education searches the biblical tradition as one means of seeing the Word of God, but it recognizes that this Word can never be identified with the literal words of scripture.

Christian propaganda regards the teaching of the Bible as a process of learning the facts and reconciling the contradictions. Christian education invites the participant to taste the spirit behind the dated and sometimes confusing words of scripture until those words become not literal symbols, but doorways into the reality of God.

The church that will live in the present and survive into the future will not be about the task of propagandizing its people. It will, however, be about the task of educating them. It will see its task not to be that of providing answers, denying doubt, and building security. Rather it will entertain questions, help people to be open to all kinds of new growing experiences, while welcoming insecurity as a virtue to be embraced, not a vice to be remedied. It will see the Christian life as a journey that is ongoing, a journey the goal of which is the undefined mystery of God, and in the pursuit of that goal no boundaries on the human spirit will be admissible.

If these principles could undergird the programs the church inaugurates each fall, the response might well be different, the decline of interest reversed, and perhaps, once again, the church would be perceived as the place where the deepest religious yearnings present in the human heart could be explored openly and honestly without fear or threat. The time has come for the church to forsake its authoritative answers of the past that were delivered inside such discredited cliches as "the Bible says" or "the church teaches." A better text for our time might come out of the Book of Isaiah, where the prophet said, "Come let us reason together, saith the Lord." A declining institution just might welcome this new possibility.

– 51 –

Can One Be a Christian without Being a Theist?

October 1996

As a person who lectures extensively across this nation and the world, I have been asked a wide variety of questions from my audiences. They have ranged from the naive to the profound, from the obvious to the obtuse. Some questions have been hostile, designed not to gain knowledge or insight, but rather to embarrass, attack, and minimize. Some have been profoundly questing, seeking in the wasteland some hint that the living water of faith might yet be available. However, no one has ever confronted me with a question at once so penetrating and modern and yet so devastating and threatening as the one with which I began this column.

To my amazement and delight this question was asked by a lay person within the Diocese of Newark. It originated inside that activity we call Education for Ministry (EFM) and specifically from a member of St. Thomas' Church, Vernon. It was posed at an EFM graduation ceremony held at St. Stephen's Church in Millburn in June. It made me newly aware of the significance of the EFM program. If that program can free this person to inquire into her faith on this level, then it has renewed my conviction that EFM is the best educational tool available for lay people in the church today.

Theism is the historic way men and women have been taught to think about God. Most people think theism is the only conceivable way to think about God. The primary image of God in the Bible is a theistic image.

By that I mean that God is conceived of as a being, even the supreme being, external to this world, supernatural in power, and operating on this world in some fashion to call this world and those of us who inhabit it into the divine will or the divine presence. This theistic being is inevitably portrayed in human terms as a person who has a will, who loves, who rewards, and who punishes. One can find other images of God in the scriptures, but this is the predominant and the familiar one.

Theism is also the primary understanding of God revealed in the liturgies of the Christian churches, including the various Anglican Books of Common Prayer. There the God we meet is described as a being who desires our praises, elicits our confessions, reveals to us the divine will, and calls us into the spiritual life of communion with this divine being.

So dominant is this theistic understanding of God that if one rejects theism, one is thought to be an a-theist. An atheist is defined as one who dismisses the theistic concept of God and, since theism exhausts most people's definition of God, an atheist by definition is one who rejects the concept that God might be real.

So when one is confronted with the question, "Can one be a

Christian without being a theist?" it opens vast doors for further thought and theological speculation.

This question becomes askable only when one lives in a world that has rendered the traditional theistic view of God inoperative. We may not like to confront that reality, but in a real sense, this is what the postmodern world forces the contemporary religious community to face. The supernatural being that we have traditionally called God has increasingly been rendered impotent by the explosion in human knowledge over the last five hundred years.

We once attributed to the will of this deity everything we did not understand, from sickness to tragedy to sudden death to extreme weather patterns. But today sickness is diagnosed and treated with no reference to God whatsoever. Tragedies like the crash of TWA Flight 800 or the rise of the AIDS epidemic are investigated by this secular society without reference to the will of God. That was certainly not the case when ancient tragedies, such as the black death or the bubonic plague, swept across the world. When death strikes suddenly today, we do autopsies that reveal a massive coronary occlusion or a cerebral hemorrhage as its cause. We do not speculate on why the external Deity, the theistic supreme being, might have wanted to punish this particular person with sudden death. Even what the insurance companies still call "acts of God" are today thought to be completely explainable in nontheistic language. We chart the formation of hurricanes from the time when they develop as low pressure systems in the southern oceans and we mark their paths until these weather systems are broken up either over land, after unleashing their fury of wind and water, or in the cold and heavy air of the extreme northern parts of our hemisphere. No meteorologist I know of refers to this phenomenon of nature as divinely caused to inflict godly punishment upon a wayward region, people, or nation. Only someone as naive theologically as American televangelist Pat Robertson would assume, as he did a few years ago, that his prayers could steer a hurricane away from his television and radio enterprise in Norfolk, Virginia. Interestingly enough, Mr. Robertson did not pray to break the storm up, but only to redirect its fury. Furthermore, there was no expression of concern on Pat Robertson's part about what might happen to those in whose path his prayers might have redirected the storm.

At least one English theologian, Michael Goulder, saw this shrinking conclusion of the theistic God destroying his faith. He became an atheist when he came to the perception that the God of traditional theism "no longer has any work to do." This God no longer explains mysteries, cures sicknesses, directs the weather, fights wars, punishes sinners, rewards faithfulness. Indeed, the idea of an external supernatural deity who invades human affairs periodically to impose the divine will upon this world, though still given lip service in worship settings, has nonetheless died culturally. If God is identified exclusively with this theistic understanding of God, then it is fair to say that culturally at least God has ceased to live in our world.

If the theistic understanding of God exhausts the human experience of God, then the answer to the question of the EFM student from Vernon is clear. No, it is not possible to be a Christian without being a theist. But if, on the other hand, one can begin to envision God in some way other than in the theistic categories of the traditional religious past, then perhaps a doorway into a religious future can be created. That is to identify what I regard as the most pressing theological issue of this generation.

Christianity has been shaped by traditional theistic concepts. Jesus was identified in some sense as the incarnation of this theistic God. It was said that he came to do "the Father's (read: that external supernatural supreme being's) will." Indeed, Jesus was portrayed as a sacrifice offered to this God to bring an end to human estrangement from the Creator. Theologians talked of original sin and "the fall," to which it was asserted the cross spoke with healing power and in which drama of salvation the shed blood of Jesus played a central role. But in a world that has abandoned any theological sense of offering sacrifices to an angry deity, what could this interpretation of the cross of Christ possibly mean? In a post-Darwinian world, where creation is not finished but is even now ongoing and ever-expanding, the idea of a fall from a perfect world into sin and estrangement is nonsensical. The idea that somehow the very nature of the heavenly God required the death of Jesus as a ransom to be paid for our sins is ludicrous. A human parent who required the death of his or her child as a satisfaction for a relationship that has been broken would be either arrested or confined to a mental institution. Yet behavior we have come to abhor in human beings is still a major part of the language of worship in our churches when we speak of God. It is the language of our ancient theistic understanding of God. It is also language that is doomed first to irrelevance and later to revulsion. The real question then becomes, "Can Christianity be separated from ancient theistic concepts and still be a living faith?" That is why this inquiry from the EFM student was such a threatening, scary question. Once it is raised to consciousness, it will never again go away. It will also destabilize forever the only understanding of God most of us have had.

The "religious right" does not understand the issues involved here. On the other hand, the secular society where God has been dismissed from life has also answered this question by living as if there is no God. Only those who can first raise this question into consciousness and who then refuse to sacrifice their sense of the reality of God when all theistic concepts fail will ever wrestle with these issues.

It would surprise many pew sitters in our churches to know how deeply this debate already rages in the theological academy. In this world of scholarly dialogue God has not been spoken of as an external supernatural being who periodically invades the world in decades. Yet the experience of God as a divine presence found in the midst of life is all but universally attested. Jesus as a revelation of this divine presence is the heart of the Christian claim. The normative language of theism by which this experience has traditionally been processed and transmitted is, however, today all but universally rejected by the academy

So perhaps the major theological task of our times is to seek a new language of faith or at the very least a new way to translate those premodern theistic categories into the postmodern, nontheistic language of tomorrow. That is not an easy assignment. It is, however, the vocation to which my mind and heart are dedicated as I begin to create the last major theological book of my active career. I cannot begin to say how much the posing of this frontier question about the relationship between the Christian faith and the theistic language of the past encouraged me. At least one lay member of this diocese is wrestling on the same frontier where my mind is now engaged; I rejoice that I am not alone.

– 52 –

Will Christianity Survive the New Millennium?

November 1996

As the romantic sounding year of 2000 C.E. appears on the horizon, people in all walks of life begin to speculate about life in the third millennium. It has clearly entered the rhetoric of politicians this election year as they attempt to build "a bridge to the twenty-first century."

But amid all the banter there is a serious concern. What will be the shape of humanity in this future? What values will survive? What issues will engage us? What new knowledge will reorganize our thinking? The leadership of the Christian church must surely ask about those things that are present on the church's horizon and seek to understand the direction in which Christianity is headed.

When this century began in 1900, the thought of Charles Darwin was just beginning to reverberate around the Western world. *On the Origin of Species* had been published in 1859, and the attack on traditional Christian thinking implicit in its pages had just begun to be felt. The literalness of the seven-day creation story was the first casualty, but the authority of all scripture was also seen to totter. An uneasy accommodation was made by the pious suggestion that each day in the biblical account of creation was really millions of years. Scripture could thus still be called accurate even as its substance was visibly eroded. It did not, however, save the church from the embarrassment of the Scopes trial in the 1920s. Periodically other versions of the same hysteria that found John Scopes guilty would erupt to play across the headlines of our newspapers as fear and ignorance masqueraded as faith and knowledge.

However, Darwin's challenge to traditional Christian concepts was far more profound than first imagined.

Darwin's revolutionary concepts destroyed forever the power of the traditional Christian myth by which this religious system had defined itself for centuries. This myth assumed that the original act of divine creation was perfect and complete and that from this perfection human beings had fallen away into a sinfulness that was both universal and inevitable. This "fall," it was said, required a divine rescue operation, and in terms of that requirement the Christ story was typically told. That is what produced the various atonement theories which stated just how it was that the divine rescue of our "fallen nature" had been accomplished by Jesus. "Christ died for my sins," became the code word. His death was even interpreted to be a sin offering that God required to be paid, a ransom if you will. Those strange-sounding theological words reflect a first-century Jewish-Christian mentality which understood Christ in his death as the new paschal lamb slain to break the power of death or the new sacrificial lamb of Yom Kippur that was believed to have taken away "the sins of the world." But Darwin has confronted this traditional understanding with the vision of an unfinished and therefore imperfect universe and of human life not fallen but still emerging out of its evolutionary past. The basic Christian interpretive myth of Jesus as God's divine rescue operation, designed to save a fallen creation, quickly becomes inoperative. As that realization dawned in religious circles, both anger and defensiveness have risen and, simultaneously, religious power has waned. The heart will never respond to that which the mind rejects.

One manifestation of this decline in religious certainty is that people today no longer have confidence in the reality of life after death. Life after death was a powerful and consoling idea in a believing age. It was this hope that kept our human fears and insecurities in check. It provided believers with the ability to embrace the radical unfairness of human life. It promised that God would rectify this unfairness in the world to come. With the demise of belief in life after death, a passion was born to bring fairness to this present world now. Heaven, as a solution for this human problem, was simply too nebulous.

That was the reality that gave birth to the revolutionary politics of the twentieth century. From the writings of Karl Marx to the legislation that launched the Great Society, the hope to build a just society was born to deal with the loss of the assurance that justice would be done in heaven. So it was that this century witnessed a variety of liberal political expressions: communism, socialism, and the New Deal. Its emergence was a kind of secularized attempt to provide what belief in a just God who promised an afterlife once provided. But the conviction that liberal politics could make fair our unfair world has also died, and with its death has come a new disillusionment. The liberal experiment died in the 1980s and was replaced by a mean-spirited politics of greed and raw power. National budgets are cut by curtailing welfare and medical resources for the poor. Homelessness increases in the richest nation of the world.

So it is that another reality the church must face as we prepare to enter the third millennium is that we do so on the wings of a dying idealism. That is why I believe we are witnessing today a growing political concern to protect the boundaries of our affluence from the surging masses of the Third World, and why we struggle to maintain our standard of living at the expense of the poor in our own country and the underdeveloped nations of the world. An increasingly cruel and insensitive world is on the horizon of the new millennium. One wonders how or if the Christ story will be heard in this world where tomorrow is rapidly approaching.

Still another factor before us as we enter the third millennium is that the twentieth century has seen the breakdown of one oppressive, dehumanizing stereotype after another. As each stereotype has crumbled, Christian anxiety, which manifests itself in both hostility and defensiveness, has increased. The nineteenth century ended slavery legally, but the twentieth century gave rise to racism's bastard stepchildren known as segregation and apartheid. The battle to end these twin evils has been won officially, but unofficially racism has demonstrated an incredible tenacity, and it still lurks just beneath the level of our consciousness. The churches of the Christian West continue to have soiled racist hands.

The traditional religious definition of a woman as a second-class human being, based upon significant literal biblical references, has also been obliterated. Only in this twentieth century have college and university educations been opened to women, have the power to vote and to serve in public life been achieved by women, and has the freedom to determine how their own bodies would be used been won by women. Only in the latter years of the twentieth century has full participation in the life of the church been accorded to women. Each of these battles divided the church into warring camps.

The traditional religious stereotype of homosexuality is also dying. This century has finally learned that gay and lesbian people are not heterosexual people who, because of their moral depravity, have chosen to live sinful homosexual lives. They are not people who need to be rescued from this evil and converted or restored to normalcy. They are simply people born with a different sexual orientation who have been inaccurately defined as abnormal and condemned as immoral by an ignorant heterosexual majority. Once again, as this new consciousness has dawned, the body of Christ has been torn between the dying stereotype and the new learning. On every front the relentless revolution in thought that has marked the twentieth century has been resisted by traditional religious voices. Yet nowhere is there any evidence that the thought revolution is being deterred by this opposition. Rather the church itself is being driven involuntarily into a new world which will require a new understanding of what we Christians believe and how we live that Christianity out. A religious system based on the dismissed truth of another age and filled with the vestiges of the rejected stereotypes of the past will hardly appeal to people in a postmodern world. These are major factors before the church as the new millennium is born.

We could cite other thinkers whose work has shattered the operative presuppositions of the religious life in the past. Despite the assumptions of the Bible, the earth is not flat. It is not the center of the universe. God is therefore not looking down on us from beyond the sky. This God does not invade our world with miracle and magic to fight our wars, destroy our enemies, or do our bidding. Virgins do not conceive. Resurrection cannot mean physical resuscitation and the restarting of bodily processes after three days of death. People cannot ascend on their own gravity-defying power into the sky of a Ptolemaic universe that is no longer believed to exist. Both human truth and traditional moral standards have been relativized. Infallibility and inerrancy do not exist any longer. These are among the changes that have created the tidal wave that now propels us into the twenty-first century. Reality is that we are destined to be third millennium Christians or we will not be Christians at all.

How shall we respond to this new reality? Can we learn to sing the Lord's song in the strange land of the third millennium? Can we be believers without denying the reality of the world? Must we park our brains outside the church door in order to worship?

Until we address these issues, all that we do as a church will be akin to rearranging the deck chairs on the great ship *Titanic!* Yet from within the Christian institution seldom do we hear a voice that speaks to these concerns. Church leaders, rather, seem content to occupy themselves by stopping the leaks, denying the storm, and pretending that things will soon improve.

My vocation as a Christian and as a bishop is to walk into this future of our faith. I prefer to walk in concert with others in the body of Christ, but if this institution is unresponsive, I am prepared to walk alone. I do it because I am a believer who lives in a world that the Christians of the past could never have anticipated. I will never sacrifice my faith, my integrity, or my citizenship in this modern world. Faith must have integrity. It must live in this age or it will not live at all. The third millennium ought to be exciting for it will be the context in which the life or death struggle for the Christian church is engaged. Stay tuned.

– 53 –

Heaven's Gate and the Death of Christianity

May 1997

Their faces were covered in purple shrouds. Their feet displayed new black Nikes. Identification was neatly placed at each side. They had voluntarily gone to what they referred to as a "higher level." It was one more bizarre incident that revealed something very strange about the human spirit.

In 1927 Sigmund Freud published a vigorous critique of organized religion in general and Christianity in particular in a book entitled *The Future of an Illusion.* There he suggested that the origins of religion had nothing to do with revelation or truth; it was born, he said, in the trauma of the emergence of a higher consciousness. Religion developed when beings emerged out of the evolutionary process who understood life's fragility, in the midst of a vast and morally neutral universe. This universe was, he argued, not organized for the benefit of human life or tribe. The ultimate end of every living thing, Freud believed, was death and decay. The inhabitants of the universe had been able to tolerate this reality for billions of years because no creature had been able to contemplate its own mortality or its own lack of ultimate value or meaning. But when Homo sapiens arrived on the stage, they saw themselves as victims, knew they would die, and even anticipated impending disasters. They also recognized that they were not capable of doing anything about their fate. Trauma was the result, and, so Freud argued, religion was developed to deal with this trauma by fostering the illusion that life was controllable.

Religion and human self-consciousness thus began their pilgrimage in human history together. The first tenet of religion was that the powers of the universe were personal and that they could thus be placated, bargained with, or appeased. Natural disasters were defined as the angry expressions of a supernatural being who ruled the universe and were designed by this deity to warn, reward, or punish, on the basis of human deservings. It was thus deemed to be essential that human beings acknowledge and reverence this powerful deity so that the divine one would control these forces for the benefit of the worshiping subjects. Since proper worship could not be accomplished unless the will of this god was known and understood, those who claimed to know the will of this god and to be able to speak for this god emerged as powerful people in primitive societies.

The professional priesthood shrouded itself in claims of magic. Its task was to organize the life of the people so that the blessing of God could be assured and the divine wrath averted. It informed the faithful how the deity must be worshiped. An analysis of primitive worship practices reveals that its rituals were not unlike those used to pay homage to the chief of the clan or the king. Like the chief the deity was thought to revel in the flattery of "his" devotees, to be angry at human failures, and to stand ready to punish unless these shortcomings were properly confessed, penances assigned, and restitution worked out. Groveling before God was assumed to be the proper posture of the penitent. In this manner, Freud declared, the human creature sought to control the anxieties of life by courting the favor of the divine power who would thus protect and defend this fragile human creature.

If religion was born in the trauma of knowing our human vulnerability, then hysteria, which is a typical human response to trauma, would surely be found in the practices of religion. If discerning the will of the deity was a prerequisite for avoiding the wrath of God, then one's security would be well-served by the assertion that absolute certainty accompanied the pronouncements of those who claimed to speak for God. Without this religious security, hysteria would be commonplace. So infallibility claims for religious leaders were born and inerrancy claims came into being for those sacred writings judged to be the place where the will of God was spelled out. These served to keep hysteria at bay.

Believers suspended their rationality and embraced these security claims. But the repressed hysteria was revealed in the rage or banishment meted out by religious traditions when a challenge to the accuracy of its claims was heard. This mentality was behind those dark chapters of religious history when heretics were burned at the stake, excommunication enforced religious conformity, and such critics of the religious status quo as Copernicus, Galileo, and Charles Darwin were threatened and harassed.

This Freudian analysis suggested that security, not truth, was the primary goal of every religious system. Security, not truth, is well-served by controlling thought, disciplining deviation, and purging critics. These tactics represent an attempt on the part of frightened people to calm their fears when confronted by a vast, impersonal, and, ultimately, a killing universe. They encourage religious zealots to surrender their freedom for the security of being told what to think. We live in a world where most religious systems are honored, where piety is extolled, and where the criticism of anyone's religious tradition is looked upon as inappropriate; yet we still see these destructive aspects of religion at work around the world. In Ireland Catholics and Protestants have killed each other for centuries. In the Middle East, Moslems and Jews are regularly at each other's throats. In India and Pakistan, the hostility between Moslems and Hindus forced the division of the whole subcontinent. Throughout the Western world a killing anti-Semitism still emanates from the heart of Christianity. This world seems to tolerate religious violence as if it is almost proper.

From time to time that violence takes a bizarre turn which cannot be ignored. A Jonestown, Guyana, episode will occur in which hundreds of people drink poison to satisfy both their cultic needs and the illusions of grandeur that have gripped their leader. Now we are confronted with a community called Heaven's Gate that combines unchallenged religious convictions with modern technology and a story line out of *Star Trek*. Its members were castrated to remove sexual desire, and they died contemplating being taken to a "higher level" by a spaceship traveling in the wake of the Hale-Bopp comet. It was one more startling revelation of the primitive hysteria that lurks in the heart of every religious system. The public was shocked as this story broke. Commentators analyzed the data from every angle. Magazines flashed the eerie portrait of the cult leader on their covers. Television played their farewell speeches over and over. Reporters scurried to discover the background of these people, to interview families, friends, and associates. The religious establishment was quick to condemn this activity as a distortion of "true religion." Few there were who would suggest that this behavior was but a slight exaggeration of those elements that are present at all times in every religious system.

When will we recognize that religion is always in the mind control business? Religion purges its critical thinkers by removing them from official positions, indexing their writings, or silencing them officially until they recant. If that does not work, eternal and God-sponsored punishment is made quite vivid. Organized religion is cultic at its core, but seeks to keep this fact well concealed. It is revealed only when its authority is questioned or when some group takes the neurotic aspects of religion to their natural conclusion. That is the final meaning of the Heaven's Gate community in San Diego.

Sigmund Freud was right in so many ways. He has described accurately, I believe, the origin of religion. Far more than most are willing to imagine, religion has been a destructive and divisive force in human history. It still tolerates such neurotic claims as papal infallibility and biblical inerrancy. Almost every religious tradition still asserts that it alone constitutes the sole channel to salvation.

Can Christianity escape the corrupting roots of its religious origin? If it cannot, then the world might well be better off without it. Yet, I am encouraged that there is no word that can translate "religion" in the Gospel tradition. Jesus did not say, "I have come that you might be religious," but rather, "I have come that you might have life and have it abundantly." I am pleased to hear Christian theologians begin to say that the creeds do not capture truth, they only point to truth. I am thrilled to hear Christian voices declare the church to be a place to go not to receive answers, but in which questions can be raised. Increasingly, the Christian life is seen as a journey toward a mystery rather than as a theological database in which the mysterious can be fully explained. The task of Christianity is not to provide security; it is to give us the courage to embrace life's insecurity without surrendering our humanity.

Insecurity is a mark of being human. No drug, including the drug of religion, should be allowed to take it away. God is not a name for the forces of the universe that stand ready to snuff out our frail humanity. God is the name of the ground of all being that is manifested when we discover the ability to live fully, the capacity to love wastefully, and the courage to be in the face of the ultimate threat of nonbeing.

We are moving into a postreligious world. I see humanity emerging out of its primitive origins, a humanity that does not need a heavenly parent figure in the sky to feel secure, a humanity that claims its grandeur by refusing to surrender the radically insecure quality of existence to any would-be authority. This humanity, I believe, can worship the God known biblically as "I Am," not by groveling, but by living. Religion, I suspect, will finally die, a victim of its own immaturity. But Christianity, if it can separate itself from the tentacles of religion, has a chance to be the song of the universe, sung by those who have come of age. It was Dietrich Bonhoeffer, a German martyr in World War II, who said, "To be a Christian does not mean to be a religious man [or woman]. It simply means to be a man [or woman]." Once, Bonhoeffer observed, Christianity had to separate itself from Judaism. Now it is called upon to separate itself from religion. The group known as Heaven's Gate makes us understand why.

– 54 –

The New Reformation: Revisiting the Meaning of Christ

June 1998

Last month I posted in this column and on the Internet the twelve theses that I believe must be addressed as part of a New Reformation in Christianity. They were drawn substantially from my newly published book, *Why Christianity Must Change or Die.* The response has been overwhelming. My mail on this topic is now averaging one hundred letters a week. The content of these pieces of communication is wonderfully mixed.

"You are an utter disgrace . . . as a bishop you are beneath contempt" — an e-mail message. "Had you been a naval officer you would have been tried for treason and shot" — from a Pennsylvania layman. An English Canon preached against my twelve theses at St. Paul's Cathedral in London. But when the BBC sent me a copy of his sermon, I noted that he had edited and distorted my theses to make them more amenable to his attack. It was yet another example of evangelical dishonesty. I suppose that attacks like this are probably inevitable. Certainly Martin Luther's life was at risk when he nailed his ninety-five theses to the door of the church in Wittenberg in 1517. Every religious reformer before and since has confronted the same hysterical fear.

More impressive than this hostility to me has been the outpouring of positive mail and the interest on the part of the media. The ratio of positive to negative mail is now about four to one. The content is also quite revealing. From Alabama: "I am a recovering Baptist and your latest book is like spiritual manna." From South Carolina: "Let me congratulate you on your newest book. My 82-year-old father was bragging about it to my superiors who called you 'that heretic.'" From Tennessee: "Where can I find a church in this area whose minister might share your views?" From Texas: "You really have nailed me down [as a believer in exile], and I am deeply touched and affected. I thought I was alone." From a retired bishop in New England: "I read your article with great interest and sympathy. I agree that we must reinterpret the faith." From a Montclair, N.J., non-Episcopalian: "[reading your book] has been a liberating experience . . . helping set me free from a childhood confusion...where I tried to believe things that were on their face unbelievable." From a Sparta, N.J., Episcopalian: "You have done for me what one of your premises was — to give those who find it difficult to have faith in the convoluted and archaic tenets of classical Christianity a way back to the truth."

From the media have come two invitations from Bill O'Reilly to appear on his Fox Network program, *The O'Reilly Factor.* I have debated Pat Buchanan on CNN's *Crossfire.* Major features have appeared in the *Philadelphia Inquirer* and in *USA Today.* I have done a radio debate on the BBC and a one-hour program for the Canadian Broadcasting Company. There is clearly an interest in things religious in our society when they are looked at openly and honestly.

I find it interesting that those who are identified with present-day institutional religion are the most eager to shut the debate down and even to purge my ideas from the church. But those who live on the edges of institutional church life and those who have abandoned Christianity itself are effusive in welcoming this debate to find a new way to God.

So to press for a New Reformation, I focus now on the dated way the Jesus story has been traditionally interpreted and on what a reformed Christology might look like.

The bedrock of the Christian experience is captured in the assertion that the holy God was present in and met through the life of Jesus. That experience was at first not explained; it was simply stated. Paul did it best when he wrote, "God was in Christ, reconciling the world." But once that assertion was made, various explanations began to develop based on the way God was perceived in the first century as a supernatural being, dwelling beyond the sky, who invaded human history to accomplish the divine will. If God was in Christ, then an explanation had to be devised about how this God above had entered the world in Jesus and how this God in Jesus returned to heaven when the work of redemption was complete. The story of the virgin birth was designed to achieve the divine entry. The story of the cosmic ascension provided the means of departure.

The virgin birth tradition, however, assumed an ancient view of reproduction which believed that the newborn lived in the sperm of the male, who simply planted it into the womb of the female. So to proclaim the divine origin of a person, one simply replaced the human father with a divine agent. It was not necessary to replace the mother since she was believed to add nothing to the new life. A virgin birth was therefore a rather sexist male misunderstanding of procreation.

But in 1724 the egg cell was discovered, and people realized that the woman was the co-creator of every life, contributing 50 percent of the genetic code of every child. Suddenly virgin birth stories became biological nonsense. The church needs to face this fact.

At the end of Jesus' life a story had to be devised to enable the theistic God whom they believed they had met in him to return to the divine abode above the sky. The ascension story accomplished that. This story assumed that the earth was the center of a three-tiered universe. The sky was the roof of the earth beyond which the theistic God lived in heaven.

But in the sixteenth and seventeenth centuries Copernicus and Galileo confronted us with a new version of cosmic reality. The centrality of the earth was obliterated and the heavens began to be demystified. Suddenly Christians had to recognize that ascending into the sky was not the route to heaven. Given our present knowledge of cosmology, such a journey would at best achieve an endless orbit, while at worst one would ultimately escape the limits of gravity and sink into the infinite depths of space. So the literal story of the ascension no longer translates to space-age people.

Perhaps the most challenging and disturbing realization of all comes when believers begin to recognize that the primary way in which the death of Jesus has been traditionally understood is in terms of human sacrifice. That is hardly an appealing concept in our day. The words so central to Christian self-understanding, like "Jesus died for my sins," or "Jesus paid the price of sin on the cross of Calvary," or "I have been saved by the blood of Christ," are nothing short of ludicrous when we recognize what they mean. They assume a literalness about various elements of the ancient Christian myth. That myth proclaimed that God, at the dawn of time, completed the act of creation, judged it to be perfect, and then turned the creation over to human beings. This myth asserted that the human creatures violated God's sacred order in an act of cosmic disobedience and fell into sin. So distorting of our humanity was this "original sin," as we called it, that human beings stained by this sin were exiled permanently from God's presence. Unable to save themselves, the myth continued, these human beings stood condemned before the throne of grace, crying out for a savior to rescue them from their self-inflicted wounds. Jesus was God's answer to these cries. He came from God to aid the fallen world only to discover that the price of rescue would be his very life. Accepting that price, Jesus became the human sacrifice which both God and sin required. In the death of Jesus, God's sense of justice was thus satisfied and the divine wrath of God was turned away from the fallen human creature, at least from those who were willing to be covered by the shed blood of this sacrificial act. Only through that human sacrifice on the cross, this myth proclaims, are human beings enabled once again to enter the presence of God from which the fall had banished us.

Christians have repeated the formulas of this traditional myth so often that we have become inured to the grotesque image of God they reveal and to the destructive definition of human life they employ. Such words may have carried the Christian message in an ancient world, but they are not likely to carry it into an enlightened future. A Reformation must redefine the function of the Christ if Christianity is to remain a viable faith system.

We begin that Reformation with the recognition that we are post-Darwinian people. We know that creation is neither finished nor perfect. Human life is still in an evolving process. New galaxies are still being formed. So the definition of human beings as fallen from an original perfection becomes unreal. Reality for us is that we emerged from the darkness of our evolutionary struggle and we have been moving for billions of years into higher and higher levels of consciousness. Thus the tale of a savior who rescued us from a fall that never happened and who has restored us to a perfection we never possessed is not likely either to communicate or to appeal to modern minds. Equally unappealing will be a liturgy designed to reenact each Sunday that saving sacrifice of the cross which required the death of the divine Son as a ransom.

The traditional view of Christology is thus no longer operative. These ancient explanations must now be seen not as the essence of Christianity, but as part of the cocoon of our religious immaturity that must be abandoned. They can never be the essence of our religious future. If these outmoded understandings of the meaning of Jesus exhaust the Christ experience, then Christianity will surely die.

Christianity clearly stands today in need of a Reformation that will recast the Christ experience in radically different ways from those of our Christian past. If God was in Christ, as I deeply believe, then a new way must be found to make sense of that incarnate presence. But surely that must be a call into the transforming love of God rather than a call into dependent gratitude. The idolatry of ancient and outmoded explanations must be broken open or we stand to lose the wonder that makes the Christ so radically important.

I welcome the pressures that will usher in this New Reformation. I will continue to encourage them. I seek nothing less than to light a spark that will ignite a movement that, once begun, will be unstoppable. I cast my vote for this kind of scary religious future because I am a Christian and I am not willing to assume that there is no way other than the way of yesterday to process the eternal Christ experience.

So the debate goes on.